WM 200 BEL

2013

D1145639

LIVING O

Tavistock Clinic Series

Margot Waddell (Series Editor)
Published and distributed by Karnac Books

Other titles in the Tavistock Clinic Series

LIVING ON THE BORDER

Psychotic Processes in the Individual, the Couple, and the Group

Edited by
David Bell & Aleksandra Novakovic

Foreword by
John Steiner

KARNAC

First published in 2013 by
Karnac Books
118 Finchley Road
London NW3 5HT

Copyright © 2013 by David Bell & Aleksandra Novakovic
All contributors retain the copyright to their own chapters.

The rights of the editors and contributors to be identified as the authors of this work have been asserted in accordance with §§ 77 and 78 of the Copyright Design and Patents Act 1988.

All rights reserved. No part of this publication may be reproduced, stored in a retrieval system, or transmitted, in any form or by any means, electronic, mechanical, photocopying, recording, or otherwise, without the prior written permission of the publisher.

British Library Cataloguing in Publication Data

A C.I.P. for this book is available from the British Library

ISBN: 978–1–85575–601–4

Edited, designed, and produced by Communication Crafts

Printed in Great Britain

www.karnacbooks.com

CONTENTS

v

SERIES EDITOR'S PREFACE

Margot Waddell

Since it was founded in 1920, the Tavistock Clinic has developed a wide range of developmental approaches to mental health which have been strongly influenced by the ideas of psychoanalysis. It has also adopted systemic family therapy as a theoretical model and a clinical approach to family problems. The Clinic is now the largest training institution in Britain for mental health, providing postgraduate and qualifying courses in social work, psychology, psychiatry, and child, adolescent, and adult psychotherapy, as well as in nursing and primary care. It trains about 1,700 students each year in over 60 courses.

The Clinic's philosophy aims at promoting therapeutic methods in mental health. Its work is based on the clinical expertise that is also the basis of its consultancy and research activities. The aim of this Series is to make available to the reading public the clinical, theoretical, and research work that is most influential at the Tavistock Clinic. The Series sets out new approaches in the understanding and treatment of psychological disturbance in children, adolescents, and adults, both as individuals and in families.

The editors and contributors to this fine volume, *Living on the Border: Psychotic Processes in the Individual, the Couple, and the Group,* have brought together their collective experience and insight to produce a comprehensive exploration of some of the most puzzling and intransigent mental states that clinicians encounter. Such states belong to the wide spectrum of different pathologies that tend to be roughly grouped together under psychiatric umbrella terms such as borderline personality disorders, and medication is often the first port of call.

Here, by contrast, we find a group of clinicians who are dedicated to trying to understand the meaning that underlies the experience of what it is like not just for someone who is struggling to live "on the border", but also for those involved in their relationships and their care.

As these pages repeatedly attest, this commitment to understanding—whether the individual, the couple, the group, or the organization—involves a profound respect for all concerned. It involves both rigour and compassion and also dedication to a psychoanalytic way of thinking that can throw an honest light on people's struggles to engage with their own troubled lives and those of others. In the process, many of the chapters draw on some of the most original aspects of Kleinian and post-Kleinian thinking as it has been absorbed into work with psychotic processes and very primitive mental states.

The chapters that the editors have chosen to include are each, in their very different ways, both fresh and unusual. Above all, however, the long-term passion for the work sings through. Such work is taxing and tough, disturbing, to say the least. Yet it is of a type that seems to nurture originality across a very wide range of encounters with the inhabitants of that "on the border" place. "Ground breaking" is often an over-used and clichéd term, and I have always used it very sparingly. But in the case of this book, it constitutes a fair description, one most unusual in the professional literature hitherto.

ACKNOWLEDGEMENTS

We would like to firstly thank Margot Waddell for her unwavering kind and real containing presence during the long work of this project. Liz Allison assisted us with very thoughtful editorial work, which was generously supported by the Melanie Klein Trust. We wish to thank the Solomon R. Guggenheim Foundation, New York, for giving us permission to use the painting *Red Balloon*, 1922, by Paul Klee, for the front cover of the book.

ABOUT THE EDITORS AND CONTRIBUTORS

David Bell is a Consultant Psychiatrist at the Tavistock Clinic, where he directs the Fitzjohn's Unit, a specialist service for serious/complex psychological disorders. He is visiting Professorial Fellow at Birkbeck College, London, and past President of the British Psychoanalytical Society. Throughout his career he has been deeply involved in the relation between psychoanalysis and literature, philosophy, and politics, and he has made numerous contributions in these areas. He is one of the UK's leading psychiatric experts in asylum/human rights. He is contributing editor of *Reason and Passion* (1997) and *Psychoanalysis and Culture: A Kleinian Perspective* (1999, revised edition 2004) and the author of *Paranoia* (2002).

Tim Dartington is a group and organizational consultant, with affiliations to both the Tavistock Institute and the Tavistock Clinic. He has directed the experiential Leicester Conference on authority and leadership in organizations and is a member of OPUS (an Organisation for Promoting Understanding of Society) and ISPSO (the International Society for the Psychoanalytic Study of Organizations). He has a PhD for his work on developing a systems psychodynamic approach to health and social care and is the author of *Managing Vulnerability: The Underlying Dynamics of Systems of Care* (2010).

James V. Fisher [1937–2012] was a member of the British Psycho-analytic Association and the International Psychoanalytical Association. He was a Senior Fellow of the Tavistock Centre for Couple Relationships. He worked in private practice with both individuals and couples. He had a particular interest in Bion and Meltzer, giving seminars on both. His writing included *The Uninvited Guest: Emerging from Narcissism towards Marriage* (1999) and articles, "The Emotional Experience of K", "A Father's Abdication: Lear's Retreat from 'Aesthetic Conflict'", and "The Marriage of the Macbeths".

Caroline Garland is a Fellow of the British Psychoanalytical Society, working both in private practice and at the Tavistock Clinic. She has specialized in the understanding and treatment of trauma and on the ways in which groups function and can be used therapeutically. She writes, lectures, and supervises on these subjects both at home and internationally. Her edited publications include *Understanding Trauma: A Psychoanalytical Approach* (1999) and *The Groups Book: Psychoanalytic Group Therapy* (2010). She is currently working on the understanding of chronic treatment-resistant depression.

Francis Grier is a Training Analyst and Supervisor of the British Psychoanalytical Society and a Member at the British Society of Couple Psychotherapists and Counsellors. He edited *Brief Encounters with Couples: Some Analytical Perspectives* (2001) and *Oedipus and the Couple* (2005). He contributed a chapter, "Lively and Deathly Intercourse", to *Sex, Attachment and Couple Psychotherapy: Psycho-analytic Perspectives* (ed. C. Clulow, 2009). "The Hidden Traumas of the Young Boarding School Child as Seen through the Lens of Adult Couple Therapy" will be included in *Enduring Trauma Through the Life-Cycle* (2013).

R. D. Hinshelwood is Professor of Psychoanalysis at the Centre for Psychoanalytic Studies, University of Essex, and was previously a Consultant Psychotherapist in the NHS and Clinical Director of the Cassel Hospital. He is a Fellow of the British Psychoanalytical Society and a Fellow of the Royal College of Psychiatrists. He authored *A Dictionary of Kleinian Thought* (1989) and other texts on Kleinian psychoanalysis; *Observing Organisations: Anxiety, Defence and Culture in Health Care* (2000, edited with W. Skogstad); and *Suffering Insanity: Psychoanalytic Essays on Psychosis* (2004), on schizophrenia in psychiatric institutions. *Research on the Couch: Single Case Studies, Subjectivity and Psychoanalytic Knowledge* is forthcoming in 2013.

David Kennard is a clinical psychologist and group analyst. He was involved in the development of the Association of Therapeutic Communities and edited its journal, *Therapeutic Communities*, from 1992 to 1998. From 2004 to 2009 he was Chair of the UK Network of ISPS (the International Society for Psychological and Social Approaches to Psychosis). His co-authored/co-edited books include *An Introduction to Therapeutic Communities* (1983/1998), *A Workbook of Group Analytic Interventions* (1993), *Experiences of Mental Health In-patient Care* (2007), and *Staff Support Groups in the Helping Professions* (2009).

Julian Lousada is a psychoanalyst with the British Psychoanalytic Association, former Clinical Director of the Adult Department at the Tavistock & Portman NHS Foundation Trust where he was also a Principal Consultant in Tavistock Consulting. He is the Chair of British Psychoanalytic Council. He trained initially as a psychiatric social worker in Lambeth and Islington, and he subsequently taught at a number of universities. He has directed and been a staff member on many group relations conferences both nationally and internationally. He is currently in private practice.

Mary Morgan is a psychoanalyst and couple psychoanalytic psychotherapist and a founding member of the British Society of Couple Psychotherapists and Counsellors. At the Tavistock Centre for Couple Relationships she is Head of the MA in Couple Psychoanalytic Psychotherapy and the Professional Doctorate in Couple Psychotherapy. She is a member of the International Psychoanalytical Association's Psychoanalytic Perspectives of Families and Couples Working Group. She has developed and led couple psychotherapy trainings in several countries, lectures internationally, and has worked for many years closely with colleagues in Sweden and the United States.

Aleksandra Novakovic is a group analyst and psychoanalyst and is a member of the London Institute of Group Analysis and the British Psychoanalytic Association. She was Joint Head of the Inpatient & Community Psychology Service, Barnet, Enfield &

Haringey Mental Health Trust. She has worked with patients with severe and complex mental health problems and facilitated staff groups for inpatient and community mental health staff teams. She is currently working in the Complex Care Services, St Ann's Hospital, and is a Visiting Clinical Lecturer at the Tavistock Centre for Couple Relationships.

Salomon Resnik is a psychoanalyst, a psychiatrist, and a Training Analyst of the International Psychoanalytical Association. He trained in Argentina and London with Melanie Klein, Herbert Rosenfeld, W. R. Bion, Esther Bick, and D. W. Winnicott. He was a Professor of Psychiatry in Lyon and Rome and was awarded an Honorary Degree in Philosophy by the University of Cosenza, Italy. He is one of the pioneers in work with psychotic patients individually, in groups, and in institutions. His publications include: *The Theatre of the Dreams* (1987), *The Delusional Patient* (2001), *L'avventura estetica* (2002), *Glacial Times* (2005), *An Archaeology of the Mind* (2011), and *L'arte del dettaglio* (2012).

Margaret Rustin is a child, adolescent, and adult psychotherapist. She was Head of Child Psychotherapy at the Tavistock Clinic for many years and continues to supervise and research in child psychotherapy and has a private practice. She has taught widely internationally and published many papers and books. She co-edited *Psychotic States in Children* (with M. Rhode et al., 1997) and most recently *Work Discussion: Learning from Reflective Practice* (with J. Bradley, 2008) and co-wrote with Michael Rustin *Narratives of Love and Loss: Studies in Modern Children's Fiction* (1987) and *Mirror to Nature: Drama, Psychoanalysis, and Society* (2002). She is an Honorary Associate of the British Psychoanalytical Society.

Hanna Segal [1918–2011] was the foremost exponent of Melanie Klein's work. Her original work on symbolism and her deepening of the understanding of psychosis continue to be extremely influential. She also made major psychoanalytic contributions to aesthetics, literary theory, and sociopolitical understanding. She served as President of the British Psychoanalytical Society and Vice-President of the International Psychoanalytical Association. She wrote six books, the last of which, *Yesterday, Today and Tomorrow*, was published in 2010. In 1992 She was awarded the Marie S. Sigourney award for outstanding contributions to psychoanalysis.

Wilhelm Skogstad is a Consultant Psychiatrist in Psychotherapy and Lead Clinician at the Cassel Hospital, a centre for psychoanalytically based intensive treatment for adolescents and adults with severe personality disorder. He is a Fellow of the British Psychoanalytical Society and a psychoanalyst in private practice. He has published papers on inpatient psychotherapy and problems of psychoanalytic practice such as the inability to mourn and the impenetrable object, as well as papers and a book, co-edited with R. Hinshelwood, on psychoanalytic observation of organizations. He also teaches regularly in Germany.

Elizabeth Bott Spillius is a Distinguished Fellow and Training Analyst of the Institute of Psychoanalysis. She was Editor of the New Library of Psychoanalysis, and her publications include: *Family and Social Networks* (1957), *Tongan Society at the Time of Captain Cook's Visits* (1982), *Melanie Klein Today* (Volumes 1 and 2, 1988), *Encounters with Melanie Klein* (2007), *The New Dictionary of Kleinian Thought* (2011). In 2012, she published with Mrs E. O'Shaughnessy, *Projective Identification: The Fate of a Concept.*

Margot Waddell is a Fellow of the British Psychoanalytical Society. She is a Consultant Child and Adolescent Psychotherapist at the Tavistock Clinic, London, and also works in private practice. She teaches and lectures both in Britain and abroad and has published many journal articles and chapters in edited books. The second edition of her book, *Inside Lives: Psychoanalysis and the Development of the personality* was published by Karnac in 2002 and *Understanding 12–14 Year Olds* by Jessica Kingsley in 2005. She is overall editor of the Tavistock Clinic Series.

INTRODUCTION

The chapters collected together in this book will be of interest to any professional working with disturbed patients, and this of course covers a very broad range of disciplines. The work presented explores the kind of situations that, although occurring in different contexts, can all be understood as expressions of primitive psychological processes, processes that impact profoundly not only on the individual patient but also on those around the patient.

When we consider severe psychological disorder, there is an inevitable pull towards focusing on the individual mental state, the main emphasis in general psychiatry. By contrast, one of the distinctive contributions of the psychoanalytic perspective derives from its engagement with the processes—that is, the characteristic anxieties and defences through which these states are created and maintained. This approach gives centrality to the *meaning* of these communications, their function within the human relationships that provide their context.

As reflected in the general progression of the chapters, one might think of the different "levels" of disturbance as somewhat like Russian dolls. At the first level, there is the individual patient's mind and the disturbing thoughts and feelings it has to manage, then there is the relationship between the patient and his or her immediate carer (usually the primary nurse), then the context of that relationship, perhaps the psychiatric team and the ward. Higher levels include the hospital/institutional structure and extend up to very broad societal levels, which would include Government policy. A further aptness of this metaphor (as discussed in chapter 13) derives from the way it suggests that each level in the system acts as a container to those at the lower levels and is, in turn, contained by those above. All these levels have important effects, and at any moment one level may have a more determining effect than others.

Our use of the term "borderline" perhaps needs a little elucidation. It is a term now very widely used to cover a broad range of psychological problems. However, one can perhaps discern two broad groups. There are those whose difficulties, because they impact so massively on those around them, are very manifest. The other group, often termed "schizoid", are quieter and tend to be emotionally isolated and are easily neglected. Both these groups of patients, though at a manifest level so different, are, at a deeper level, struggling with similar underlying profound anxieties, such as fear of fragmentation or claustrophobic terror. The term "borderline" also captures an experience familiar to staff working with these patients. With one group, there is a characteristic feeling of losing one's moorings in the ordinary realities of life and finding oneself living on a kind of edge, where it feels that, at any moment, things might go catastrophically wrong. Alternatively, with the more schizoid patients, staff feel a strange lack of contact or emptiness. These disturbed states of mind can not only affect the staff's relationships with the patients but spread to contaminate their work more generally. The term "borderline" also refers to characteristic social and institutional processes that, though presenting themselves as rational, soon reveal themselves to be profoundly irrational and very maddening for all concerned.

We hope that the work presented here can help establish a framework for the understanding of this kind of disturbance, be it on the level of the individual, the couple, the group, or wider social and institutional processes, and so make a contribution to the care of this patient group.

FOREWORD

John Steiner

In this volume, David Bell and Aleksandra Novakovic have brought together a collection of impressive chapters dealing with the problem of working with seriously disturbed patients in a variety of settings. These patients are not only disturbed in themselves but, as many of the authors point out, are also very *disturbing* to the people they come into contact with. Part of the difficulty arises from the fact that these relationships are dominated by psychotic processes and primitive mental mechanisms that have to be tolerated and coped with *before* they can be understood.

A psychoanalytic approach offers a unique way of grappling with this problem, bringing an attitude in which meaning is given a priority. This is very rare. It is so often the case that, because the patient and those around him or her are so overwhelmed, their capacity to process these difficulties is severely undermined and so they can seek only action to try to put things right. The current medical preoccupation with drug treatment adds a further dimension as most doctors/mental health workers and many institutions seek only to eliminate rather than to tolerate signs of madness. It is thus very refreshing to find a group of psychotherapists who, through their capacity to contain their reactions to the disturbance, are able to prioritize understanding. Never could this need be more urgent than at our current juncture.

The "border" referred to in the title of the book can have a variety of meanings, many of which are elucidated in the chapters that follow. In its usual meaning, the term refers to those patients who function through the use of psychotic mechanisms and who occupy a position somewhere between psychosis and neurosis. However, as the editors make clear in their Introduction, it also refers to the subjective experience of patients who have lost their identity and so find themselves "living on the border" between intense and conflicting states of mind. Such a borderline existence means that there is not only personal distress and suffering, but great difficulty in being integrated into a family or social group—yet such integration is vital to their rehabilitation.

The editors have collected together a variety of approaches to the subject. Some describe psychoanalytic work with patients, whereas others are more concerned with the application of these concepts to other settings, in particular to couples and groups. But all are concerned with understanding this difficult but rewarding area of work. *Living on the Border* is a major contribution to the care of this patient group.

CHAPTER ONE

The psychoanalytic approach to the treatment of psychotic patients

Hanna Segal

The psychoanalytic approach to the treatment of psychotic patients is based on the general assumption underlying all psychoanalytic thinking that psychological phenomena are amenable to understanding. The beginnings of psychoanalysis are in a way very modest. It starts with Freud listening to the communication of his neurotic patients. Up to that time, the patient was classified, manipulated, maybe treated, but his communications were listened to in a cursory manner only and were not considered material for examination. Psychoanalysis starts with Freud's conviction that the verbal and non-verbal communications of his patient could be understood and should be examined with the intention of understanding. The pre-Freudian attitude to mental illness partly continues in many psychiatric approaches to psychosis. That is, they can be classified, diagnosed as schizophrenic or manic depressive, given treatment, and so forth, but their communications are considered either as not understandable or as only marginally relevant to the understanding of the patient. In fact, it is often considered to be a diagnostic point that the content of the schizophrenic patient's psychotic communication is not understandable.

From the historical point of view, Freud tried to extend his attempts at understanding psychological manifestations beyond neurosis and into the area of psychosis, as evidenced by his well-known analysis of the memoirs of Senatspräsident Schreber (Freud, 1911c [1910]). However, he never deliberately attempted an actual psychoanalysis of a psychotic. Since psychoanalysis depends on working with the patient's transference, and since psychotics are, as Freud understood it, wholly narcissistic and form no transference, he could not visualize how psychoanalytic work could be done with them. However, for many who worked with psychotic individuals in their ordinary psychiatric practice, Freud's conclusion did not seem to fit the facts. To begin with, no one is completely psychotic—there are always areas of personality that function in a more neurotic way and so are capable of forming an object relation, however flimsy. So a number of analysts did undertake treatment of psychotic patients provided that the healthy area was sufficiently in evidence, and they tried to work on this healthier part of the patient's ego, mainly in the positive transference with the aim of strengthening it enough to enable the healthier part of the ego to become dominant in relation to the psychotic part, a state of affairs that obtains in remissions. Frieda Fromm-Reichmann, Edith Jacobson, Harold Searles, and others in the United States continued and developed work with psychotic disturbance on a similar basis.

A completely different line of development was initiated by Melanie Klein, who continued Abraham's pioneering work in the analysis of psychotic patients—namely, manic depressives. This work was pursued by analysts trained by her. Bion (1967b), Rosenfeld (1965), and myself (Segal, 1950, 1956, 1957), among others, have produced a number of papers relating to the treatment of both acute and chronic states, and this is the approach I shall concentrate on in this chapter, since this is the area in which I have direct experience.

Melanie Klein's contribution to the theory and practice of psychoanalysis is rooted in her work with children. As a pioneer of child analysis, she had discovered that small children can develop a transference, both positive and negative, of great intensity. In her work with small children, she was impressed by the prevalence of the mechanisms of projection and introjection, more active and dynamic in the small child than the mechanism of repression. She also discovered that the infantile neurosis was a defensive structure, defending the child against primitive anxieties of a paranoid and depressive type bearing an obvious resemblance to those found in psychotic states. She herself did not analyse psychotic patients. However, she did analyse a 6-year-old child who today would be diagnosed as autistic, an analysis she described in the paper on

"The Importance of Symbol Formation in the Development of the Ego" (Klein, 1930). In this paper, she shows how psychotic anxiety can block the process of symbol formation and the development of the ego and how the resolution of that anxiety can lead to a re-establishment of symbolic processes and ego development.

It is our contention that psychotic illness is rooted in the pathology of early infancy, where the basic matrix of mental function is formed. By projection and introjection, by splitting of the object into good and bad, followed later by integration, by introjection and identification with good objects, the ego is gradually strengthened and so acquires a gradual capacity to differentiate between the external and the internal world; the beginnings of superego formation and relation to the external objects are laid down. It is at this time also, in the first year of life, that symbol formation and the capacity to think and to speak develop.

In psychosis, all these functions are disturbed or destroyed. The confusion between the external and the internal, the fragmentation of object relationships and of the ego, the deterioration of perception, the breakdown of symbolic processes, and the disturbance of thinking, are all central features of psychosis. Understanding the genesis of the development of the ego and its object relationships and the kind of disturbance that can arise in the course of that development is thus essential to understanding the mechanisms of psychotic states.

In order to undertake a psychoanalytic investigation of a psychotic patient, certain requirements of the setting and management must be satisfied. The management of the patient outside the sessions must be assured. The patient has to live between the sessions, and his minimum needs, at least, must be satisfied. It is very helpful and at times essential that the management should be friendly to the analysis or at least neutral. It is part of a good management situation, for instance, to ensure that should the patient need hospitalization, the analytic treatment will not be interrupted just at the moment the patient needs it most—it is often because of a failure to arrange a sufficiently stable management that the analytic treatment comes to grief. The analytic setting must provide for the patient the kind of holding environment in which his relationship to the analyst can develop without being broken up by the patient's psychosis. This obviously necessitates reliability and regularity of the hours, a certain uniformity of the setting, a feeling of physical safety if the patient is violent, and so forth. But the analyst himself is a very important part of the setting. He must remain constant and not vary his role, so that the patient's phantasies of omnipotent powers over objects can gradually undergo reality testing. With secure management of the background and a proper analytic setting, the analysis can proceed.

Far from failing to develop a transference, the psychotic patient develops an almost immediate and usually violent transference to the analyst. The difficulty with the psychotic transference is not its absence but its *character*—the difficulty both to observe it and to stand it. The apparent lack of transference or its peculiar nature when it manifests itself is due to the fact that the psychotic transference is based primarily on projective identification. By the term "projective identification" I am referring to an omnipotent phantasy of the patient that he can get rid of unwanted parts of himself into the analyst. This kind of transference is both violent and brittle. The psychotic transference tries to project into the analyst his terror, his feelings of badness, his confusion, and his fragmentation. Having achieved this, he perceives the analyst as a terrifying figure from whom he may need to cut himself off immediately, hence the brittleness of the transference situation. The violence of this projective identification gives rise to a variety of phantasies and feelings. The patient may feel completely confused with the analyst and feel he is losing such identity as he still possesses; he may feel himself trapped or that the analyst will invade him in turn, and so on. As the transference is experienced concretely, interpretations are felt as actions. A familiar scenario is the experiencing of the analyst's interpretation as projective identification in reverse—that is, to feel that the analyst is now putting into him, the patient, his own unwanted parts and in this way driving him mad. This concreteness of experience, in which he feels that he is omnipotently changing the analyst and the analyst concretely and omnipotently changes him, is a technical point of utmost importance. It is essential for the analyst to understand that, when he interprets an anxiety, the patient may feel that he is in fact attacking him, or if he interprets a patient's sexual feelings, the patient may experience it concretely as the analyst's sexual advances towards him or her.

At this point I cannot discuss further the various mechanisms that underlie this concreteness of experience, which arises from the failure of the patient's symbolic function (see Segal, 1957, where I have elaborated this further). I emphasize this point here, however, in order to make clear that it is useless to interpret to the psychotic patient as though he suffered from a neurotic disturbance. For instance, ordinary interpretations of the Oedipus complex are so easily experienced as a sexual assault and thus make the patient worse. It is the schizophrenic patient's language with its concrete symbolization and its confusion between object and subject—his psychotic transference—that has to be the subject of the analysis.

In the space of this chapter I cannot give a complete picture of the theory and practice of the analysis of a psychotic patient—the nearest I can come to it is to provide a model derived from Melanie Klein's (1946) concept of the paranoid-schizoid position and Bion's (1963) concept of a mother capable of containing projective identification. In this model, the infant's relation to his first object can be described as follows: when an infant has an intolerable anxiety, he deals with it by projecting it into the mother. The mother's response is to acknowledge this anxiety and do whatever is necessary to relieve the infant's distress. The infant's perception here is that he has projected something intolerable into his object, but the object was capable of containing it and dealing with it. He can then reintroject not his original anxiety but an anxiety modified by having been contained. Furthermore, through repeated episodes of this type, he also introjects an object capable of containing and dealing with this kind of anxiety. The containment of the anxiety by an internal object capable of understanding is the beginning of mental stability. This mental stability may be disrupted from two sources. The mother may be unable to bear the infant's projected anxiety, and he may introject an experience of even greater terror than the one originally projected. It may also be disrupted by excessive destructive omnipotence of the infant's phantasy.

From this perspective, there are two conflicting trends of development from the very beginning of mental life. One is based on the good container–contained relationship leading to growth, the other on a very disturbed relationship leading to psychosis. The two are in constant struggle—no one is quite mad or quite sane. In this model, the analytic situation itself provides a container. Into the setting, the patient projects his intolerable anxieties and impulses, but the setting itself cannot produce a change. The analyst, who is capable of tolerating and understanding the projected parts, responds by an interpretation that, at its best, is felt by the patient to contain the projected elements made more tolerable and understandable. The patient can then reintroject these "made more tolerable" projected parts, plus the functions of the analyst with which he can identify. This provides the basis for the growth of a part of himself capable of containment and understanding.

This is the ideal progress. But the countertransference is very hard to bear. Over and over again the power of the patient's projective attacks shake our state of mind and we fail to function adequately. But such failures in themselves give us precious information about the nature of the interaction, if we can bear it long enough to understand it.

I shall give one short example from my paper "Depression in the Schizophrenic" (Segal, 1956). The patient, who came to see me aged 16, had suffered from schizophrenia from the age of 4 when her persistent hallucinations started. She had some remissions, but when she started analysis with me she had suffered for many years from chronic hebephrenic schizophrenia. In her first session she rushed around the room gesticulating, muttering, or shouting incessantly. I caught some references to vomiting and to ghosts. I suggested to her that she was trying to get rid of all the bad thoughts in her mind and body by leaving them in my room. Typically, the next day she was silent, obviously paralysed by fear. She hadn't spoken in weeks, mostly lying on the couch and tearing threads from the couch cover. I want to report material from the second year of treatment.

The sequence that I want to describe occurred in October. She had come back from the summer holiday remote and hallucinated. From her behaviour I could gather that she was hallucinating God and the devil; they represented the good and bad aspects of the patient's father, who had committed suicide when she was 15. At times it was clear from her gestures and expressions that she was having intercourse, now with God, now with the devil. There was a great deal of screaming, shouting, and attacking; at times she looked terrified. She was also continually picking threads from the cover of the couch and breaking them off angrily. I had interpreted to her mainly her relation to her father in terms of splitting, idealization, and persecution, and I related this to the transference, particularly in connection with the long summer holiday. I also paid a great deal of attention to her breaking off the threads from the couch cover, interpreting this behaviour according to the context as breaking the threads of her thoughts, the threads of analysis, the threads connecting her internal world with external reality. Her violence gradually subsided, and although she was still picking off threads and breaking them, and as usual she did a lot of biting, grimacing, and angry shaking, the change in her mood was noticeable. As time went on there was more skipping and dancing, more grace in her movements, less tension, and there was about her a general air of half-gaiety, irresponsibility, and remoteness. Then one day, as she was dancing round the room, picking some imaginary things from the carpet and making movements as though she was scattering something round the room, it struck me that she must have been imagining that she was dancing in a meadow, picking flowers and scattering them, and it occurred to me that she was behaving exactly like an actress playing the part of Shakespeare's Ophelia. The likeness to Ophelia was all the more remarkable in that in some peculiar way, the more gaily and irresponsibly she was behaving, the sadder was the effect, as though her gaiety itself was designed to produce sadness in her audience, just as Ophelia's pseudo-gay dancing and singing is designed to make the audience in the theatre sad. If she was Ophelia she was scattering her sadness round the room as she was scattering the imaginary flowers, in order to get rid of it and so make me, the audience, sad. As the patient in the past had often identified with characters in books or plays, I felt on fairly secure ground in saying to her: "It seems to me that you are being Ophelia." She immediately stopped and said, "Yes, of course", as though surprised that I had not noticed it earlier, and then she added, sadly, "Ophelia was mad, wasn't she?" This was the first time she had admitted that she knew about her own madness.

I then connected her behaviour with the previous material and with my interpretations about her relation to her father and showed her how she had felt guilty about the death of her father-lover whom she wished to kill and whom she thought she had killed for his having rejected her. I also explained to her that her present Ophelia-like madness was a denial of her feelings about his death and an attempt to put these feelings into me. As I was interpreting, she threw herself on the couch and let her head hang down from it. I said that she was representing Ophelia's suicide and showing me that she could not admit her feelings about her father's death, as the guilt and distress about it would drive her, like him, to suicide. But she did not agree with this and said Ophelia's death was not a suicide. "She was irresponsible, like a child, she did not know the difference. Reality did not exist for her; death did not mean anything."

I then interpreted to her how putting into me the part of herself capable of appreciating the fact of the death of her father and the reality of her own ambivalent feelings and guilt resulted in her losing her reality sense, her sanity. She then became a person who "did not know the difference" any longer.

She came back the next day very hallucinated and persecuted, externally and internally. She was obviously having unpleasant hallucinations, and she also turned away from me in an angry and frightened way. She did a lot of grimacing, muttering, and biting. She again picked up and broke off threads. I reminded her of the previous session and how she was trying to get rid of her painful feelings by putting them into me. I drew her attention to the breaking of the threads and told her that in getting rid of those painful feelings she felt she was trying to break off and get rid of her sanity. At the same time she felt that I had become a persecutor because she put her painful feelings into me and, as a result, she felt that in interpreting I was trying to push those feelings back into her and persecuting her with them.

The next day she came looking sad and quiet. She started again picking threads out of the couch, but instead of breaking them off completely she was intertwining them. When I made some reference to her Ophelia-like feelings, she said, "You know, when Ophelia was picking flowers it was not, as you said, all madness. There was a lot of the other thing as well. What was unbearable was the intertwining." I said, "The intertwining of madness and sanity?" She said, "Yes, that is what is unbearable." I then told her that my interpretations about how she tried to put her sanity into me made her feel that she had regained the sane part of herself, but she felt it was unbearable because now that sane part of herself could appreciate and feel distress about the disintegration of the rest of herself. In the previous session, she had tried to make me into the sane part of herself who knew about and so was distressed by her, the patient's, insanity. I pointed out to her how she was intertwining the threads that she was picking up and contrasted this with the earlier session in which she was breaking the threads. I interpreted to her that the breaking of the threads represented her breaking her sanity because she could not bear the distress, sadness, and guilt that sanity seemed to bring into her mind.

In the next session she looked at me very carefully and said: "Do you ever smile or laugh? My Mummy says that she cannot imagine you doing either." I pointed out to her how much laughing and giggling she had done during the last weeks and said that she felt that she had stolen all my smiles and laughter and put into me all her depression and guilt, thereby making me into the sad part of herself, but in doing that she made me into a persecutor because she felt I was trying to push this unwanted sadness back into her; then she could not experience her guilt or her sadness as her own but instead felt it as something pushed into her by me in revenge and punishment. She felt that I had lost my laughter but she herself had lost the meaning and understanding of sadness.

Whenever the patient could be put in touch with her emerging depression she became communicative in a sane manner, sanity and depressive feelings returning together to her ego. Whenever the depressive feelings became intolerable, re-projection occurred with the corresponding loss of reality sense, the return of mad behaviour, and an increase of persecutory feelings.

For the schizophrenic mind, the guilt and distress are intolerable, and so the steps that the patient has taken towards sanity have to be reversed. The patient immediately projects the depressed part of the ego into the analyst. This constitutes a negative therapeutic reaction. The saner part of the ego is lost and the analyst becomes again the persecutor, since he is felt to contain the depressed part of the patient's ego and is experienced as forcing this unwanted depression back into the patient. In order to control this negative therapeutic reaction and to enable the patient to regain, retain, and strengthen the sane part of the personality, the whole process of the emergence of the depression and the projection of it has to be followed closely in the transference.

This is, I think, as much as I can say in the context of this chapter to try and indicate what I as a psychoanalyst see myself as doing when confronted by a psychotic patient. The question arises—of what value is this procedure? Quite clearly, psychoanalytic treatment, so very time-consuming and lengthy, does not give the answer to the social problem posed by schizophrenia. If all the psychoanalysts in the world were expert in the analysis of schizophrenic patients and devoted themselves solely to this task, it would statistically do very little for the world problem of the treatment of psychosis. What, then, is the value of psychoanalytic treatment? I think we have to differentiate here between the value to the patient and the value to the community. To take the patient first. It is my conviction that in the rare cases where all the conditions are right, psychoanalytic treatment is the treatment that gives the most hopeful therapeutic prognosis for the individual patient, and that when successful, it is the treatment that deals with the very root of the disturbance of this personality. I would not refrain from recommending it to an individual patient on the grounds that it is not a social solution, any more than I would withhold kidney machines or grafts from patients to whom they may be available just because they are not universally available. From the more general point of view of society, the value of psychoanalysis of psychotic patients lies mainly in its research aspect. Since psychoanalysis is basically an investigation, it is a method that elucidates the psychopathology of the illness. All other psychotherapeutic endeavours, such as psychiatric management, group therapy, individual psychotherapy, community care, and so forth, should be based on such knowledge of the psychopathology. Psychoanalytic research can also make important contributions to methods of prevention, which we hope one day will take precedence over treatment. Another important aspect of psychoanalytic research on psychosis is the deep understanding it brings to mental phenomena in general. In every analysis of neurotic disturbance and even more so the borderline or delinquent, we have to deal with psychotic anxieties and mechanisms, and it is in the treatment of manifestly psychotic patients that one can observe these phenomena at their most intense. But the research aspect and what we derive from it is not confined here to the treatment of illness. Just as Freud's psychoanalysis of neurotics enabled him to formulate a general theory of mental development and function, so it is analysis of psychosis with its characteristic disturbances of thinking, perception, symbolic function, object relations, and so forth that have enabled us to have a much deeper understanding of these psychic functions and their development.

CHAPTER TWO

Reflections on "meaning" and "meaninglessness" in post-Kleinian thought

Margot Waddell

Although not a psychoanalytic concept as such, "meaning" has always been central to the theory and practice of psychoanalysis. But even those theoretical concepts that could be described as "traditional" or "classic" evolve, not only over the course of time but also in various frameworks for thinking, so that they acquire different resonances and significances and throw light on different areas of human thought and interaction, ones that may have previously fallen outside the compass of the original formulations (Sandler, 1983).

"Meaning", and its psychologically equally significant correlate "meaninglessness", are such concepts. In his "Short Account of Psycho-Analysis", Freud (1924f [1923]) summarized his major findings, among which he included: a theory "which appeared to give a satisfactory account of the origin, meaning and purpose of neurotic symptoms" (p. 197) and which emphasized the fact that "even the apparently most obscure and arbitrary mental phenomena invariably have a meaning and a causation . . ." (p. 197).

My purpose in this chapter is not so much to trace the history of meaning and meaninglessness within psychoanalytic thinking generally, but, rather, to focus on what I understand to be the role and function of meaning in the work of some of the thinkers who have extended and elaborated on the theories of Freud and Klein—

primarily Wilfred Bion and Donald Meltzer and those influenced by their ideas. These writers have also opened up a rather different model of the mind and some radically new ways of understanding the nature of human development. Needless to say, in this paradigm, what is not meaningful is not therefore meaningless. Between the two there resides a broad spectrum of human relationship which gets by on the intermediate territory between what can be designated mind-creative—the stuff of genuinely intimate relationships—and, by contrast, mind-destructive.

In this latter way of thinking, the predominant interest was not only in the more traditional psychoanalytic concerns with, for example, defensive operations and the territory of what Meltzer refers to as casual and contractual relationships—in Bion's terms, the proto-mental (Bion, 1961). Rather, the focus was on the properly "mental" and, beyond that, on the very nature and origin of the mind's capacity to grow through the generation and deployment of meaningful emotion and therefore on imaginative and creative capacities more generally. As Meltzer (1986) says, the emphasis shifts from correct interpretations of the myriad ways we find of evading the impact of life around and within ourselves: "the focus moves forwards, as it were, into the interaction, the relationship from which interpretive ideas emerge. [Bion's] model of container–contained places a new value on receptiveness and the holding of the dynamic situation of transference-countertransference in mind" (p. 208). This last comment defines the crux of the matter and its difference from psychoanalytic thinking thitherto. For clearly, Freud's interest in the defences was in the name of enabling people to be freer and more creative. And analysts like Ella Sharpe and Marion Milner were certainly, in those early days, working on issues of symbolization and the growth of the mind. But what Bion, Meltzer, and others were trying to get at was a process prior to the areas that these analysts were theorizing, and this quest took them into as yet uncharted territory.

I shall start with Meltzer's 1983 accounts of the position. He describes the inner world as the place where meaning is generated. In his view, "everything that is evolved in the mind through [what Bion called] alpha-function such as dreaming, verbalizing dreams, painting pictures, writing music, performing scientific functions—all these are *representations* of the meaning" (p. 44). By placing emotional experiences as the first step in thinking processes, Meltzer believed that Bion had, for the first time in psychoanalytic formulation at least, placed "emotion at the very heart of meaning" (p. 44). Drawing on clinical and non-clinical examples, I shall be trying to clarify what this position really is. But one of the difficulties of unpacking the kind of passage just quoted is that we are attempting to put into verbal prose-form, or at least to evoke by some kind of lexical arrangement, a set of processes that belong in the unconscious mind, in psychic reality, and in the intuitive capacity that both Bion and Meltzer thought of as belonging to the aesthetic level of experience. Poetry, with its combination of words and music, fares much better here, as does music itself and the other arts. Bion, in particular, felt himself to be working at the very edge of language, and he sought a range of different ways to convey his meanings, nowhere more forcefully than in his final trilogy, *A Memoir of the Future* (1975).

Some of the confusion around the term "meaning" in the psychoanalytic field, as opposed to, say, in the linguistic, philosophical, or literary, is that the more ordinary use of it, as in "this means that", is quite the opposite of what Bion and Meltzer were trying to get at. What Bion, like Meltzer and others, was fundamentally interested in was the dawning of meaning in the *unconscious* processes that underlie and make possible what we can see, or know, or consciously symbolize. As Fernando Riolo (2007) so clearly put it: "In this theory, the work of analysis is conceived as a process not only of deciphering symbols, of revealing already existing unconscious meanings, but also of symbol production—of a process for generating thoughts and conferring meaning on experiences that have never been conscious and never been repressed because they have never been 'thought'" (p. 1375). In other words, in this realm we are using the same words but as if they function in different registers. For example, "thinking", "symbol formation", indeed "meaning" itself represent both recognizable, conscious processes and attributions and also the most primitive, unconscious exchanges between self and other, in which Bion's (1962a, pp. 6–7) raw *sensa* of experience can be received and responded to in such a way that slowly a pattern emerges—a sense of coherence, a feeling of continuity, of integration, and, only eventually, of representability. This is different from the ordinary symbolic world where meanings are, according to Bion, pinioned.

In Bion's way of thinking, "meaning" finds a much more internal position. For the generation of this kind of meaning to begin, one has to posit that an interactive process must be occurring, at least some of the time, whereby an infant, or a person of whatever age, may be enabled to engage with, and begin to make sense of, the emotional, indeed passionate, experiences that impinge upon him or her. This model of the mind is one of a thinking and learning apparatus for coming to know oneself as truthfully as possible through the capacity to learn from experience. Such a capacity begins when the earliest and most basic meaningless elements of physical and emotional experience (which Bion terms "beta-elements") are transformed by the receptive inner capacities of the other. How this unconscious process really works is mysterious and is left notional by Bion—it is simply "alpha-function". Thus "meaning", as Meltzer (1986) put it, can be reserved "for the representation of emotional states by the symbols created by alpha-function for use in the construction of dream-thoughts" (p. 10). "It seems likely . . . that the process of alpha-function is always attempting to find representations for our emotional experiences, if we can tolerate them" (p. 11). Elsewhere, Meltzer (1983) makes the process absolutely clear:

> . . . the baby, being in a state of confusion and having emotional experiences about which it cannot think, projects distressed parts of itself into the breast. The mother and her mind (experienced by the baby as the breast), has to perform the function of thinking for the baby. She returns to the baby those disturbed parts of itself in a state that enables thinking, and particularly dreaming, to come into existence. This he called alpha-function. [pp. 42–43]

The evolving "truthfulness"—that is, the true meaning of a person's emotional experience—is what is being sought. That will be, at best, "relative", as Bion states in the Preface to his autobiographical volume *The Long Week-End* (1982). But, like Meltzer and others, he finds himself focusing on the congruences between what he calls "aesthetic" truth and "psychoanalytic" truth (Bion, 1967b, p. 131). By way of clarification, I shall take the early pages of *The Long Week-End* itself as one of the most painful, poignant, and honest expressions of the agonies of a young child who simply cannot make sense of the world he inhabits, either externally or internally. During those first latency years in India under the Raj, Bion desperately sought to allay his confusion and persecutory terror by turning for answers to his well-meaning, busy, and baffled parents. But answers there were none. Though incessantly questioning and searching for explanatory facts and certainties, this little boy never manages to find some-thing that would convey the meaning of his own experience in the form of any felt emotional linkages between himself and others. He describes himself as having almost no capacity for the kind of Nega-tive Capability noted by Keats as that of not *having* to "know", a capacity that Bion was to be so struck by later on in life. He literally could not think: "Think—I couldn't." One has the chilling sense that not only the conscious but even the unconscious thinking processes had become paralysed by meaningless fragments of emotional and physical terror, ones lacking any shape or form, lacking, that is, the wherewithal that could enable them to cohere.

One can only infer that, for whatever personal or circumstantial reasons, Bion's parents were unable to be sufficiently in touch with their child's anxieties and experiences of unbearable frustration to contain them; unable to make them more manageable by register-ing and emotionally "digesting" the states of panic by which their young son was so painfully beset. (As we know, it was these very capacities, of "reverie", and of "alpha-function", which were to become central to Bion's theory of thinking, to his model of how a mind can develop through, initially, the generation of embryonic thought.) One may also infer that he himself was, dispositionally, an exceptionally sensitive and vulnerable boy, forever shifting between intense imaginative depths and utter mental paralysis, crippled, as he says, by guilt, persecution, and incomprehension—states of mind that rushed back to him in all their extraordinary detail and vividness as he recounted them in much later years (Bion, 1982). For instance, with the typical jumbling of prayers and hymns with his own extreme emotional experiences, he recalled, as of yesterday, his feelings towards his parents. "From that day on I hated them both, 'with all my heart and all my soul for ever and ever. Amen'. A few minutes? Seconds? Years?" (1982, p. 11). Where the internal world is concerned time is not linear. These are the catastrophic "internal events" that shape development. The future is contained in time past.

Deeply impressionable as Bion clearly was, his early experiences remained indelibly present within, subsequently to be re-echoed or re-awakened in the various alien, terrifying, and mentally scarring settings in which he subsequently found himself, especially, as described in *The Long Week-End*, at school, and in the army during the First World War. But for the ever-recurring and terror-inducing versions of "Arf Arfer" (a horrifying derivative of the "Our father" of the Lord's Prayer), Kitchener's "Your king and country need you" being thundered from the hoardings might, he writes, have meant "something different". Would he have signed up, effectively to be a boy soldier, but for Arf Arfer? For Arf Arfer belonged to the meaningless, persecutory incomprehensibility of the adult world in general, and especially of his father.

At the very beginning of *The Long Week-End*, Bion recounts a chilling incident. The fervid commitment to hating his parents occurred in the aftermath of a typical scrap with his much hated younger sister, an occasion when, as he puts it, the full force of Arf Arfer descended. Bion's original and typical question had been: "Is golden syrup really gold?" (p. 9). His mother couldn't explain, we are told, and his father went into too much technical detail for the boy to understand.

> The climax came when I asked my question about golden syrup for the "hundredth time". [My father] was very angry. "Wow!" said my sister appreciatively.
>
> Later, when I wanted to know what "persona non grata" meant, I kept it and similar problems to myself. I developed a sixth sense about the "hundredth time" long before I learnt enough mathematics to count up to one hundred. [pp. 9–10]

When he next goes to find his mother she was "busy". "This was another word like 'hundredth time', which it was well to regard as precautionary" (p. 10). Frustrated and hurt, he takes his feelings out on his sister, who has just goaded their mother by deliberately using rude words. With her feet apart Edna had, reportedly, stood before her mother and loudly intoned the word "lavatory" three times. The mother restrains herself from boxing her daughter's ears. Surreptitiously Wilfred obliges instead—one of his many insistent efforts to discharge his own sense of persecution into his sister. Edna screams the place down. Wilfred denies any guilt but

> Arf Arfer—as I knew him from now on—had turned up. Someone else had been "busy" and was therefore also in an explosively unstable condition. My mother was shaking me.
> "I don't know *what* to do with the boy" she said.[1]
> "Let me have him", said my father sternly.
> "Oh God, not that!", I felt wordlessly, mindlessly. [pp. 10–11]

In the face of his son's mental paralysis when being asked the facts, "The storm burst; he turned me bottom up and gave me 'a good beating'. But this I did not know about; I only heard of it as I heard him telling my mother later. He was still angry and his eyes were turned fiercely on me" (p. 11). (This episode, in other words, had been so terrifying that Bion had had to split off any conscious or even physical awareness of the beating as it actually happened.)

Candidly, he speaks of his intolerance of frustration (also to become central to his epistemological theory) and of his perpetual questioning as ruining his parents' experience of reading aloud to him. He cites *Alice in Wonderland*, in particular. He describes his need for answers as blocking the potentially shared experience by precisely the two factors that he was later to identify as blocking the capacity to think and therefore to develop: the omnipotent and omniscient incapacity *not*-to-know which was a consequence of absence of reverie. And yet we have such a vivid sense of why answers were so necessary for this child—quite simply, the belief, which was of course mistaken, that they would allay his unendurable anxiety. But beneath this belief would surely have lain the unconscious hope that answers would offer a shape and a form to otherwise meaningless emotional experience. Bion lacked precisely the kind of "linkage" that he was later to establish as central to the mind's capacity to grow. Embedded in that emotional linkage was to be "meaning".

His own bafflement about a world of puzzles he could not share—for they found no echoing resonance in his parents' minds— was overwhelming at times. Encased in what he described as a "carapace of misery", he tries to work out the meaning of the "Simply City" (of one of his prayers) or the "Electric City" (of the promised toy train) or of that "poor green hill far away" that had no city wall (of the Easter hymn). You would have thought that he might, in those days, rather have taken to Humpty Dumpty's attitude: "Words mean what I choose them to mean. Neither more nor less." Humpty Dumpty, you will remember, relied on omnipotent assertion to manage the experience of his life, being, in fact, very precariously balanced, held together with the thinnest and most fragile possible shell of pseudo-integration. A fledgling self had never hatched, let alone grown up. Bion describes his own vulnerability during his ghastly schooldays when in "my fledgling period, religion provided me with a soft mental down. Such hardness of character that I had was more akin to bits of shell that continued to adhere than to the development of a character that was a 'spine'" (p. 81)—that is, a character that had an endoskeleton and was not reliant for a sense of integration, indeed survival, on an exoskeletal structure. Small wonder, perhaps, that "meaning" became the heart of the matter for his life's work. This was precisely what Bion had so desperately needed in his childhood.

I have been describing guilt and confusion concerning not-knowing and also deriving from emotional experiences not being linked up in such a way that it could create a basis for learning about the self in any meaningful way. Yet one can infer from the account just given that the kind of receptivity and reciprocity that Bion and Meltzer were to formulate required an experiential and theoretical foundation at a much earlier stage than those more familiar to psychoanalytic discourse.

Clinical illustration 1

I have been describing mainly content. But what I am especially interested in is the process whereby, as I said earlier, thought and meaning can be generated and deployed such that learning from experience can occur from the very beginning. It seems to me that some such process took place in a session with 6-year-old Ben. He had been referred to child and adolescent mental health services (CAMHS) for a wide variety of emotional and behavioural disturbances, stemming from his early abused and chaotic years in a number of failed foster placements. Until early November, towards the end of his first year of once-weekly therapy, he had never opened his toy box nor made use of his crayons and paper.

His behaviour in the consulting room was consistently oppositional, avoidant, and largely non-verbal. He kicked and spat, he jumped around the furniture, and he was pretty much set on getting out of the door at all costs. His therapist described him as seeming to have no sense at all of any kind of symbolic register, whether in words, play, drawings, and so on. He nonetheless took to Ben and struggled hard to find some way of engaging with him. Ben tended to stay in his therapist's mind outside clinic hours, we were told, and more recently there was a sense that there was some growing trust between them, although the only apparent manifestation of this was a bit more willingness, after the first summer break, to stay in the room. In retrospect, it may have been that Ben's relief at his therapist still being there for him after so long a break, and at the evidence that he, Ben, had stayed in his mind, had something to do with the shift that I am about to describe.

One early November day, Ben, unprecedentedly, went straight to his box, took out paper and crayons and feverishly traced huge arcs and vertical lines all over the paper, mainly in red, yellow, and orange. He eventually paused, surveyed his work as if with satisfaction, and quietly murmured "fireworks". At that point, his therapist noticed that, amidst the apparent random chaos of scribbles, Ben had managed to leave blank a rectangular space at the top of the page. Without hesitation, although afterwards he could not piece together why, the therapist said that the space seemed to have been left on purpose, perhaps to write the *word* "Fireworks". Ben cast him a look that seemed a combination of gratitude and terror. For the first time, it occurred to the therapist, in an unexpected flash, that Ben might not be able to read or write and that his unacknowledged incapacity to communicate meaningfully was constantly catapulting him into enactments of unbearable states of shame and frustration. This sensitive therapist somehow intuited an emotional readiness on Ben's part to entrust to him not only a primitive and excited experience of movement, colour, and light, but also, more importantly, a gap—the gap that needed to be filled in by a receptive other, with some kind of symbolic representation of the emotional experience. Ben had already, and uniquely, given a verbal representation of his visual achievement, in murmuring "fireworks". His therapist now gave him a written representation as well. It was an almost palpable moment of tension and recognition. Ben's slow recovery seemed to begin from there. He was able to start freeing himself from the chronic and oft-repeated enactments of the story-of-his-life-so-far, one in which he had been stuck from the earliest days. Perhaps the gap was also for Ben's name: "'Fireworks' by Ben". The important thing here was that the therapist had been able to fill a deeply significant gap, not just the one on the paper. In fact, of course, that moment was indicative of a completely hidden process that had surely been going on beneath the surface relationship between himself and his therapist well before that early November day. It was evidence of the beginning of "the thinking principle", to use Keats's term.

Clinical illustration 2

The case of an 8-year-old adopted girl, Susan, seemed to offer a contrasting example. Susan had only recently been referred because of her difficulty in maintaining friends at school, her sense of isolation, and the suggestion that some quite cruel bullying had probably been going on for some time. Her general affect was very flat and two-dimensional, exhibiting what Meltzer (1986) described as a "pallor of meaning" (p. 205). Although adopted into a relatively affluent family, it seemed as though Susan's upbringing had been marked by plenty of material resources but very few emotional ones. Latterly she had been primarily in the care of a nanny with whom she had become, for her, unusually trusting and close. Out of the blue, I was told that this nanny was unexpectedly about to leave the family to go to live in France. On what was to be Susan's last day with this kindly person, she appeared in the consulting room with a badly broken arm. Usually particularly agile and dextrous, Susan had unaccountably and awkwardly fallen over.

The nanny's sudden departure for France was matter-of-factly announced by Susan near the beginning of the following session. Any suggestion, on my part, of sadness or of loss was contemptuously rebuffed. While chatting about the humour of a show recently seen, which was, I gathered, mainly about guillotining and mass execution, a picture was emerging, literally emerging, as Susan sat carefully constructing what she described as her "art". The construction began with three lambs' heads being stuck, collage-fashion, onto another piece of paper. Additions were made—camels' humps, a cow's body, a lion's mane, a horse's hoofs, a mouse's tail, a dog's ears, three elephants' trunks—a "devilish whole" she said, with satisfaction, on completion. She called it a "lamb-cow-camel-horse-devil-mouse-lion-tree-trunk-elephant". The finished piece seemed to represent the experience of a fragmented inner world, one that could not, in effect, be thought about coherently because of an inability either to digest her indigestible experience of loss or to take in the notion of "sadness", raised by me at the beginning of the session—one that threatened to put her in touch with her unbearable feelings. The body's broken limb had to replace feeling states that could not yet be symbolized, nor, therefore, be thought about. The collage was a representation not so much of meaningful experience but precisely that of, as yet, "no-meaning".

What could I have said that would have brought such dissociated phenomena into any kind of meaningful relation in the mind? I found myself silent, struggling, unable to formulate any words that could genuinely engage with Susan's inexpressible and unacknowledgeable pain and also with the gap between that pain and the activities going on in the room. I later reflected on whether my empty-headedness on this occasion might be related to an absence in Susan of much experience of, or expectation as to the availability of, some kind of reverie or containing function, whether as an infant or as a young child (Susan was adopted at 6 weeks).

The juxtaposition of this "creature" with the series of "portraits" that came next confirmed, I thought, some such way of thinking. Five "elephant portraits", as Susan put it, were produced. Different moods were quickly attributed. As one was completed, Susan moved swiftly on to the next. There was no lingering, no looking (especially at the emphasized eyes of each portrait, some but empty and depressed outlines). There was little apparent content, and yet how powerful a caricature of joy, of sadness, of worry, of the shakiness of potential disintegration those portraits seemed to express. This glimpse of the emotional reality that was being so robustly defended against conveyed, all too eloquently, the unspeakable necessity to keep such an area, for the moment at least, thoroughly sequestered, unavailable to thought.

Susan's unspeakable loss brought home to me, with renewed impact, how hard it is to manage the incipient knowledge of our own or another's pain, and also of everything that we put between undergoing that degree of suffering and finding any way of living with the truth of it. Self-deception, evasion, ambition, pedantry, shallowing out, whatever it may be, are so much easier as lived options and yet so impossible to settle for. In a letter written in 1875, George Eliot speaks of the most difficult heroism being that of "the daily conquest of our private demons" (Eliot, 1879).

In Ben's case, it would seem that his therapist's tentative description of his own unexpected and perhaps, as he feared, "unanalytic" suggestion about the label "fireworks" actually betokened a capacity for a particular quality of attention or mindfulness, indeed of "reverie", that had been going on, unnoted, over the previous weeks or months. The unconscious process of alpha-function had, one might surmise, been working on the raw and hitherto unprocessable sensory and meaningless chaos of Ben's early emotional experiences in such a way that they could become available, to both therapist and patient, to be thought about. A kind of mental digestion had been taking place, analogous, as Esther Pelled (2007) suggests, to "the digestive enzymes, which function in the stomach, a container which renders the material arriving in the digestive tract digestible" (p. 1510). Attentively, one might even say "intuitively" (as the word that captures the kind of looking inward that we are describing), this therapist felt some kind of anticipation of an emotion not yet formed, not yet thought. He offered a verbal representation for Ben's pictographic attempt to communicate his experience, the colourful scribbles and arcs being a statement of an unconscious process, already in train, but also a beginning of a capacity to participate in a shared communication, which enabled him increasingly to be able to tolerate the meaning of his experience. Unconscious primitive thoughts and embryonic meaning had been generated. In this session they found their first expression, as mere excitation was transformed into felt emotion.

In a paper that captures well the processes I have been describing, Neville Symington (2007, p. 1409) quotes from one of Picasso's biographers, writing about the act of perception:

> Picasso has always been amazed at the discrepancy between seeing an object and knowing it. Its superficial appearance is to him absurdly inadequate. Seeing is not enough, neither is the aid that the other senses can bring. There are other faculties of the mind which must be brought into play if perception is to lead to understanding. It is somewhere at the point of junction between sensual perception and the deeper regions of the mind that there is a metaphorical inner eye that sees and feels emotionally. (Penrose, 1971, p. 122.)

This kind of internal connection required by mind-building—that is, the investment of emotion with meaning—is itself generative of the particular kind of thought. In turn this is drawn upon for the continuation of this process of thinking and seeing with the "inner eye".

The psychoanalyst Esther Bick (1962) puts it another way:

> One may have to sit with children for a long time completely in the dark about what is going on, until suddenly something comes up from the depth and illuminates it. . . . It imposes on the child analyst a greater dependence on his unconscious to provide him with clues as to the meaning of the child's play and non verbal communications. [p. 330]

While explicitly drawing on "meaning" in the Freudian sense referred to earlier, my feeling is that, here, Esther Bick is referring to precisely the kind of intuition of the prior workings of the metaphorical "inner eye" that I am trying to describe.

So far, what I have been describing has been essentially focused on the post-Kleinian picture of the dynamics of the potential for the emergence of incipient meaning such that thoughts can find a thinker and psychic growth can occur. In a book such as this, we need further to consider the implications, in terms of psychotic states of mind, of a breakdown of this process in infancy. The absence in the potential container of a capacity for alpha-function, and, in the yet-to-be-contained, of a capacity to bear frustration without dismantling the perceptual apparatus itself (to avoid contact with the consequent, unbearable mental pain), is a combination that has a disastrous impact on the individual psyche. In this psychic scenario, an internal catastrophe occurs, which plays havoc with any potentially reciprocal unconscious communication between self and other.

In the cases of Ben, Susan, and, indeed, Bion himself, we encounter, respectively: areas of frantic enactment; the dismantling and somatic localization of potentially meaningful emotional states; and the panicked frustrations of the craved-for certainty, certainty that, it is thought, would assuage the horror of an existence without meaning.

Bion's epistemological theory, which, as we have seen, puts emotion at the heart of meaning, was the outcome of years of work with very disturbed patients, suffering psychotic or schizophrenic illnesses. He observed that frequently, in these states, there was an extreme aversion to emotion itself, together with decimating attacks on any mental interaction or linkage that might make such emotional experience possible. Meaninglessness here is preferable to meaning.

This new way of thinking not only made a huge clinical contribution to the understanding of psychotic states of mind, but was also, as I have been suggesting, a fundamental epistemological contribution to an understanding of the development of the human mind more generally.

At whatever age or stage mental and emotional problems reveal themselves, and under whatever circumstantial pressures, the fault-lines tend to have been in place from the earliest times. As Freud (1933a) so memorably put it:

> If we throw a crystal to the floor, it breaks; but not into haphazard pieces. It comes apart along its lines of cleavage into fragments whose boundaries, though they were invisible, were pre-determined by the crystal's structure. [p. 59]

The post-Kleinian theorists I have been discussing have been elucidating these fault-lines in the structuring of the personality. The situation can hardly be put more clearly than by Edna O'Shaughnessy (2006) whom I shall quote at length:

> . . . we know too that the nature of the baby's "give and take", its reciprocity, interacts with all that comes from the mother. If the experience is "good enough" the baby will feel psychologically contained and internalise the experience. The pieces of his personality will then be held together internally with an orientation to the satisfying object. As we also know, the infant oscillates between such replete, connected states and states of persecution from hunger, discomfort, delays in attention and the like. All are bad objects that threaten him with disintegration, even annihilation, which he fights by getting his good object to come to his aid.
>
> An infant who is not active in this way in both gratification and distress, an infant who is persistently passive has, I believe, suffered, and continues to suffer, some huge adversity. Maybe the mother cannot love him and even hates him, or perhaps she is psychically withdrawn and does not receive or modify his emotional projections and communications. Perhaps he is nearly starving and she does not know it, or it might be that she cannot do other than project her disturbance into him. All these events, as we know, affect the infant grievously, in both specific and different ways. Or it is possible that the infant suffered some intra-uterine trauma or had a difficult birth. Or perhaps he suffers from a constitutionally adverse or overly fragile temperament, and instead of a strong, active push towards life—"the instinct to preserve living substance and join it into ever larger units", that is, the life instinct (Freud, 1930a, p. 118)—the infant has a strong instinct "to dissolve these units", to attack links (Bion's terminology) within himself and without—the death instinct—which in Klein's view is the original inner source of anxiety. Such a temperament has small capacity to want or sustain contact with new experience, and even a normal birth, its journey and the change of life circumstances from being in the womb to being in the world where there is a gap to a new external object, will be intolerable and terrifying. [pp. 154–155]

Psychic development, then, occurs in the fine balance between the baby's disposition and the mother's capacity for reverie. When this balance is not achieved, for whatever reason, the baby is at risk of adverse states of mind and being that may, in extreme cases, border on psychotic dysfunction. Elizabeth Bott Spillius (1994) adds an interesting dimension to this:

The process can, of course, go wrong, either because of the mother's incapacity for reverie or the infant's envy and intolerance of the mother's being able to do what the infant cannot. If the object cannot or will not contain projections—and here the real properties experienced in the external object are extremely important—the individual resorts to increasingly forceful projective identification. Reintrojection is effected with similar force. Through such forceful reintrojection the individual develops an internal object that will not accept projections; that is felt to strip the individual greedily of all the goodness [and potential meaning] the individual takes in; that is omniscient, moralizing, and uninterested in truth and reality testing. With this willfully misunderstanding internal object, the individual identifies, and the stage may be set for psychosis. [p. 343]

Yet latterly at least, Bion focused less on the psychopathology of thought than on the genesis of thought and the factors that impeded it. Psychoanalytically, this was new territory. How did sense data become organized and thus eventually become meaningful? Meltzer's view was that lacking the container–contained fit, people can drift into a life of mindless social adjustment or, more destructively, into a variety of empty and emotionally dishonest states. He elaborates on Bion's concept of "reversal of alpha-function" producing beta-elements with traces of ego and superego. By this he means something like a format for the breakdown of incipient thought: symbol formation commences but meets with such mental pain that it cannibalizes what has begun to form, and the debris of this has shreds of meaning clinging to its fragments. He likens this to the breaking up of a model Lego car. There may be traces of carburettor or whatever, but this is neither a car nor an individual piece of Lego (Meltzer, personal communication).

Such a psychic situation is beautifully conveyed in Bion's (1954) own description of the way in which a schizophrenic patient is both himself split, and also splits his object:

The patient comes into the room, shakes me warmly by the hand, and looking piercingly into my eyes says, "I think the sessions are not for a long while but stop me ever going out". I know from previous experience that this patient has a grievance that the sessions are too few and that they interfere with his free time. He intended to split me by making me give two opposite interpretations at once, and this was shown by his next association when he said, "How does the lift know what to do when I press two buttons at once?" [pp. 24–25]

Here Bion gives clear expression to the way in which apparent meaninglessness can mask what is deeply and inarticulably meaning*ful*. Beneath the evidently psychotic state lies the non-psychotic meaning, if only it can be found.

The place of meaning in post-Kleinian thought is, I believe, closely related to literary understanding—for example, in Shakespeare, in the Romantic poets, and in the novels of George Eliot and others. That is, all cognition/"knowing" is essentially an imaginative experience. By establishing the need to place emotions at the heart of the matter, this way of thinking focuses attention on recognizing the place and value of meaning in human affairs. Indeed, it establishes the absolute import of a meaningful engagement between two minds, first unconsciously then consciously, as a *sine qua non* for any significant emotional growth to occur. And it also stresses the catastrophic consequences of the absence of meaningful communication—the scrambling of mental and perceptual processes.

I hope that these examples will have shown the centrality of the need to draw on our own internal capacities actively to meet with the unconscious thought processes of another mind—this is *not* settling for some kind of passive state of receptivity. There must be an inter*action*. The baby has its mental chaos received, made sense of, and returned to it in a form that has been rendered meaningful through the mother's internal capacity for unconscious symbol formation. This is what alpha-function *is*. It makes things "thinkable", as with dream images. The process involves an inwardness of feeling, something akin to the "passion" of which both Bion and Meltzer speak. These precursors of meaning coalesce in the formulation of interpretations, in the clinician's attempt to express the result of unconscious work in a shape fit for analytic "publication" (the "Fireworks" of Ben's case, or perhaps the replacement, in that instance, of a "gap" with a reassuring "no-gap").

In her definition of imagination, George Eliot (1879) gives a vivid description of the best of her own writing, where the symbolic representations of experience are expressed in decreasingly discursive and more idiosyncratic, active and passionate ways. These words could be taken to express the nature of the kind of psychoanalytic process that I have been exploring in this chapter:

> . . . powerful imagination is not false outward vision, but intense inward representation, and a creative energy constantly fed by susceptibility to the veriest minutiae of experience, which it

reproduces and constructs in fresh and fresh wholes; not the habitual confusion of provable fact with the fictions of fancy and transient inclination, but a breadth of ideal association which informs every material object, every incidental fact with far reaching memories and stored residues of passion, bringing into new light the less obvious relations of human existence. [p. 197]

Note

1. As another mother—cited as an example of lack of a containing capacity in Bion's 1959 paper "Attacks on Linking"—was to do.

CHAPTER THREE

Rigidity and stability in a psychotic patient: some thoughts about obstacles to facing reality in psychotherapy

Margaret Rustin

This chapter is an attempt to think about a particular kind of rigidity in a post-autistic patient, Holly, who lives simultaneously in a psychotic private world and in the world of relationships and shared meanings. I worked with her for nine years, and I discuss here the material of a session some months prior to the end of her therapy. In considering the meaning of our interchange, I wish to distinguish between the changes that have been achieved and the ongoing obsessional ruminative power of the psychotic process. I shall try to consider these from two perspectives: the patient's continuing partial addiction to delusional defensive structures, which she experiences as protective, and the analyst's countertransference difficulties in facing the limitations of the work. Both of us needed to struggle with anxieties about facing reality; the reality of the approaching end of the treatment brought these into clearer focus.

I shall begin with some details of the patient's history. Holly is the first child of a middle-class couple and is now 22 years old. She has a sister three years younger than herself. When I met her parents to explore the possibility of Holly beginning psychotherapy, they told me with the most intense outpouring of feelings about her early life. The pregnancy had gone well, and Mother was waiting with happy anticipation for the arrival of a much-wanted baby. This mood was massively disrupted by what seems to have been a traumatic experience of labour and childbirth, when Mother felt overwhelmed by pain and unsupported and criticized by medical and nursing staff. After a very long labour, Holly was delivered by forceps and was said to be at risk; the parents felt that this was due to oxygen deficiency, but the details are not clear.

The baby was not given to Mother to hold but nursed initially in intensive care. Subsequently, breastfeeding was established and continued for three months. The outstanding memories of the early months which Mother communicated were two. The first of these was the sense that, whatever she did for Holly, the baby cried. She could not satisfy or calm her and felt persecuted by the baby's distress. As in the hospital at the birth, she felt criticized and found wanting as a mother. The baby's misery was not something she could take in and bear, but something she felt hounded by. She told me, with startling and moving honesty, that there was something I needed to know from the start: "You will never understand Holly unless you bear in mind that I hated her. I feel guilty about this, but I really did hate her." She went on to describe a second crucial event, which occurred when she showed the new baby to her own mother. Here I need to include some of the history of Mother's family of origin. She herself is the younger of two sisters. Her older sister, Jane, was a severely autistic child who began to deteriorate markedly at age 12 and has been institutionalized since then. Grandmother looked at the new baby and said "Good heavens! It's Jane." I do not know whether Holly did resemble Jane, but what this remark heralded was a difficult struggle between Mother and Grandmother over how to treat Holly, and it aroused acute terror in Mother that this baby would indeed have a similar history.

Holly cried less after breastfeeding was abandoned, and she found solace in playing on her own for hours at a time. She showed very little interest in her parents or in anyone else. Mother's sense of rejection and uselessness increased. At an early developmental check, deafness was suggested, but this turned out to be a false trail. Mother was terribly worried about Holly and tried to get her anxieties taken seriously. It is hard retrospectively to understand the absence of professional concern about Holly, but what probably played a part was that Mother's own intense anxiety, guilt, and upset was so palpable. She seems to have felt trapped between a kind husband, who tried to reassure her by dwelling on all positive signs in Holly's development, and her own mother, who was committed to the notion that history was repeating itself.

When Holly was 2 years old, the family consulted a child psychiatrist because of her peculiar language development—instead of responding or replying, she would repeat what was said to her. He advised treatment for Mother, and this was arranged. Nearly two years later, on seeing Holly for review, he was very alarmed and said help for Holly was now urgently required. The family was referred to a hospital for psychotic children quite some distance from their home. Holly, Mother, and her younger sister Caroline, aged 1, were admitted together. After a brief time, Mother and Caroline returned home, and Holly remained an inpatient for a further seven months, with weekends at home. She was diagnosed at this time as autistic. I heard many terrifying memories of her time in hospital during her therapy. My overall impression was that there may have been chronic emotional abuse by the staff. Certainly, Holly was driven mad with terror. For years, this revived when approaching any break in therapy, which she would experience as my sending her back to the hospital.

When she returned home, she was placed in a small school for autistic children. Holly herself gained a good deal from this school, and she progressed to be able to manage three and a half days a week in mainstream primary school, with children one year younger than herself by the time she was 11 years old. However, Mother was extremely upset by the attitude of the school staff, who, she felt, viewed mothers as responsible for their children's autistic condition. The active involvement demanded of the parents was thus a torture to her. When the school had to close down, there was a crisis about Holly's future education, since mainstream secondary school full-time was clearly not an option. Eventually she was placed in a school for children with moderate learning difficulties, and when I became involved this placement was at risk, since Holly was very difficult to manage in a class of low-IQ but otherwise fairly ordinary children. As I came to realize, Holly was being subjected to verbal and sexual abuse by the other children and had retreated behind a non-stop flow of psychotic talk, which was driving the teachers mad with frustration.

A brief account of the therapy

When I first began to see Holly, I encountered a completely mad child. She never stopped speaking, but it was possible to detect in the flow of crazy talk that she had hopes of me. She communicated a desperate wish that I might be able to bear her projections and an intense fear that she would be too much for me as she felt she had been for everyone else. I was shocked at the bizarre discrepancy between what she herself memorably described as "verbal diarrhoea"—a flood of words with frequent bodily references and confusion of body parts—and her actual physical presence. She looked uncannily like her mother, with the same hairstyle, and even shared a similar ultra-middle-class tone of voice, though with added decibels and absence of range. She had a sophisticated vocabulary and an additional private language to refer to her "autistic objects" (Tustin, 1981). She always carried with her a bag full of small items to which she gave idiosyncratic meanings—for example, the empty boxes in which camera films arrive. These she called "cylinders", a correct description of their shape, but to her the reference was to faecal stool. For years she held in each hand throughout her sessions one or other of these precious objects, which she said were her protectors. Her awareness of the need for protection of the vulnerable parts of the self seemed an indication of her preconception (Bion, 1962b) of the protective function of a good object and her need to locate such an object. Much later, when she discovered she had bones and thus an internal structure that did not melt when she was flooded with emotion, she was able to leave her bag closed on the table and, eventually, to lie on the couch for her sessions.

She lived a life of terror—she was afraid of falling to pieces, fragmenting in body or mind, and desperately tried to protect herself from a cruelly invasive object that was intent on wounding her. She always wore trousers because she needed the reassurance of layers of clothing over her vagina and anus to prevent hostile assault. For a long time, she insisted that she possessed a penis (she constructed hundreds of phallic models, e.g. of lighthouses or windmills, to represent this). Eventually, she could talk to me about her dread of the "hole", of being and having nothing if she gave up this delusional penis. She could not bear contact with her mother and never used female nouns or pronouns during this period. Eventually she was able to acknowledge her femininity and have a much warmer relationship with her mother.

The most important thread of her therapy was the wish to drive me mad and thus rid herself of the unbearable psychological pain and confusion of feeling mad herself, and the simultaneous hope that I would survive this onslaught. For the first year or so, I spent virtually whole sessions with no idea of what was going on. The one thing I could reliably manage was to maintain the setting of the beginning and end of the session. Sometimes I could observe and describe meaningful sequences and we could have a conversation, but at other times the bombardment of nonsense was so exhausting that I was dulled into virtual inactivity or stale repetition of interpretations that had previously meant something. I felt immured in the atmosphere of a hospital ward for severe schizophrenic patients without the benefit of medication.

When I realized that the point was to test my sanity, Holly became able herself to tell me with flagrant enjoyment that she was trying to drive me potty. An infinite variety of formulations appeared. "I want to drive you crazy, up the wall, round the bend", and so forth. The usual method of doing this was to indulge in verbal masturbation. She quickly understood this idea and spoke about "rubbing with my words". However, this initial understanding did little to abate her frantic activity when she was anxious.

Over time, there was a lessening of her haunting terrors, which she had spent a lifetime avoiding through obsessional rituals and thoughts. One such manoeuvre was to "close the doors in my ears", which she would act out when she did not want to hear what I was saying. As the conviction that I was not to be trusted and would abandon her was replaced by a growing belief in my truthfulness—I seemed not to forget her, to return after holidays as promised, and so on—so the need to close her ears to reality receded. The working-through of these persecutory anxieties in her therapy enabled her to reduce her interminable efforts to control the members of her family. This lessening of omnipotent control allowed a more normal family life to develop. The terror she feels at each tiny step towards relaxing her omnipotence is extreme, and for years the family felt constrained by the fear of evoking her frightening tantrums. She once tried to force me to accept a ring from her for my wedding-ring finger (she felt she could thus bind me to her as if in marriage), and when I did not allow her to do this she was distraught with rage and fear.

When Holly was 18, plans had to be made for her future. She had attended a small school for autistic children. The only local possibility was for her to attend a work-centre for learning disabled adults and to live at home. This was unsuitable, since the family, especially her younger sister, needed some opportunity for ordinary life, and Holly needed support for further social development. Most fortunately, an unusual place was found. An ordered, humane, and down-to-earth institution with good community links offered her a long-term home. It was agreed that Holly could be brought for continuing therapy once a week. Holly could attend further-education classes and be part of a large community, where she became liked and respected. She is on the residents' committee and is not seen as a mad person at all. The contrast between the Holly I know and Holly "the resident" is quite dramatic.

Introduction to the session

This is the last session before an Easter holiday, and it is planned to end the therapy in the summer. This decision was made by me and was something Holly seemed to understand. She seemed able to tolerate it as an idea as long as we could speak about her wish to keep in touch with me from time to time. She felt this link to an external Mrs Rustin would keep alive what she called "the inside Mrs Rustin", with whom she often had conversations. Perhaps it was also felt it would keep alive the importance and reality of her experience of madness, which she had shared so starkly with me. In the last period of a long analysis, there is often a revisiting of old themes.

With Holly, this process has had the effect of making me feel full of doubt about how much has been achieved. Sometimes it seems I have only succeeded in helping her to elaborate fundamentally narcissistic structures, which do enable her to function with less anxiety and in more socially acceptable ways, but which also render her very difficult to reach. The energy required to go on with the struggle to draw her out of her retreat (Steiner, 1993) and into more lively contact with reality is phenomenal. This is true with reference both to her internal reality—her contact with emotional experiences—and to external reality. In the session to be discussed, I attempt to speak to her from outside the ongoing psychotic flow that occupies so much of her mental space.

As a preliminary, I would like to explain some references in the material. First, the people Holly speaks about. Gwen was her key worker when she first went to live away from home. When Gwen became pregnant she left her work, so she represents Holly's anxiety about being abandoned in favour of another baby. Maureen, an older woman of very calm temperament, replaced Gwen. She is extremely important to Holly, who in Maureen discovered the quality of "motherliness". Holly is possessive of Maureen and believes that she and Maureen will always live in the same house. Granny is a sinister figure from the point of view of her prospects for psychic change. In reality, her grandmother indulges Holly's obsessions and tends to blame everyone else for Holly's problems. In Holly's internal world, she is an ally in all her masturbatory phantasies as Granny is always in favour of the avoidance of mental pain. Sally is one of the older women who accompany Holly to the Clinic. The muffin man is a character in a children's song—"Do you know the muffin man?"—and has become a fixture in her imagination, representing the idea of a man who would protect her against the terrifying anxieties aroused by anything female. He is a man who can feed her muffins and sweets and help her to avoid contact with the feeding breast.

Holly uses some private words in this session. I understand the meaning of these as follows:

1. A "shuddle" is a masturbatory phallic object, which has the qualities of a shuttle (always moving), of muddle, of shit, and of shuddering, or shivering with dread.

2. A "wally" in children's slang is someone stupid, out-of-touch—this word is used as a form of abuse of other people. For Holly there are many types of wally, and she is very frightened of them, especially brown or black wallies. She has no doubt heard other children call her a wally.

3. A "wibble" has reference to a nipple-penis confusion, to an intrusive object, and one which is wibbly-wobbly—that is, in permanent motion, unstable and excited.

4. A "hamihocker"—these are the most frightening creatures in Holly's dreams and phantasies. Her perception of the external world used to be full of hamihockers. They now occur only in her dreams. They have a quality of ruthless machines, with an intention to hurt her. They are very complicated conceptions, somewhat like Bion's idea of "bizarre objects" (Bion, 1967b). They are conglomerates of persecutory fragments.

The session

In the corridor on the way to my room Holly said "The shud-dle made me laugh in the toilet. I was worried he would pick me up, and poke my bottom." When she lay on the couch she added, "Gwen was like a shuddle when she was my key-worker." I said she wanted me to know she was frightened. This was the last ses-sion of the term and this is the last holiday before she stops coming to the Clinic to see me. She is worried that I am going to turn into a Gwen-person in her mind who is hurting her by leaving her to look after another baby. "Mm. That's it", Holly said. "Yesterday in the café Jane told me off. The strange man upset me. He took no notice. I said 'Please may I have a cream carton' [repeats *sotto voce*], and he did not listen. I was going on and on. He was Mr Rustin. He was an ignoring Daddy." After a brief pause she added, "I've come to talk to you." I said that she felt that the Daddy aspect of Mrs Rustin was not listening and understanding how hard it was for her not to go on having therapy every week, like more and more cream cartons, but that she hoped that she could talk to me about this problem of not feeling understood. Holly said, "He told me not to ask silly questions. The strange man mocked me." I said that she felt mocked instead of understood, but that she hoped to find in me a Daddy who could think about her endless desire for milk. "That's right."

Holly went on: "Maureen [present key-worker] told me to pack it in. The man made me miserable." I said she was miserable that this was the last session this term. "Maureen made remarks about me." I said she was letting me know that even Maureen gets fed up with her sometimes, and she is worried that I do too. "It was at McDonalds. Maureen made me feel offended. She made me blush. She made me feel pink. She made me red in the face. . . . I love Maureen O'Dowd. In the restaurant I laughed about the yellow potty-boat. The Granny-boat." Holly giggled and imitated a sickly-sweet old lady cooing over a baby. "The black man reminds me of a shuddle." I said she was preferring to be mad now instead of sad. Holly replied, "Yesterday I was kissing the skeleton spoon." I said she was agreeing with me: she wanted to pretend that frightening ideas about dying, and especially about the Mrs Rustin inside her turning into a skeleton, could be turned into an exciting joke. Holly responded, "I like the bottom of a yoghurt carton and saying I'm not a magician." I said that she often tried to believe she was a magician.

Holly then told me she was going home on Sunday. "Tomorrow it will be two nights until I go home, then it will be one night, then it will be Sunday." I said she liked to be clear; it helped her to wait. I explained that she was also thinking about the three sessions she will miss during the holidays, and that she has quite a clear picture of this in her mind and knows that she will then be returning to see me. Holly said, "Yes, I have a clear picture." Pause. "Sally told me to wait." I said she feels everyone is expecting her to be able to wait. Holly said, "I find it very difficult. I had to talk to Maureen." I said she was thinking about two different ideas she has about me. Sometimes she feels I am asking her to manage something that is so difficult for her, to learn how to wait, but she is also pleased to be able to tell me about this and feel understood. Holly said, "I've come to talk to you." I said she was finding it helpful, and Holly replied with real feeling, "Yes, I'm finding it very helpful."

She went on: "The strange man made me sad." I said she was feeling jealous of the Daddy who she felt I would be with during the holiday. "He mocked me." I said she was afraid of an idea of a Daddy who would laugh at her sadness. "He had black eyes. A white nose. He was pale. I was homesick." I said "You felt you had lost the friendly understanding Daddy inside you." "Sally told me to stop demanding. I don't like you taking away my blue spoon. I'm afraid you will throw it away." I asked her to tell me about this spoon. "Maureen gave it to me from Disneyland. It goes purple in the water." I said she felt I would be jealous of something special that she had as a present from Maureen, so jealous that I would want to take it away from her. Holly explained: "Sometimes I bang the spoon on my mouth . . . I've come to talk to you." I talked more about her hope that I could bear her having something that she liked that was nothing to do with me, and how important it was to her to remember that Maureen is fond of her when she knows she made Maureen feel irritated with her in McDonalds.

"I'm going shopping tomorrow. I shall buy Nivea, shampoo, bubble bath. Then next time I shall buy spoons, white ones to play with. I play with them in my hospital. I give myself a tonic. I'm going to buy toothpaste on Saturday." I said she had lots of ideas about how to look after herself during the holiday. "I shall be nice and clean and look pretty."

"I dreamt about the yellow potty in the passageway. The music made me laugh. It reminded me about the muffin man who I held onto when I was little." I said there were different ways of holding on: old ways like in her dream, and new ways like the plans to take care of herself and think about the part of her that wanted to get better and stronger. Holly said, "like holding on to the melamine round the thermos that I got from Mummy." I said she was thinking about her different ways of holding on. Holly continued: "Going back to square one. Using the base of a yoghurt carton as a shuddle. The red pointer I was scared of, digging into me. It was wibble shaped."

I said she understands that her old ways of holding on hurt her, were not good for her. The new ways make her feel better. "In my dream I held the pointer to stop it digging into me. The bird was in my dream. I want to kiss the black bird that flies. I use the yoghurt carton as a pet, a bird, and I kiss it. I think that kissing the yoghurt carton is a joke." I said she was getting into a muddle now. Holly went on: "I use it as a nipple. I kiss it and say 'you said the creed'. It's perfectly natural." This last phrase was uttered in a different voice, and I asked whose voice it was. Holly replied, "I want to trick you." I said the trick was to get things in a muddle. Holly continued: "I use it as food . . . as a hamihocker, as a foot." I said she was showing me that the trick is that a bit of plastic can be made into anything she fancies in her mind, that there is then no difference between anything at all. Holly said, "The noise in the distance reminds me of a creamy white wally. I want to rub on the white wally. But the grey wally scares me." I said she knew that all these imaginary things changed quickly in her mind, that she could not get hold of anything solid to keep herself feeling safe. "They turn into shuddles that frighten me. When Maureen is my key-worker I rub on the shuddle. I want you to do that and be the same as me and get excited." I said she wanted me to be lonely like her, not to have a Daddy to be with, so that I would really understand why she tries to rub away her unhappiness. Holly added: "I want to comfort in my bottom. I kiss the shuddle in my dream. Then it smells of my bottom."

I said we were near the end of the session now and that Holly was trying to distract herself from her sad feelings, and that we both knew that when she filled up her mind with these bottom-thoughts it was hard for her to think of anything else. I wondered if there was anything she could do about it. "Clear it up", she said. I wondered if she wanted to. "I want a window-catch to let the fresh air in. It will take the stale smells away." I said she was tired of the old stuff. Holly said, "I am. I am tired of shit as well. I want fresh air instead of shit. Shit makes me sick. The man of shit kicks me inside me and makes me feel sick. The bottom man. The chocolate man." I said she was telling me that her faeces in her bottom have sometimes felt to her to be just like a penis and this idea made her feel very muddled. "Black men and children remind me of shit." I said she was afraid that I was sick of her and would only remember the messy, muddled Holly. She replied, "I've come to talk to you." I said she now believes I could also keep the other aspects of Holly alive in my mind. "I don't like going back to the shuddle." I said she was afraid of the part of her that creates muddle and terror. "I've got the base of a yoghurt carton at the convent. I find it unbelievable! [shouted]. I want it to be a bosom. I shove it on my mouth."

I said she did not believe it actually was. It was very painful for her when at the end of the session she felt that I was the mother she needed who had good things that could feed her in my mind. Now it was time for us to stop. Holly said goodbye as she left. This is not a very frequent occurrence.

Discussion

This session reveals forces in conflict in Holly's mind. There are moments of contact with creative potential, but also evident is the power of the undertow of her autistic thinking. Keeping her feet on the ground, being grounded in reality, is extremely difficult for her to sustain because it involves so much pain, but in this session there are a number of moments in which she moves towards reality. The many references to colours in Holly's associations might be considered an indication of her growing interest in distinctions and potential transformations, and her growing awareness of ambivalence in contrast to extreme splitting between good and bad. Images of hope in her material have been sustaining to me, and her attacks on her own and my capacity to see something good or beautiful have been the counterpart. She has a recurrent phantasy of taking my eyes out of their sockets so that all I would see would be dark emptiness. This is a terrible but clear description of her attempts to destroy my hope.

At the beginning of the session we are on familiar territory. She resorts to the shuddle to deaden feelings and projects disgust and despair into me, which is intended to obscure from herself and me her anxieties about loss. When this situation is contained, she goes on to speak about her possessiveness and greed. I have a vivid image of a bowlful of little cartons of cream, and of Holly's desire for the whole lot. Also implicit is the problem she has of getting stuck on one particular thing, the need for sameness and repetition. This is a continuing difficulty for her parents, who try to introduce her to new experiences, while Holly demands always to have the same food (scrambled eggs, chocolate pudding, etc.) and the same treats (going for a bus ride to a place where she can go shopping for smooth round objects of some kind) and the same conversation (she bullies her mother to speak the script she provides and Mother needs a lot of courage to deviate from this). Important in contrast to this passion for repeating something comfortingly familiar is the reference to the strange man. This is the strangeness of the unknown, which stimulates in Holly not curiosity and interest, but panic. She projects her harshly critical superego into the man. On this occasion, I did not enquire about the reality of what had happened, but sometimes I have done, and it has become quite clear that Holly knows she is talking to me about what is going on in her mind, and she can distinguish quite well between that and actual events.

The first shift in the direction of tolerating reality is when she tells me that Maureen got fed up. She has previously maintained an unpunctured idealization of Maureen, and I registered a shock of excitement and hope as she dared to acknowledge a change. A second surprise is when I heard the everyday fact that she was in McDonalds. I do not think I have ever before been allowed to know that she has been in a particular public place, a place I, too, could know. We are always stuck together in a world lacking specificity of time or place; I am rarely allowed to share Holly's real life activities, and I felt a thrill to catch this glimpse.

As she struggles with the mixed emotions evoked by Maureen who has shamed her, but whom she loves, an intolerable situation develops. If she were to bring together the shame and the love, she would experience guilt, which she cannot bear, so there is a defensive retreat from this threshold.

But with some support from me, she rejects the magic solution and emerges to locate herself very firmly in time. The clarity of her thinking is impressive, and there is a further development when she describes seeking help from Maureen with the problem of waiting instead of resorting to magic. This is a firm choice for dependence on an external object, which is a real and non-idealized object, and against the narcissistic evasion. This is followed by a real gift to me when she tells me I have been very helpful. Holly has felt that she has been given something good, and she experiences and expresses gratitude. This is linked with being able to stay, for a few moments, in a sad rather than mad state. She is "homesick", in touch with missing something essential to feeling that she has a psychic home. This home is both a place in my mind and her internalized capacity to think about herself, which so often gets destroyed. The problem of mourning all that has been lost in the years of her deluded existence is frequently too much to bear, even briefly.

At this point she is more able to feel her own desire for something outside herself, and she can acknowledge her demandingness. This experience is terrible for her, both because she fears overwhelming a weak object and because she has so little capacity to bear the frustration of not possessing all that she desires. So the insupportable need is projected into me, and Holly investigates, as so often before, whether I can stand such emotion.

When I made the link back to Maureen, I think this revived her hope of having the capacity to sustain her loving feelings for Maureen, but at this moment there is an explosion of envy at the creative work we have been doing together. The retreat to the yellow potty is a vicious attack on the part of herself that can take in caring capacities. The introjective identification has been quite fully experienced, and the bitter disappointment and despair evoked in the dependent part of the self that is now being betrayed is projected wholesale into me.

In such circumstances, it is hard to believe in the reality of what has just been happening. The slough of despond (Bunyan's *Pilgrim's Progress*) sucks one in. I have found that to describe the destruction, which I have done many, many times, is not enough to bring about a shift. This is because Holly is no longer aware of any hope at all, but is entirely in the grip of the counter-system of narcissistic object relations, with all the false friends aiding and abetting this disavowal. So I have learnt to speak about the projected sane part of her.

I believe that my incipient mindless despair mirrors my patient's problem and that it is my task not to become hopeless and confused, but to speak up for the temporarily abandoned, dependent infantile self. The therapist's problem, with a psychotic patient, is often echoed by the way in which parents and teachers get stuck in very low expectations and cannot remain responsive to the possibilities for change and development. Much of my work with Holly's parents has been to try to pull them out of this state of numbed passivity in the face of her destructiveness.

The next part of the session illustrates Holly's struggles with psychic truth. In her dream, there is contact with reality; the bird flying away is a well-known image for us of my freedom to leave her, which hurts and threatens her. She substitutes for this the pet, the autistic object that can be manipulated in any way she wishes. But she is aware that a trick is being played. The trick is the claim that we are exactly the same, in which case she could not miss me, for I would have nothing to offer her. As the trick is elaborated, and everything is reduced to an anal world, depression wells up in me, depression about her vulnerability to psychotic delusion and about the tremendous limitations of my work. At this point, I think I felt that I could not do any more. She had to do something. But I could remind her of her capacity to make such a choice, as I did in quite an explicit way, by asking her if she could do anything about the overwhelming anal stink. The idea of fresh air has been an important discovery for her, as the image of opening a window involves a recognition that the inside world so impregnated with her rubbish can be improved by contact with an alive outside world if she allows it in.

The last minutes of the session are a tremendous struggle between her mad system of confusing, useless, manipulable things (an empty yoghurt carton—she used to have literally dozens of these at any one time) and the quality of contact she can have with a real person. She is fighting for her sanity when she protests about the unbelievable nature of this way of looking at the world, and the fight enables her to say goodbye to me because she has allowed my existence to continue after her departure.

Discussion

I think Holly is always battling with the painfulness of facing what Money-Kyrle (1978) describes as "the facts of life". These are three fundamental truths to be faced if we are to achieve mental stability. There is, first, the difference of the generations—adult and child, analyst and patient do not have the same responsibilities or capacities. Second, the difference of the sexes—male and female can have complementarity, but they are distinct. If we have the physical attributes of one sex, we must lack those of the other. Both these distinctions are a source of mental pain because they give rise to envy and jealousy. Third, there is the reality of the passage of time and of our own mortality.

Holly struggled to deny the difference between herself and her parents: she tried to blot out her mother and to create a world in which there were only Daddy and herself, no mother and no sister. Externally this has greatly changed, but in the transference it has to be confronted again and again. She also tried to maintain that a delusional penis was equivalent to a real one, and that she could be a boy if she wanted. This idea too has given way to a knowledge of her longing for a boyfriend, but as in this session, there is a frequent retreat to equating faeces and penis, and thus denying difference and lack.

But perhaps most central in this final phase of work is the issue of the termination of the treatment. Time is now of the essence. We have had a lot of time together, and its coming to an end raises for both of us problems of mourning. Most urgent for Holly is the question of whether she has enough strength in the sane part of her mind to provide a continuing bulwark against madness. In particular, will she be able to forgive me enough for leaving her to remain in touch with me internally and thus converse with herself? There is the problem of the rage and envy with me when I am not her possession, and the cruelty with which she can take revenge both on me and on the part of herself that is deeply attached to me. Insofar as these destructive processes unravel in our work, her stability is undermined, and she then resorts to obsessional rigidities to prevent a psychotic breakdown. These rigid structures are serviceable in a certain very limited way, but they prevent any real relationships developing, and they have their own fragilities too, since they are impervious to reality and therefore vulnerable when change forces its way into consciousness. So the question is whether she can achieve acknowledgement of the end of our work and mourn both what it has offered her and what it cannot do. For both of us, this involves bearing my limitations. Holly has often seen me close to my wits' end. Distinguishing between what I have failed to understand or bear and what I could and did provide for her can be the basis for her continued internal contact with an imperfect but valuable object. She once told me that the inside Mrs Rustin was telling her in a horrid hissing voice that she would never come back and see her because she was "fed up to the back teeth". Then she acted out unlocking the doors in her ears and announced, "Now I can hear the outside Mrs Rustin." When I asked what she could now hear, she said, "You are talking sense in a kind voice."

For the therapist of such a patient there is also a painful process to face. Therapeutic zeal or omnipotence takes a massive bashing in work of this sort, although the awareness of one's dependence on one's own internal good objects to withstand the loneliness of working with a psychotic patient is both tested and deepened. My patient is still a very fragile and limited person, though she is now a human being who can give pleasure and contribute to life, and receive pleasure through relationships. She remains very vulnerable to external circumstances, which may not always be as supportive as they now are.

I think there has been a tendency for me to experience in the countertransference a reluctance to face the facts of life. The pervasive atmosphere of being in another world, not at all the same as the everyday world, created in such therapies interferes with realistic thinking. I have certainly had the idea that I could never end Holly's treatment but am needed on a life-long basis. The patient's difficulty in internalizing a good object is colluded with once one starts to think that only an external analytic presence can make a difference. One is also in danger of agreeing with the patient's view that such a specially needy baby must never be faced with the reality of there being other babies to consider.

There is a particularly seductive quality in the weird understandings achieved—no one else can make sense of the details of her rituals, for example, and this tends to generate ideas of therapeutic self-importance. There is a pressure to go on elaborating interpretations of the autistic defences and to lose sight of the need to pull the patient out of them. There is a dulling of necessary anger at the cruel waste of her life and the potential waste of the therapist's time. Holly has always made it difficult for me to mobilize my justified anger with her because she experiences resistance to her manoeuvres as physical and mental assault, and because she then attempts to twist the straight talking into a sadomasochistic exchange.

The setting for psychoanalytic therapy, with its emphasis on structured reliability, is a double-edged matter with such patients—the regular sessions can become part of the patient's organized evasion of life unless one is very attentive. From this point of view, it is crucial that the setting of an analysis is understood to include its termination. Working towards ending has helped me to reflect more constructively on ways in which I have sometimes been co-opted to maintain a psychotic equilibrium rather than consistently challenging it.

CHAPTER FOUR

Forms of *"folie-à-deux"* in the couple relationship

James Fisher

In this chapter I want to consider some aspects of the theoretical structure underpinning my view of psychoanalytic therapy with couples, which I have described in terms of a struggle to emerge from narcissism and move towards marriage (Fisher, 1999). In working with couples, it may appear to be overstating the challenge we face as therapists to talk in terms of the psychiatric diagnosis of a *folie-à-deux*. The phenomenon of a shared psychosis is a well-known, although relatively rare, psychiatric condition. However, I want to suggest that, from a psychoanalytic perspective, getting to grips with pockets or extended moments of shared psychotic states constitutes the heart of the challenge in psychoanalytic therapy with couples. A couple's capacity to recognize and to find their way out of such extended moments is a mark of the developmental process I am describing as emerging from narcissism and moving towards marriage.

This chapter is not concerned with those couples in which one partner has been diagnosed with some form of a psychotic condition. Therapeutic work with such patients and their partners is an important mode of couple therapy, in which the dynamics I discuss in this chapter may play a critical role. However, such couples also present challenges that I do not address here.

45

The theoretical framework I am exploring is based on a view of narcissism in which the expression *narcissistic object relating* is not the oxymoron it might appear to be in a different approach. That is, in my view, narcissism is not an object-less state but, rather, a particular way of relating.

In reconsidering the idea of narcissism as a form of relating, I want to take us back to the myth from which the term derives—that is, the story of Echo and Narcissus. Here we encounter an intriguing portrait of a familiar but disturbing dilemma. How is it that the choice of a beloved, what we typically picture as a *falling-in-love*, can turn out to be more like a demand that two become one? While the picture of "two becoming one" may sometimes reflect the experience of deeply emotional moments in which each feels genuinely at one with the thoughts, wishes, and desires of the other, it can also reflect the unconscious expectation, often leading to a conscious demand, that the Other should reflect my thoughts, wishes, and desires. The myth of Narcissus faces us with the latter uncomfortable possibility, where the longing for the beloved is permeated with an unconscious expectation that the beloved become my mirror image, to save me from having to be aware of unwelcome difference.

The myth of Narcissus portrays something that echoes through our own personal experiences, as well as what we experience in our consulting rooms. Certain poets have articulated a wish for two to become one that I think we would all recognize. Consider, for example, Eliot's poetic dedication of his last play, *The Elder Statesman* (1969), to his second wife, Valerie. With her he appears to have found the contentment and happiness that he had found so elusive in his first marriage. Eliot describes the shared experience of the lovers as they breathe in "unison", a couple who think the same thoughts and babble the same speech "without the need of speech", "without the need of meaning".

Eliot's poetic description of what it is like to fall in love, with its moments of passion marked by a sense of oneness, offers us a memorable picture of one dimension of the intimacy we imagine at the heart of marriage. A breathing in unison, a thinking the same thoughts without need of speech—these and other such moments mark the passion that is so precious in the experience of falling in love and in the subsequent moments in which two people discover, and rediscover, their capacity to be in love as they make a life together.

However, this ideal oneness becomes problematic when it is seen as *defining* the relationship. Though it is an essential moment in the experience of being in love, this can only be so when it is one pole of a *dialectic* moving between that sense of oneness and moments of awakening to the reality of separateness. I am picturing marriage as a state in which the experience of otherness is not the antithesis of the experience of oneness *but, rather, a necessary complement to it.*

We might say that at either pole of this state of marriage there is an experience in which either the sense of oneness or the sense of otherness can be felt as absolute. Thus, we can have, on the one hand, a narcissistic demand that the Other be the same, identical, with no difference tolerated. And, on the other hand, there can be an experience of the Other as so completely other as to be alien.

In *The Uninvited Guest* (Fisher, 1999), I suggested that the oscillating tension of this dialectic, adapting one of Bion's well-known notations, could be pictured as *"narcissism ↔ marriage"*. However, since we are characterizing marriage as a state in which there is a developing, and increasingly enriching, oscillating tension between an experience of oneness with the partner and an experience of his/her otherness, we might want to alter the notation by which we picture this dynamic. That is, we could picture marriage as the state in which not only is it possible to tolerate *"narcissism ↔ alienation"*, it is also possible to thrive in this dialectical drama as there is an almost continuous emotional movement between these polar experiences.

At first glance, it might seem that, just as the term *narcissism* is too extreme a term for the sense of oneness that Eliot pictures, so the term *alienation* exaggerates the sense of otherness one experiences in marriage. Those who have worked in therapy with couples, and even those who have closely observed not only the marriages of others but also their own, will not be startled by the idea of narcissism as the relation between two people enacting the phantasy of two being one, or by the idea of alienation as the relation between two people that appears to enact a phantasy that irreconcilable differences mean that the other is literally an alien.

This chapter will proceed from a brief consideration of the Narcissus myth itself to some reflections on a kind of identification which is more like mimicry or imitation. This kind of relation can be pictured as a "being stuck to the Other" and consequently described as a form of *adhesive identification*.[1] Following this, I discuss the notion of "intrusive projection" as a kind of identification, a concept that has been the pivot for much of the psychoanalytic thinking about disturbed couple relations. Complex permutations of these forms of narcissistic relating lead to the most disturbed couple patterns where two people can live neither together nor apart. Finally, I want to look at the "living hell" of sadomasochistic *folie-à-deux* relationships, which have the quality of what Donald Meltzer (1992) terms a "claustrum".

These disturbing patterns mean that psychoanalytic therapy with couples can be a formidable enterprise. Yet some couples may respond to a psychoanalytic approach that addresses itself to challenging and unravelling these interlocking narcissistic defences. A psychoanalytic understanding allows us to appreciate how intransigent these patterns can be, reflecting as they do, albeit in very exaggerated form, a universal desire and persistent struggle to achieve intimacy.

Narcissus: a longing for the other and a hatred of separation

Freud said he borrowed the term "narcissism" from Havelock Ellis's discussion of the myth of Narcissus and Echo, although he credits Paul Näcke with coining this term (Freud, 1905d, p. 218, fn. 3). Subsequently the word has found a place in the vocabulary of today far beyond the technical meaning it has in psychoanalytic theory. It will be instructive to return for a moment to the myth of Narcissus itself. I am calling it a "myth", although Robert Graves makes an interesting distinction by referring to it as a "sentimental fable" rather than what he called a "true myth", because it lacked a connection with public ritual, which for Graves is essential to "true myths" (Graves, 1955, p. 12).

This myth gives representation to one of the most fundamental human dilemmas and, in that sense, is universal. As such, it has taken on a critical importance in contemporary psychoanalytic clinical theory, particularly in the object relations tradition influenced by Bion, and complementing the Oedipus myth. In fact, the two myths are, I suggest, intimately related and, perhaps, even interdependent.

At the heart of the story of Narcissus and Echo, we have the picture of an attractive young man with whom, as Graves has it, "anyone might excusably have fallen in love". Having heartlessly rejected many suitors of both sexes, including the nymph Echo, Narcissus finally falls in love with someone he sees as he gazes into a still pool, apparently unaware, as we might imagine an infant might be, that he was looking at his own reflected image. In the end, Narcissus is consumed by his unrequited longing, distraught at possessing and yet not possessing this beautiful young man who awakens in him a passion he cannot bear. Echo, who has been condemned by Hera to be unable to use her own voice except to repeat the words of others, can only watch and repeat his final cry of "Alas!, Alas!" as he plunges a dagger into his breast (Graves, 1955, pp. 286–288).

Surely in this myth we see Narcissus as *longing for* someone he sees as the Other, not *wanting to be* the Other. We might say that the mystery of the state of mind of Narcissus in this myth is like the mystery of the state of mind of Oedipus. Does Oedipus know that this desirable woman whom he would marry is in fact his mother? Does Narcissus know that this beautiful young man for whom he longs is in fact his own reflection?

We have some idea why Oedipus would not want to know what he appears not to know, as we understand the wish to deny the reality of the divide between the generations. At one level the story of Oedipus is the drama of the little boy who wants to be his father's equal. Hating his smallness and inadequacy, his vulnerability and dependence, he unconsciously achieves his wish to be identical with his father. Unnoticed, apparently by him or anyone else, he takes his father's place. One uncomfortable aspect of the awareness of the difference between the generations is that it marks the reality of procreation, that we are determined by forces outside our own control: we are the *outcome* of our parents' intercourse. We enter the world helpless, life itself continuing to be precarious but for those on whom we depend *absolutely*.

This familiar story is complex enough, but we must ask what it is about dependence on those who give us life that makes it emotionally so difficult to tolerate. Through an almost incomprehensibly arduous reorienting of our framework of assumptions, Bion has shown that apart from the difficulties of managing the experience of frustration there is a problem that is "meta" to this—

that is, the difficulty in acknowledging emotional experience itself (see, e.g., Bion, 1962a). Dependence can lead to either frustration or satisfaction, both of which can be felt to be unbearable. We know that frustration is linked with mental pain, but it is only with difficulty that we have come to acknowledge Melanie Klein's insight that satisfaction can also lead to the mental pain of envy. In *The Apprehension of Beauty* (Meltzer & Williams, 1988), the aesthetic impact of the primal object on which we are dependent, the mother, is itself an overwhelming experience, as if beauty itself were too painful to look at.

If we were to approach the story of Narcissus in the spirit of Bion and Meltzer, what might we imagine that he wishes to deny? Why would he harbour an unconscious ambition to be the equal of the one for whom he longs, equal in the sense of "identical to"? Or could it be said that unconsciously he wants this other to be a version of himself? It could be said that here we might be reading our own assumptions about narcissism as a kind of infatuation with oneself into the myth. But if we suppose that a myth like this carries an unconscious wisdom in the very shape of the story and the images, then it seems reasonable to take seriously the picture of the *longing for the Other* at the heart of the story.

The second great reality that we find so unbearable, the difference between the sexes, carries a universal meaning quite apart from questions of heterosexuality and homosexuality in a conventional sense. Like the difference between the generations, the difference between the sexes is a *locus* of both the unbearable beauty of and the unbearable dependency on an *Other*. Awareness of these differences brings an emotional experience the reality of which is difficult to tolerate. Where it cannot be tolerated it is attacked and undermined.

Compare this picture with the distinction about the "direction" of identification made by Laplanche and Pontalis in their discussion of this most critical of concepts in psychoanalysis:

> In everyday usage, identification in this last sense [identification of oneself with] overlaps a whole group of psychological concepts—e.g. imitation, *Einfühlung* (empathy), sympathy, mental contagion, projection, etc.
>
>   It has been suggested for the sake of clarity that a distinction be drawn within this field, according to the direction in which

identification operates, between an identification that is *hetero-pathic* (Scheler) and *centripetal* (Wallon), where the subject identifies his own self with the other, and an *idiopathic* and *centrifugal* variety in which the subject identifies the other with himself. Finally, in cases where both of these tendencies are present at once, we are said to be dealing with a more complex form of identification, one which is sometimes invoked to account for the constitution of a "we". [Laplanche & Pontalis, 1973, p. 206]

Echo presents us with an image of someone condemned to being able to give voice only to the words of others, while Narcissus offers us an image of someone who seems able to love only an Other who is a reflection of himself. They represent the "heteropathic" and "idiopathic" directions of identifying with an Other. What I want to call attention to is the fact that these are pictures of "object-relating", albeit object-relating of a peculiar kind. This corresponds with Freud's first use of the term "narcissism" to account for homosexual object-choice:

[They] pass through a phase of very intense but short-lived fixation to a woman (usually their mother), and, after leaving this behind, they identify themselves with a woman and take *themselves* as their sexual object. That is to say, proceeding from a basis of narcissism, they look for a young man who resembles themselves and whom *they* may love as their mother loved *them*. [Freud, 1905d, p. 145, n. 1 (added 1910)]

Note that in this picture Freud includes identifications in both directions in reference to the self–Other link. The object chosen resembles the self, while the self in this relationship resembles the mother whose love the self seeks to re-create. Whatever one makes of this as a description of the unconscious dynamics of same-gender object-choice, it is a description of narcissistic object-choice. It retains the formal structure of a genuine object relationship, in that we have both lover and beloved. To put it into the form of a simple children's drama, it is as if I were to say to you,

I'll teach you about true love. You be me and I'll be my mother. I will love you (playing me) as you (remember, that's really me played by you) should be loved, something I know about since I know how I should be loved. And you will love me (playing my mother) as I (of course, I mean my mother) should be loved, again something I know about since I loved my mother, and I am (playing) my mother and you are (playing) me.

As director, producer, scriptwriter, and one of the two actors in this scenario, mine is the only authentic voice, the only point of view. Constructed in this way, there is no need for an imaginative attempt to picture anyone else's experience or point of view. Creative imagination, in the sense of my needing to imagine someone else's point of view, is not necessary because the only experience and point of view represented is mine, and that I can know, or believe I know, with absolute certainty.

When we encounter certainty in our patients, or indeed in ourselves, about the experience, the feelings, beliefs, points of view, of the Other, we must consider the function of a need for certainty. The person who is subjectively so certain about something *apparently outside* him/herself is in one sense right in that certainty, at least insofar as one can be certain what one feels, thinks, or believes. However, if one is so *certain* about something in the mind of another, this certainty can only derive from projection—for one can only be certain about what is in one's own mind, here misattributing this mental content to another instead of to oneself. In this situation, the reality of the "Other" is ignored or denied.

The distinction that characterizes relating to a genuine Other is the moment "when an object can be given its freedom to come and go as it will", as Meltzer puts it so evocatively (Meltzer, 1978b, p. 468). In this brief but remarkably evocative paper, "A Note on Introjective Processes", Meltzer links this capacity to relinquish the need to control one's objects with a process that results in a different kind of identification: introjective identification. I believe that this concept is at the heart of an understanding of what Klein captures in her concept of the depressive position (Klein, 1935, 1940), which Britton (1989) elaborated as "triangular space". It is a remarkable idea, and an even more remarkable experience when one discovers in one's patients, or more importantly in oneself, the capacity to allow the object "its freedom to come and go as it will". This is surely one of the aims of the psychoanalytic process and thus a primary criterion for determining when to bring the formal phase of therapy with couples to an end.

Imitation and adhesive identification

To allow one's external objects their freedom requires a relationship with one's internal objects in which their freedom is a genuine possibility, something that narcissistic defensive structures necessarily prevent.

I want to look more closely now at a form of narcissistic relating that makes use of clinging, imitative attachment. I previously explored a vivid picture of narcissistic relating to be found in T. S. Eliot's *The Cocktail Party* where Eliot suggests the other side of the experience of "two becoming one" (Fisher, 1999). The character Edward despairs of the relationship with his wife, Lavinia, in that he "cannot live without her" because, as he puts it, "she has made me incapable of having any existence of my own" (Eliot, 1950, p. 101).

In their description of the phenomenology of a form of narcissistic identification characterized by this "being stuck to the Other", Bick (1968) and Meltzer coined the term "adhesive identification". Meltzer (1967, p. 14) suggests that "intolerance to separation can be said to exist when there is present an absolute dependence on an external object in order to maintain integration". He gives a graphic description of this serious psychopathology in children:

> This can be seen in autistic and schizophrenic children in whom the need for physical contact, or constant attention, or to be held in contact by constant verbalisation, reveals the absence of the psychic equivalent of the skin. [Meltzer, 1967, p 14]

It is important to keep in mind that in this kind of relating there is no emotional experience of a genuine, external Other. In this case, the external object functions as virtually a *part of the self*, a containing *skin*, so to speak, that holds the self together.

Edward gives voice to this sense of the Other, not as a genuine Other, but instead functioning as a "second skin". Without his wife, he says, he "began to dissolve", "to cease to exist".

It is this form of identification that plays a significant role in the disturbed relationships we see in the couples who turn to us for therapy, in some ways as significant as the role played by the now more familiar (and certainly more discussed) process of projective identification. Little attention has been paid to this adhesive form of identification in the literature of psychoanalytic psychotherapy with couples, and yet it can help us to understand some of the dynamics we see so often in this work.

In his description of the phenomenon of adhesive identification, Meltzer directs attention to an important observation. Some children and adults seemed to lack a sense of internal space and, instead, created the impression of "two-dimensionality". Objects are related to primarily through contact or lack of contact. He suggests that a "two-dimensional" self would, in the language of Bion, "have no means for distinguishing between an absent good-object and the presence of a persecuting absent-object" (Meltzer, Bremner, Hoxter, Weddell, & Wittenberg, 1975, p. 225).

Related to this would be the failure to distinguish between a present object "with a mind of its own", unwilling (or unable) to do what was wanted or needed by this self, and a persecuting absent-object. But even though an *independent* object may feel particularly persecuting, it may be clung to, for in desperate situations *any* contact is preferable to no contact at all.

Gaddini (1969) argues that, in these adhesive states, the aim of imitation "seems to be that of re-establishing in a magical and omnipotent way the fusion of self with object" (p. 21). But it is important to note that this state of mind is linked with the obverse state. On the one hand, separation anxieties are countered by being "stuck to" or "fused with" the object in unconscious phantasy, but on the other, there is no door that can be closed to prevent this fusion from happening.

This can be seen more clearly when we consider what constitutes the capacity for internal space—that is, for three-dimensionality. The move from a two- to a three-dimensional structure of mental functioning is linked not only with an awareness of orifices but, more importantly, with the struggle to guard or close those orifices. This is experienced firstly in the encounter with an object that can protect itself against intrusion, closing its orifices against an intrusive attempt to penetrate, an experience that can lead to the development of a similar capacity in the self.

> The potentiality of a space, and thus the potentiality of a container, can only be realized once a sphincter-function has become effective His material [the child patient "Barry" under discussion] shows with particular clarity that the capacity of the

object [Barry's therapist] to protect and thus to control its own orifices is a precondition for the self to make a move in that direction, of continence as well as of resistance to aggressive penetration. [Meltzer et al., 1975, p. 226]

It often happens in therapy with a couple that one finds one or both partners in a state of mind that in some ways resembles that of those young patients so vividly described in *Explorations in Autism*, especially in this characteristic lack of a "skin", some door that can be closed, so that one does not feel defined by the Other. And this is true both for the self and for the self's objects. If my object cannot preserve its difference in the face of my passionate intrusion, how can I be myself without the Other becoming my reflection? If I cannot preserve my difference in the face of the Other's passion, how can I avoid becoming only a reflection of my object, or my object's desires?

One might be tempted to picture adhesive identification as a defence against separation anxieties, a way of remaining "stuck to" an object that is threatening to disappear. But what one sees in couples in therapy is a picture of what it is like to be "successfully stuck" to the object or to have the object "stuck to" oneself. This is one version of the sadomasochistic *folie-à-deux* relationship. This brief description of one couple is typical of such an "adhesive hell":

Mr and Mrs M both protested desperately against the feeling that the other "defined" them. Although this is one of the most common complaints from couples in therapy, there was a special intensity in the way Mrs M would interrupt whenever Mr M described, from his point of view, something about her, what she had said, or done, or meant. Whenever I or my co-therapist would comment that of course he was speaking from "his point of view", we discovered through many painful exchanges that these words had no emotional meaning for her. Especially in moments of intense emotions, the notion of "a point of view" was a meaningless abstraction for her. It was as if she were open and exposed, with no adequate protection from what he said.

At times she would literally put her hands over her ears as if to close those orifices to block out his words. And there was one particularly shocking time when she actually began to scream, pleading for him to stop talking, as if his words were painful missiles assaulting her through her ears. It was not an aggressive, hostile scream, but the scream of someone in the kind of intense pain caused by a high-pitched piercing sound.

It was also gradually possible to talk with her about her belief that my co-therapist and I were as open and exposed to his omnipotent, defining words as she was. What he said at those moments seemed to her to have the capacity to define what was real for us. Clearly she could not entertain with any emotional conviction the possibility that we might be able to listen carefully and sympathetically to him, while thinking for ourselves and having our own point of view. His words simply were an "aggressive penetration", although "penetration" perhaps gives the wrong impression. It was not as if his words got inside her, but that they simply were her.

But I do not mean to give the impression that she was alone in this experience of having no idea of the concept of "a point of view". If her version of this relationship had an almost hysterical quality, an endless flow of words defining him to stop him from defining her, his version had an empty, passive quality. The only way he could keep her from defining him was to absent himself, either physically or emotionally. He was able in the session to act almost as if he were a robot, puzzled about what it was that she wanted of him and trying to feel whatever it was that she was wanting him to feel.

If anything it was even harder for him to entertain the possibility that he might listen to her without being defined by her. He never quite understood what was expected of him, only that nothing he did satisfied her. Yet it was so obvious to him that she must be right about all this "emotional stuff" that his only question was how to avoid igniting her touch paper. "Keep a low profile" was his motto, since he could not begin to understand "what she was on about". You can imagine that his capacity, as she put it, to "blank her", left her infuriated, while he stared at her uncomprehendingly when she erupted in desperation. Often at such moments he would catch my eye or that of my co-therapist, surreptitiously raising his eyebrows and tilting his head in a gesture of contempt. It never occurred to him that, not only was his contempt not hidden, but his "blankness" conveyed his contempt in a most sadistic way.

When he did make an effort to listen and to accommodate her and her feelings—which he felt was most of the time—his role seemed to be to decipher what he was supposed to do, or say, or, insofar as he understood what it meant, to feel. He felt that when his attempt at compliance was successful, things went along reasonably well between them. This would last, he would tell us ruefully, until in a moment of forgetfulness he would say something from his own "point of view", and the explosive cycle would start all over again. For the most part, however, his watchful caution prevailed, as he chose his words carefully, saying what he thought she wanted to hear.

This makes for an interesting comparison with the exchange between Edward and Lavinia in *The Cocktail Party* concerning his passivity, a passivity to which she forms the perfect complement (Eliot, 1950, pp. 92–93, I.3.279–298). Edward's repeated "fitting in" with his wife, his "giving in" to her, mirrored by her "giving in" to him, conveys a humorous and all-too-familiar exchange, repeated almost daily by couples in consulting rooms and so reminds us of the ordinariness of these dynamics. When we discuss severe psychopathologies, pockets of autism, and narcissistic object-relating, we can forget this ordinariness. Although we find that the scene with Edward and Lavinia makes us laugh, perhaps wryly, it is difficult, even impossible, to find anything humorous in the scene with Mr and Mrs M. Instead of humour, the presence of which might mark the possibility of some emotional distance, the room is at times electric with tension, as his passivity sets off a firestorm in her.

In order to develop a sense of humour about their dilemma, these couples would have to be in a very different state of mind. We might hope that couples in therapy gain opportunities to stand back and see themselves the way the audience can see Edward and Lavinia. However, to do that requires a sense of internal space, which in turn requires a capacity to observe oneself and the theatre of one's internal world. When Edward says he doesn't mind where they go on their honeymoon, and thinks he means it as a compliment, or when Mr M watches his words in a desperate attempt to say and be just what he thinks his wife wants, there seems to be no sense of space in either of them. For each, there is only a relationship, or, better, a "connection", with an Other to which he can more or less happily adapt and attach himself—or not.

In couples where each partner has this kind of adhesive connection with the Other, the resulting relationship can be described as a kind of adhesive *folie-à-deux*. In fact, some of the most intractable couple dramas that we see often in our consulting rooms are those in which there is a mixture of this two-dimensional adhesive *folie-à-deux* with aspects of more three-dimensional intrusive projections. These underlying dynamics constitute a sadomasochistic *folie-à-deux*.

The claustrum of intrusive projections

In this section I would like to think further about the complex phenomena of projective identification. Bion's concept of *container–contained* has so coloured our use of the notion of projective identification that it has become common in some quarters to assume that this unconscious phantasy of splitting off parts of the self and projecting them has *as its aim* the wish to communicate. But there can be communication only if the person acting as a "container" can bear to be the recipient of the disturbing projections and still sustain an ability to think about the experience. The more intrusive the projections, the more difficult it becomes to achieve and maintain this state. The *identificatory* aspects concern transformations of the self—for example, grandiosity, psychotic depressive states, hypochondria, confusional states. Meltzer's contribution to our understanding of the phenomenon of these intrusive processes is particularly relevant to those couple relationships where intrusive projection dominates the clinical picture.

The so-called projective aspects concern the nature of the experiences when *inside* that phantasy world into which one has intruded, the "claustrophobic" aspects. What is it like in there? What are the unconscious phantasies about the inside of the object into which the self or part of the self has been projected? These projective aspects of the intrusiveness create a major problem for the recipient of the projections, in that it is difficult, sometimes virtually impossible, to escape being drawn into the "claustrum".

Meltzer has proposed a modification of our terminology, moving from a *quantitative* distinction in terms like "massive" projective identification to a *qualitative* distinction. Thus, he proposes some definitions that are helpful to consider, although they have not entered the mainstream of psychoanalytic discourse:

> *Projective identification*—the unconscious phantasy implementing the non-lexical aspects of language and behaviour, aimed at communication rather than action (Bion)
>
> *Intrusive identification*—the unconscious omnipotent phantasy, mechanism of defence (Melanie Klein).
>
> *Claustrum*—the inside of the object penetrated by intrusive identification.
>
> *Container*—the inside of the object receptive of projective identification. [Meltzer, 1986, p. 69]

For our purposes here, I will assume that projections into external objects fundamentally depend on projective processes that are taking place internally with internal objects. The critical "arena" for our understanding of these intrusive projections is the *interior of internal objects*, specifically the internal mother. Meltzer uses the term "geography" to describe this "interior", emphasizing the spatial quality of experience in unconscious phantasy—that is, that the "internal world" and "internal objects" necessarily have a psychic reality that is "spatial".[2] Rosenfeld (1987a) recognized phantasies of living in an unreal world that has qualities of being the inside of an object, the mother (pp. 168–169). Steiner (1993) makes a similar point: "Sometimes it is possible to get information about deeper phantasies in which psychic retreats appear as spaces inside objects or part-objects. There may be phantasies of retreating to the mother's womb, anus, or breast, sometimes experienced as a desirable but forbidden place" (p. 8). Steiner also reminds us of Rey's discussion of the "claustro-agoraphobic" dilemma and the "marsupial space" (Steiner, 1993, pp. 52–53).

The geography that is *central*, therefore, to the "phantasy geography" of the self is the geography of the internal regions, the "compartments" of the internal mother. The view of the inside of the internal mother (and, critically, the means by which this view is arrived at) forms a template for all relationships. Thus, in his exploration of the "projective" aspects of projective identification, Meltzer is suggesting that the *mode* of entry *in phantasy* into the mother's body determines the quality of the experience, the phantasy of the nature of what is found *inside her body*. This contrasts with the respect for the mother as an Other who is known *only* through imagination rather than through omnipotent intrusion in phantasy.

This omnipotent "knowledge" of the internal mother—and consequently, because it is a "template" for important relationships, of the "interior" of the Other in all intimate relationships—creates the sense of living, through intrusive identification, in the *claustrum*. When the part of the personality ensconced in the claustrum gains control of consciousness, marked changes occur:

> . . . the experience of the outside world becomes dominated by the claustrophobic atmosphere, meaning that the person, in whatever situation he finds himself, feels trapped. Job, marriage, holiday, on trains, buses or lifts, in personal or casual relations, in restaurants or theatres—in every area there is a tangible atmosphere of catastrophe immanent and "No Exit" (Sartre). [Meltzer, 1992, p. 119]

The reference to Sartre's play *No Exit* has particular relevance to the above discussion of *The Cocktail Party*, for what Eliot provides in this play is a picture of the content of Sartre's "hell is [that is] other people". When Edward cries out that "hell is oneself / the others merely projections", this could be understood as representing the experience of being trapped in a *claustrum*. A question here arises as to how describing Edward's dilemma in this way adds anything to our understanding of him, or of the relationship between him and Lavinia, or for that matter, that between him and Celia.

As I understand it, Meltzer is suggesting a correlation between the experience of the outside world as dominated by a "claustrophobic atmosphere" and the hypothesis of a deeply unconscious process of intrusive identification. We are often presented in sessions with couples with "enacted dreams", which take the form of narrated stories about their experiences. The therapists' job here is to infer or re-create the unconscious phantasies that underlie and are expressed in these stories which can so vividly convey the couple's experience of each other and of their shared world. I propose, then, that what we primarily observe in these more disturbed situations is the claustrophobic atmosphere of their shared world, and that what underlies this is intrusive identification.

With a fictional character like Edward in *The Cocktail Party*, we have no access to any unconscious phantasies, whether of intrusive identification or whatever. Similarly, we have no reliable access to Eliot's state of mind as he created this character and this dialogue.

But this is the same situation that we find ourselves in with couples in therapy. Here, too, we are limited to what we observe, and we do well to let modesty rule our speculations about the underlying unconscious processes. *But* we are at liberty to let our imagination roam over the text (or the material that couples present to us). When we choose to share some of our imaginings with our couples, we aim to stimulate their own capacity for curiosity and imagination, which in turn may create a sense of space between them and their different versions of shared experiences.

A major characteristic of intrusive projections is that, necessarily, they leave no space for the imagination. This allows us to differentiate between a genuine intimacy with the Other and a "pseudo-intimacy" that is actually a narcissistic form of relating. The former is based on the reality that the Other is known *only* from the outside. The latter is based on the phantasy of getting *inside* the Other. Seen from the "outside"—that is, through the use of imagination—the primary quality of this region of the internal mother is richness, understanding, and generosity. However, when "experienced" from the inside and influenced by the motives of intrusion, a very different picture emerges:

> Generosity becomes quid pro quo, receptiveness becomes inveiglement, reciprocity becomes collusion, understanding becomes penetration of secrets, knowledge becomes information. . . . [Meltzer, 1992, pp. 72–73]

The *imaginative knowing* of the Other, inspired by an imaginative knowing of the internal mother, is constructed out of elements of experience of the external world, respecting the privacy of the interior of the mother. It is characterized by an attitude that Bion has brought into our vocabulary from his reading of the letters of the poet John Keats—namely, *negative capability*, "that is, when [one] is capable of being in uncertainties, mysteries, doubts, without any irritable reaching after fact and reason" (quoted in Bion, 1970, p. 125). No matter how intimate the "knowledge" of the Other, it is always characterized by these uncertainties, mysteries, and doubts.

However, in many of the couples seen in couple therapy, there is a sense of *certainty* in the so-called knowledge of the Other, a "certainty" often characterized by boredom and complacency, or persecution and tyranny, depending on what is omnisciently "known". This near-delusional certainty is a frequent occurrence in more disturbed couples and is closely related to the complaint of intrusive attack on privacy and integrity that one partner makes against the Other. Ultimately I believe it is central to the physical as well as psychological violence seen in many such couples.

These are couples with whom it feels almost impossible for the therapist to maintain the capacity to think for him/herself. Therapists are not only the "recipients" of this intrusive projective identification, but are also *in the presence* of the couples' intrusive identification with their own internal objects. Both these processes exert a powerful lure in the nightmare worlds in which the couple are trapped.

In such a nightmare world, the countertransference experiences are sometimes almost too much to bear. These could be called *claustrum transferences*,[3] and they are very difficult countertransference experiences.

Complementary intrusive projections

In an interview in 1995 , Meltzer suggested that "*mutual projective identification in action*" is an important couple phenomenon, which is distinct from the schizoid mechanism that Melanie Klein described (Meltzer, 1995, p. 111). I quote him at length here again because the implications require us to re-examine some of our fundamental assumptions about primitive processes of projection and identification in the couple relationship. Meltzer observes:

> I think there is also a phenomenon that has a strong resemblance to [projective identification] that is really mutual projective identification in action, and it seems to give rise to what we call a *folie-à-deux* relationship. In the case of couples, it can give rise to sadomasochism, which is probably its most frequent phenomenology (Phillips et al.). This form of fusion by projective identification seems to be different from the schizoid mechanism that Mrs Klein was talking about. It seems to be really a rather sophisticated mechanism and much more closely connected with hysterical and obsessional phenomena than with schizoid mechanisms, as far as I can tell. [Meltzer, 1995, pp. 110–111]

In couples like Mr and Mrs M, each tries futilely to control the Other, although Mr M's emotional withdrawal seems more closely linked with an overt obsessionality. But Mrs M's hysterical response to this blankness may be related to her experience of him as an "impenetrable Other". Here I have in mind the model of an infant, faced with an object that cannot take in its desperate projections, who makes increasingly violent attempts to get through to this impenetrable object or, alternatively, withdraws to the blankness of a hopeless situation that cannot be faced. Mr and Mrs M seem to represent both poles of this dynamic situation.

At this point in my attempt to give more content to the idea of a *folie-à-deux*, I will turn to consider the experience of the recipient of intrusive projections. In Melanie Klein's original description of projective identification, projection and control are at the core of the processes she describes. She writes of "excrements and bad parts of the self", which were meant, in unconscious phantasy, "not only to injure but also to control and to take possession of the object" (Klein, 1946, p. 8). Although one can see why one might want to get rid of parts of the self, whether these parts are substances or emotions felt to be poisonous and dangerous, it is not clear why there is a need to "control and take possession" of the object into which these substances or emotions are projected.

Projective identification is a dynamic of the pleasure-ego, to use Freud's idiom, the unconscious aim of which is to "gerrymander" the boundaries of self and Other. As Melanie Klein put it: "In so far as the mother comes to contain the bad parts of the self, she is *not felt to be a separate individual* but is felt to be *the bad self*" (Klein, 1946, p. 8, my emphasis). The anal quality of this dynamic is clear.

Bion's introduction of the concept of the container–contained relationship gives us a way of thinking about these intrusive projections which allows for the possibility that they can function as a primitive form of communication. But that is true *only if* the person who is the recipient of these projections can bear to be the recipient of the disturbing projections and so sustain a capacity for thinking. As Joseph (1989) has put it, projective identification "*can* act as a communication whatever its motivation"—that is, "whether it is 'aimed' at communicating a state of mind or at entering and controlling and attacking the recipient" (p. 175).

Meltzer captures some of the flavour of what it is like to be on the other end of intrusive and unwelcome projective identification. This can be schematized as a three-part experience for a therapist: (1) "the experience of having been manipulated to play a role in someone else's phantasy"; (2) "the realization of [it] which is accompanied by *anxiety* and *humiliation* leading to *retaliatory* impulse" (Meltzer, 1978a, Book III, p. 14; emphasis added); and (3) *not* acting on that impulse while remaining able to think about what is happening to me and how I am feeling.

Retaining a balanced outlook and *not acting out* these retaliatory impulses is a central part of our responsibility to be an adequate emotional *container* for our patients. In these couples, there is not only a lack of this capacity to acknowledge the truth of the Other's experience without retaliation, but also a counter-projective process of unconscious retaliation. Recognizing the impulse to retaliate when it feels difficult or even impossible to tolerate intrusive projections raises the question of the form of the retaliation. Feldman's (1989) notion of an "impenetrable" object is helpful in this respect—that is, a form of retaliation that simply rejects the intrusive projection (Feldman, 1989; Fisher, 1993). Although at least at a conscious level the aim here may not be retaliation, it can result in an escalation of more and more violent projections. In this way, impenetrability can be a form of retaliation, and, even where this is not the case, it can still be experienced as such.

Sometimes the response to intrusive projections goes beyond impenetrability; the dynamic can be even more insidious. Responses to intrusive projections or projective identification are, of course, an important component of countertransference experience.

Racker's elucidation of the range of countertransference is very germane to the issues being discussed here. He distinguishes two kinds of countertransference response to a transference experience: "concordant" and "complementary". In the former, the analyst identifies "each part of his personality with the corresponding part in the patient's personality—his id with the patient's id, his ego with the ego, his superego with the superego" (Racker, 1968, p. 134. In *complementary* countertransference (a term Racker credits to Helene Deutsch) "there exist also highly important identifications of the analyst's ego with the patient's internal objects, for example, with the superego" (p. 134).

Racker suggests that the complementary identifications "are produced by the fact that the patient treats the analyst as an internal (projected) object, and in consequence the analyst feels treated as such; that is, he identifies with this object" (Racker, 1968, p. 135).

He goes on to discuss the relationship between concordant and complementary identifications:

> The complementary identifications are closely connected with the destiny of the concordant identifications: it seems that to the degree to which the analyst fails in the concordant identifications and rejects them certain complementary identifications become intensified. It is clear that rejection of a part or tendency in the analyst himself—his aggressiveness, for instance—may lead to a rejection of the patient's aggressiveness (whereby this concordant identification fails) and that such a situation leads to a greater complementary identification with the patient's rejecting object, towards which this aggressive impulse is directed. [p. 135]

The countertransference reactions that Racker describes here are related to the dynamics of intrusive projections or projective identification described above. Projections of this kind will tend to find objects that are unconsciously receptive to this projective process. That is, when one splits off and projects an aggressive part of the self, the projection tends to resonate with something in the object, a "hook" on which it is hung. The recipient of the projection here *identifies* with the projection. There will also be circumstances where the individual in the couple who is the recipient of the projection rejects it. The same person might even both accept and reject what is projected in a confusing way. These projective processes can be manifestations of an unconscious wish to be the same, a desire to avoid separation and separateness.

In analysis, when the analysand projects a feeling of aggressiveness, the analyst who is made to feel aggressive is unlikely to be inclined to identify with the patient, as Racker points out. In his language, the "concordant identification" fails and so the patient does not feel understood. What is worse is that not only does the analyst in this sense become an "impenetrable" object but, Racker suggests, unconsciously the analyst becomes identified with the rejecting object against which the aggressive feelings had been directed. Thus, the failure of the concordant identification leads to the unwanted success of the complementary identification.

I want to emphasize just how insidious as well as complex such a dynamic is. Even in the best of hands, it can lead to subtle and sometimes not so subtle forms of retaliation, which can be very damaging. One has somehow to find a way to "step aside" from this dynamic. This requires an actual external person to facilitate the creation of sufficient mental space. A psychoanalytic training does not mean we will escape falling into these retaliatory patterns. The question is really how well we can recover from them.

Conclusion: interlocking intrusive and adhesive dynamics in the folie-à-deux

In conclusion, I will bring together the dynamics of adhesive identification and intrusive projective identification explored above. Given that adhesive identification is a two-dimensional experience and intrusive identification takes place in three-dimensional space, it might seem that these processes are mutually incompatible. However, my experience with couples suggests to me that there can be an interlocking of adhesive and intrusive dynamics that function together to produce a profoundly sadomasochistic manner of relating. I believe that this sadomasochism is inherent in the narcissistic "solution" to the anxieties of separateness in the context of a wish for intimate closeness with the loved Other.

I suggest that the various forms of *folie-à-deux* constitute particularly insidious shared defensive patterns motivated by an intolerance of both separation and closeness in the couple relationship. An intimacy premised on the reality of separateness exposes the couple to separation anxieties that are unbearable because they make the Other appear to be alien. But if the narcissistic "solution" is premised on a oneness, fusion soon becomes intolerable when there are such contradictory feelings, as we have seen. At times, couples trapped in this structure can join forces to project negative feelings and hostile internal objects into a figure external to the couple relationship (such as a family member, a sibling, a parent, or even a child, a friend, or a professional such as a GP), creating a shared paranoid defence. Where the couple cannot join in this kind of shared projection, the negative feelings ricochet in an escalating fashion. As a result, the adhesive dynamics exacerbate masochistic tendencies and the intrusive dynamics exacerbate sadistic tendencies, mutually reinforcing each other as each partner in the couple feels increasingly locked into intensifying spirals of retaliation. This *folie-à-deux* offers no way out. As Edward says: "There was a door / And I could not open it; I could not touch the handle." Some couples do not see that there can be a door out of their "hell", their "claustrum", and coming to therapy may be a first step in establishing this possibility.

I experienced one of the most dramatic illustrations of this dynamic with a couple who sought help in a state of turmoil and desperation because of their inability to separate and to end their relationship. They both claimed that they wanted—and, worse yet, that they needed—to separate. However, in spite of numerous attempts, using different devices, to help each of them, they had always come back together in unbearable panic; they were addicted to the relationship. They simply could not understand this and described their experience vividly as being emotionally like "Siamese twins", as though joined physically. When they separated, it was as if it left an open wound. It was as if part of the self was torn away, like a ripping of the skin, and it was impossible to survive alone, with what was felt to be an incomplete self. They were "claustrophobic" *inside* the relationship but "agoraphobic" when contemplating life *outside it*.

I want to conclude this chapter with a brief look at another couple. I am presenting them not because the specifics of their version of narcissistic relating are so common, but because they offer us yet another picture of a *folie-à-deux* that I have encountered in my consulting room.

Mr A described their relationship as a perversion of Proust, the kind of relationship that has no beginning and can have no ending, only a middle. It began, so to speak, when he lost his accommodation and found himself staying with Ms Z. Why not, she said. From the beginning they were "soul-mates" and could be together for hours on end without speaking, as each knew what the other was thinking. In this they reminded me of a cross-cultural couple who had an idyllic relationship at first when neither spoke the language of the other, not needing to communicate. When that couple began to speak each other's language, they could not believe, nor could they tolerate, how different they were.

And Mr A and Ms Z both agreed that really it was never a genuine relationship. They spent session after session recounting and arguing over all the ways each was not what the other wanted, ironically betraying their unconscious assumption that the other ought to conform to exactly what they had expected of each other. Each described how they had been drawn in by the other, each felt defined by the other, the other holding an essential part of the self which could not be recovered. Ending the relationship, therefore, was felt to be tantamount to disaster.

Both had been in therapy—as they described it, "forever"—and both continued in therapy throughout the time they were seen as a couple. Their individual therapists both said they were pleased for the two of them to be seen as a couple, and one could imagine the frustration of these therapists because the couple's exchanges were full of psychological jargon. In the sessions with them, there was a feeling that what they offered apparently for understanding was just another way of becoming entangled in a meaningless and endless enmeshment. Either of them could talk for a whole session, and they filled the sessions with words, although most of the time there was no sense that either speaker or listener understood what was being said or what was going on. This felt particularly shocking as both were talented and intelligent and were doing jobs that demanded real creativity. Nevertheless, it required considerable presence of mind for me not to become lost with them in a caricature of therapy.

In the face of this chaotic, tense environment, I found myself becoming increasingly forceful and bold with them, in a way that was very different from my usual style. It felt as if I had to assert myself or we would all be overwhelmed in a whirlpool of confusion. It became essential to focus on what was happening in the session rather than on the content of what they talked about, although, on the face of it, the content often seemed rich with potential, if confused, meaning.

In my notes at the time I wrote: "This couple functions on a more primitive level than almost any couple I have seen in therapy." In working with such a disturbed couple, what I said was much less important than the fact I was there relating to them as a couple and to each of them as separate individuals, something the reader will easily imagine was not easy. And yet they (especially Ms Z, since she was so compliant as to almost never be able to hold on to her own view) cared desperately that I get it right in that there was hell to pay when I got it wrong. It was as if words were things and misunderstanding was akin to being physically mishandled (as a baby).

The challenge for this couple was to form a relationship with me that might allow them to "tear themselves away", as they put it. The difficulty was for them to feel they could do this in a way that felt emotionally genuine, without having to enact it literally—that is, by walking out of the therapy. For them, it was an intolerable paradox, and we were always on the cusp of this impossible possibility. Each at different times would gather the strength to make a move to feel like a separate person, finding the emotional reserves and the psychic space to allow them to remain together in therapy until their separation could become something other than annihilation for both.

These two people could at times get enough psychic distance to describe their experience in an "as-if" language, although even those moments felt tenuous. In the heat of the moment, they entered psychotic-like states that were sufficient to immobilize both of them in their desperation. She would become blank, sometimes unable to remember what she was saying either to him or to me. He often became correspondingly aggressive, insisting that she understand his complex and convoluted theories about their relationship, sometimes reaching such a pitch of excited agitation that he would resort to shouting.

This *claustro-agoraphobic* dilemma represents alternating poles of their narcissistic "solution". On the one hand, the claustrophobic feelings represented the intense and unbearable anxieties of the narcissistic fusion as the couple tried to be "one". On the other, the agoraphobic feelings represented the experience of their attempts to separate, which both felt as an abandonment inevitably leading to annihilation.

It is only when the therapist working with such couples can recognize and tolerate the anxieties that each partner feels to be unbearable, through imaginative identification with each partner, that the couple can begin, together and separately, to imagine that there might indeed be a door leading out of the hell of their claustrum.[4]

Notes

1. This term originates in the work of Esther Bick (1968) and describes a very early form of relationship where the skin is experienced not only as a material object but as a psychological function. In adhesive identification, the individual clings to the outside of objects in order to feel held together. This concept has been developed further particularly by Meltzer et al. (1975).

2. The etymological origins of the word geography are of interest in this regard. It derives from "geo-graphy", the charting of *Gaea*, the "deep-breasted earth" whom Hesiod described as the most primitive omnipotent source and mother of all life—mother of the universe, the gods, and the human race. This is confirmed in the Homeric hymn in which the poet says: "I shall sing of Gaea, universal mother, firmly founded, the oldest of divinities" (Larousse, 1959, pp. 87–89) The etymology of the word "geography" conveys well the sense that it is in some fundamental way the "mapping" of the inside of the *internal mother*.

3. I recognize that this idea involves some reformulation of the understanding of transference.

4. [The author has further developed the concept of a "shared proleptic imagination" (see J. Fisher, 2009).]

CHAPTER FIVE

Psychotic and depressive processes in couple functioning

Francis Grier

M uch has been written about the differences between the psychological universes of the paranoid-schizoid and depressive positions for the individual. In this chapter I wish to explore how these differences affect couple relationships, especially when their shared paranoid-schizoid frame of mind is extreme, bordering on psychotic functioning. I wish to give special attention to the way these differences express themselves in their impact on couples' ideals, and the results of the betrayal of those ideals. I also wish to emphasize how couples' different experiences of the passage of time fundamentally affect their psychological functioning.

Ideals

Couples in trouble often themselves bring up in the initial consultation the centrality of ideals in their view of what should constitute the core of a relationship. They will often say how sad or angry they are that the hopes and ideals they cherished at the start of their relationship have now become so dim, or spoiled, or lacking. Although it may not be conscious, at the start of a relationship each partner tends to have an ideal, often absolute, of a specifically desired relationship to which he or she feels entitled. When a relationship with a real partner does not meet the requirements of the ideal, typically the partner is blamed for betraying the ideal relationship (and he or she is expected automatically to share an identical version of this relationship). An essential development in couple relationships entails the psychological separation and movement of the partners from a more or less fused, conglomerate unit towards a more flexible couple structure, consisting of two separate partners who can move in and out of combined and individual psychological functioning. The less this development can occur, the more the couple will remain in the orbit of narcissistic, paranoid-schizoid functioning, where the reality and the consequences of the difference and separateness of the partners will not be tolerated. A defensive clinging to the ideal that the couple should function as a single, almost undifferentiated unit can push the couple towards very disturbed modes of functioning.

Many couples also cling to an ideal of perfect and perpetual harmony, unable to perceive that they are thereby insisting on forcing each other (as well as, often enough, their children and other close relatives, and, where they are in treatment, their therapist) to try to realize an ideal that, however superficially attractive, is in reality tyrannical and destructive. This is ironic, given that the motive driving this ideal is the desire, often manic, to maintain a vigorous defence against facing destructive impulses within the couple relationship. This can also be seen as a couple variant of Melanie Klein's description of the infant's relationship to the "good breast", which

> [it] tends to turn into the "ideal" breast which should fulfil the greedy desire for unlimited, immediate and everlasting gratification. Thus feelings arise about a perfect and inexhaustible breast, always available, always gratifying. [Klein, 1952, p. 64]

It is important here to distinguish between ideals (in the sense of us all needing ideals) and something that, although denoted by the same term, is quite different, more in the realm of the unreal and fuelled by the pleasure principle. Klein's use of the term is in this latter sense. And it is in this sense that ideals become so problematic for couples who, when functioning in paranoid-schizoid mode, cannot perceive that they have idealized an ideal and, in doing so, have transformed it into something so demanding, tyrannical, and condemning that it has become persecutory and so cannot promote growth. Klein, commenting on a paper of Heimann's (1942), had something like this in mind when she wrote: "When the ego serves its good internal objects excessively, they are felt as a source of danger to the self and come close to exerting a persecuting influence" (Klein, 1946, p. 9 fn.).

The couple, in this joint state of mind, cannot discriminate between this kind of ideal, spoiled by its own idealization, and ideals that can be approached and understood in quite a different sense, as expressing an invitation towards an uplifting vision and goal. With depressive-position awareness, these latter ideals are recognized as tyrannically absolute and therefore unattainable. The tyrannical demand for the ideal is balanced, in the depressive world, by toleration of limitations. Here I am focusing principally on the ideals that have themselves been idealized in their most problematic, intolerant aspect.

One "solution" for a couple facing the dilemma of how to remain "ideal" is to draw even closer together into a kind of fusion, denying and ejecting differentiating and problematic aspects of their own relationship into others—for example, children, relatives, therapist. The very notion of being less than perfect can evoke catastrophic anxiety and also hatred, and correspondingly extreme defences.

It is this conflictual relationship between fear of persecution and consequent defensive idealization that marks out the psychological territory of many couples in serious difficulty. The idealization partly derives from a jointly conceived primitive and ferocious superego that threatens terrible persecution unless the partners are able to maintain the ideals. Since these ideals are unachievable if taken literally (e.g., that the couple and their family should be able to maintain perfect harmony at all times), sooner or later they are bound to plunge the couple into crisis. The couple then feel that the only way to protect themselves is through renewed manic denial of the possibility that their combined psychologies contain anything negative, such as jealousy, envy, aggression, hostility, or covetousness. They are then forced to disown and project these (ordinary and universal) qualities into others. This is the couple version of the terrible infantile dilemma set out by Klein:

> . . . the infant's feeling that both an ideal breast and a dangerous devouring breast exist, which are largely kept apart from each other in the infant's mind. These two aspects of the mother's breast are introjected and form the core of the super-ego.

Splitting, omnipotence, idealization, denial and control of internal and external objects are dominant at that stage. [Klein, 1952, p. 70]

In this situation, it is hardly possible for the couple to have genuinely loving relations with each other, since their relationship is permeated by suspicion and fear, even though this situation is highly camouflaged by defensive attempts to adhere to ideals of perfect harmony.

On the level of the couple relationship, adherence to an idealized relationship is destructive to the libidinal, loving, couple relations. These ideals may be defensive against any experience of vulnerability and dependence on the partner, which has to be denied or at least highly controlled.

It is the mark of a developmental advance when a couple can start to bring their ideals to consciousness and subject them to scrutiny. If a process of thoughtful examination can take place in a relatively benign emotional atmosphere, the couple may begin to move towards the kind of "third-position" reflectiveness described in current psychoanalytic theory—for example, in individual analysis by Britton (1989) and in the context of couple work by Ruszczynski (2005) and Morgan (2005).

But this is easier said than done. The whole area is overlaid with such intense emotion that, in the attempt, couples regularly find themselves in serious conflict. The very act of falling in love has, of course, a kind of madness about it, and, although most adults may try to relate to others in more or less mature forms in non-domestic areas of their lives, when it comes to their partner or spouse things are often very different. Many couples unconsciously keep their relationship as a sort of reservation in which much more disturbed forms of relating are, implicitly, deemed permissible. Sexual intercourse involves the loosening, if not abandonment, of normal physical and psychological boundaries and inhibitions, and many couples share an ideal that dictates that they ought to be allowed to go in and out of each other's minds, sharing their most intimate thoughts, feelings, and impulses, in much the same way that, on a physical level, their relationship entitles them to go in and out of each other's bodies.

Such intimacy is meant to deliver ecstasy, and it may sometimes fulfil this promise; but it is equally bound to deliver pain. For those couples who simply cannot tolerate depressive pain and guilt, the journey to the depressive position is especially difficult, particularly if they have made huge investments in defences against just such pain, coupled with addictions to excited states of mind, paranoid-schizoid "highs". They may be very invested in "enjoying" these highs to the full and be hostile to any threat of their being spoiled, undermined, or contaminated by depressive-position doubts.

Arguments and conflicts are inevitable in a close relationship, and couples need to be able to accept this as a fact of life. However, the emotional quality of such arguments is crucial. For example, does respect for the partner vanish? Do memories of their loving relating effectively disappear—frequently the case in the more disturbed situations? Or can more loving and constructive dimensions remain? In the latter situation, even serious and hurtful differences may be marked by a much more depressive quality—for example, of concern. Ironically, it is usually those partners who appear to have the highest ideals of harmony who are likely to drive each other towards a destructive, at times psychotic relationship through their non-comprehension and intolerance of disharmony.

The experience of time

In all of this, the dimension of *time* is crucial. The journey from predominantly narcissistic, paranoid-schizoid to predominantly depressive couple relating inevitably takes time, usually many years, and so the couple's basic unconscious attitude towards time itself is involved and fundamentally affected. In the depressive position the partners become conscious of the passage of time, in various ways. The ideal of perfect harmony goes hand in hand with living in a kind of timeless zone, where nothing changes because nothing should need to change, since everything should be perfect. Sooner or later, when this totalitarian ideal comes to be experienced not as liberation but as denial and suffocation of individuality, the partners will feel confused, resentful, accusing, and guilty.

The partners can only genuinely begin to try to repair their relationship if and when they can begin to face their depression and guilt, moving on to an awareness that the relationship cannot right itself magically and instantly, but that repair will require them to take real steps—which takes time—to help the relationship move out of its malfunctioning and depressed state. This involves becoming thoughtful about the past, and concerned and realistically anxious for the future. The awareness of the passage of time, its importance in making developmental changes to the quality of the relationship, is therefore a crucial psychological dimension of development.

This is true not only for the couple, but also the therapist. Therapists and analysts, too, are usually caught up in unconsciously aiming to achieve, in the course of treatment, various unrealistic ideals, perhaps camouflaged behind quite legitimate, conscious hopes and goals. A typical example would be the ideal that the partners learn to reciprocate more evenly, emotionally, and sexually, alternating between positions of giving and receiving, initiating and responding, and that this should manifest itself in the transference, the partners openly expressing themselves to the therapist—you might say, willing to penetrate him—and taking an interest in and being open to receiving his interpretations. Another ideal might be that bad feelings would be owned, worked through, mourned, and repaired by all parties equally—and with insight. As is obvious when this is spelt out, although these are perfectly legitimate aims, we learn from experience that such neat, ideal situations are highly unlikely to transpire so flawlessly in the real world. A crucial dynamic of the therapeutic process is, therefore, whether the therapist, too, is able to temper an idealization of analytic ideals, without dropping them entirely, honing them more tolerantly to the specific couple in their specific emotional context. This process, too, which we could understand as a kind of benign disillusionment, can happen only over a period of time.

Clinical examples

I shall use two clinical examples to illustrate how easy it is for a couple to get stuck in the paranoid-schizoid position. I shall attempt to highlight the deadly and destructive transferences partners get caught up in when they get fixated on and cling to unrealistic, highly persecutory ideals and to a psychotically eternal present, resistant to developmental, chronometric time. In one case, the inability to give up and move on resulted in destruction of the relationship, though one partner regarded the result as a liberation; in the other, the couple was narrowly able to avoid disaster and to change tack, and so begin a developmental journey towards a more depressive mode of joint functioning.

Mr and Mrs X

In the case of Mr and Mrs X, the wife had had an affair, and so, understandably, the husband appeared aggrieved. She had ended her affair, racked with guilt. The husband was voluble about his sense of betrayal, but he said he now forgave his wife. The couple had got back together again, but they explained that the problem was that they could not just forgive and forget and settle down. The harmony, peace, and happiness that they felt had been the hallmark of their previous "ideal relationship"—their phrase—had deserted them. The hopes and aims of the early stages of their relationship, which they felt they had to a large extent achieved, were now proving horribly elusive. Each felt constantly irritated with the other. Eventually they sought therapy.

They had been married for many years, and, for a considerable period, each had been happy enough with their choice of spouse. But Mrs X had begun to chafe at the bit, experiencing her marital relationship as claustrophobic and infantilizing. This remained the case after the couple's formal reconciliation. Mr X angrily experienced his wife's feeling this way as a breach of contract.

The couple gave the impression of being very enmeshed, as if they were living inside each other's pockets. I soon felt quite anxious and claustrophobic myself when meeting with them, and I found it difficult to think my own separate, different thoughts in their presence. The atmosphere between them was constantly tense. Mr X needed to know and control as much as he could about his wife as much of the time as possible—her dealings with her professional colleagues, with any social engagements, with relatives, and with her thoughts and feelings. He would taunt her for having, many times in the years before her actual affair, flirted provocatively with various men. She would exasperatedly respond that it was he who had often set these meetings up—all she had done was to flirt. But, in the face of his dogged insistence on his hurt and anger, she would eventually backtrack and apologize. The couple seemed, therefore, to operate in such a way that the husband could constantly be reassured not only that he could control when his wife was attracted by a rival (threatening him with rejection), but also that he could control her subsequent rejection of the rival and her turning back repentantly and obediently to him. He could not allow her to have her own separate existence. Mrs X, in other respects a confident woman, seemed to have been willing to be inordinately manipulated by her husband. They operated as a single unit: he dominated and she colluded.

Salient features of their history were that Mrs X, an only child, felt that her father had consistently sought her out to form an intimate couple with her (though nothing overtly sexual had occurred), relegating her mother to a denigrated background position. Mr X, also an only child, had slept in his parents' bed until he was about 9. When his father eventually complained, it was he, the father, who left the room.

Although Mrs X gave a superficial impression of receiving a measure of excitement and satisfaction from tantalizing her husband sexually with her flirtatious advances towards other men, myself included, the bigger picture was that she would always reassure him (and herself) by compliantly moving back under his control. She seemed as invested as her husband (= symbolic father) in keeping her primary identification as daughter rather than woman. This seemed to serve the purpose of defending herself (and him) from their joint anxieties about developing psychologically and sexually, given the alarming unconscious phantasy that, if Mrs X became a sexual woman, like her mother she might well lose her husband's interest. Mrs X's personality and relationship to her husband seemed to be powerfully stuck in an eternally present tense, deriving from her past and hostile to development. This hatred of development in almost any dimension, whether to do with time, ageing, or sexual development, had a psychotic quality in its utter refusal to recognize and make realistic accommodation to the ordinary "facts of life".

Both Mr and Mrs X had been very caught up in nearly actualized oedipal relationships with their parent of the opposite sex. For Mr and Mrs X, then, their unconscious ideal appeared to have been to continue to enact these archaic, enmeshed relationships, in which each spouse almost perfectly fitted the projective identifications of the other, each quite happy to unconsciously introject what the other projected. Mrs X was to be dominated and never quite to be respected as an autonomous, adult woman. Mr X, too, would never grow psychologically into an adult male, but would retain the gratification of remaining always a boy, controlling his wife's (= mother's) sexuality, keeping her for himself and away from other men, who were feared and/or mocked as representing father. The couple's avoidance of having children was in part the outcome of these powerful, joint phantasies.

Eventually, Mrs X began to tire of this arrangement. The balance of conflicting drives and desires appeared to alter, so that frustration and anxiety over her psychological stuckness began to affect her more strongly than the gratification she experienced through her masochistic submission to her husband and triumph over any possibility of their development. Real, chronometric time began to impinge on her, as she began to be aware that, although time was passing, she was not developing. The almost servile quality of Mrs X's attachment to her husband was soon repeated towards me in the transference. However, when I had interpreted how I was apparently meant to find this flattering and seductive, she started to wake up to what she was doing and so began to find a freer, more autonomous relationship to me. Mr X resented and resisted this development. When his wife had been servile to me, I think he felt that he had not only his wife but also me under his control. From his point of view, an unnervingly chaotic situation was now threatening to unfold: his control was waning.

Mrs X now began to turn away from Mr X in earnest. Her flirting changed its character, both towards me and also, as I heard, towards other men, growing into more genuine, if initially desperate, attempts to seek out a more adult, autonomous relationship. This entailed opening her eyes to what she had been involved in. She found this very painful. It was also very distressing for her to understand the historical antecedents of her present predicament in her childhood relationship with her parents, particularly as she began to grasp her own part in perpetuating it. She began to experience herself as a person with a past, a present, and a future, whereas, by contrast, Mr X seemed to have only a superficial comprehension of these dimensions of time. In other words, she began to withdraw her projections from her husband and to see the reality of his omnipotent, triumphant immaturity. This also enabled her to look at herself more dispassionately and to begin to see and experience the couple much less as an agglomeration and more as a relationship between two different people.

Mrs X's developmental drive did not succeed in triggering a corresponding effect in her husband. Had that been possible, their shared marital ideal might have changed. Mrs X might have discovered her "real" husband—that is, a separate, adult man, in her actual husband. Mr X, too, might have moved towards exchanging someone who symbolized primarily a mother for a real, separate adult woman, a wife. But he was quite fixated in his clinging to the old ideal, the old arrangement.

As Mrs X began to move towards more depressive functioning and became more autonomous, Mr X began to realize that "the party was over" (his words), at least with regard to this wife. From this time on, he quite consciously began to plan to re-marry when—not if—he could find someone else to restore his former happiness to him. He thus began to let Mrs X go, although, as might be expected, this more reality-oriented attitude oscillated with thinly veiled emotional blackmail, whether along the lines of anticipating his own overwhelming grief, which seemed intended to stimulate maximum anxiety and guilt in Mrs X (and me), or of threatening her by placing before her an imagined scenario of his future happiness with another wife while she was pictured as forever pining for him.

Mrs X then began to mourn not having had children. Until then, the prospect of children had only signified to them the mad idea that they would voluntarily create siblings as rivals for their exclusive (child–parent) relationship. Having never experienced ordinary oedipal defeat in his childhood, Mr X could only conceive of it as catastrophic, not survivable, and thus to be avoided at all costs. As Mrs X's ideal of a marital relationship shifted towards an adult woman to adult man, if possible with Mr X himself, Mr X experienced this as a betrayal.

Mr X had remained consistent in his belief as to the couple's original contract with its underlying psychotic, anti-reality, anti-developmental ideal. This allowed him to be quite clear about what constituted betrayal. For Mrs X, things were starting to be different. As she developed, she was able to start reconsidering her history and now came to feel that her father had betrayed her, no longer excitingly, but on a much more serious level. She began to speak more sadly about how she wished that her parents had been happier with each other, and that her father had been less caught up with her and less dismissive of his wife. In other words, she began to have intimations of what she had lost through not suffering ordinary oedipal defeat as a child.

Maintaining an analytic stance became increasingly difficult in this therapy. It could so easily seem as if I were siding with Mrs X and against Mr X. I communicated this and tried to balance my understanding of Mrs X's difficulties and hopes with empathy for Mr X's tragic situation. However, because this did not lead to a change of heart in Mr X, and I did not push Mrs X to re-submit to her husband, Mr X inevitably felt let down. I had to bear the anxiety that, far from containing this couple, I might have exacerbated the split between them. And yet it is a maxim of couple psychotherapy that a couple resolving their differences and remaining united is not the only possible good outcome: sometimes a "good" outcome consists precisely in the partners coming to recognize their differences as insurmountable and choosing to separate, rather than remaining locked in a mutually destructive and hateful relationship.

This therapy ended with the couple separating. Although both spouses found this traumatic, Mrs X experienced relief in breaking away from her husband's control and from their joint collusive system. Mr X also felt relief. If his partner could not repent and submissively rejoin him in the "ideal", archaic relationship, he felt it was better for her to go. He was confident that he would find someone else to replace her, which was his defence against anxiety about being abandoned. But he clearly felt betrayed by myself and the therapy, as well as by his wife.

The ending seemed to me to express the elemental difficulty, sometimes insurmountable, of achieving a "healthy" oscillation between paranoid-schizoid and depressive components of couple relating. In this couple, the paranoid-schizoid current had intensified to a more psychotic level, which lived in unremitting enmity with a depressive mode of functioning/psychological reality. When the couple's commitment to enacting their jointly structured archaic phantasy broke down, through one of the partners reneging on the original unconscious contract, an un-healable split developed between the spouses, one spouse representing the belated acceptance of developmental reality, while the other remained implacably hostile to it.

In terms of ideals of marital or couple functioning, Mr X remained true to his idealized ideal. Though it was rigid and defensive, he clung to it as an essential part of his character structure; its dismantlement threatened him with catastrophic anxiety. Mrs X could let go of this idealization and was free to begin to look for a more tolerant and pragmatic ideal. The therapist had to give up an ideal of "curing the couple"—that is, keeping them intact and delivering them to a happy future together, a seemingly innocuous but powerful idealization of an ideal that, in consequence, was bound to make any other outcome seem like failure.

Mr and Mrs Y

In some fundamental ways, Mr and Mrs Y presented similarly to Mr and Mrs X, but the dynamic differences were strong enough to enable this couple to move towards a different outcome. Mr Y's fecklessness and unreliability were immediately presented as the main problem. In this marriage, it was the wife who came across as very controlling, constantly nagging her husband, while the husband was presented not only by his wife but also by himself as little more than an irresponsible boy. While he had not actually had an affair, nonetheless an unmistakable aura of potential infidelity emanated from him. His wife felt keenly undermined by this, as well as feeling betrayed by his inability to support her psychologically when she had become a mother to twins a few years earlier.

It came as no surprise to learn from Mr Y of a very troubled childhood relationship with his mother, of whom he had been very critical for not being able "to get her life together". His father, who he professed consciously to admire greatly, had left the family home when Mr Y was a young boy. Following analysis of his idealization of me, a much more critical, private attitude was revealed. Following my cancellation of a session at short notice, it soon surfaced that, for a long time, Mr Y had been attempting to suppress and deny bitter, internal criticisms of his father, who he felt had betrayed him by not staying at home. He resented his father for not helping him to cope with either his mother or with growing up, except at a safe distance. His memory of a strong father defended and camouflaged an internal image of a weak father and husband, hiding behind a veneer of charm, serving to deny his pattern of fleeing from psychological difficulties. Mr Y seemed to be identifying strongly with this internal paternal object as well as with the maternal object, becoming a person who could not "get his life together".

Nevertheless, these feelings overlaid and disguised another scenario of oedipal triumph over his rivalrous father, who had left, defeated, leaving Mr Y in sole "possession" of his mother. After the cancelled session, this emerged very clearly in the transference: Mrs Y had felt extremely unsupported and upset by my sudden absence; by contrast, Mr Y's concern for his wife barely concealed his greater pleasure in grasping the opportunity to show up my failings and successfully take over my role.

Mrs Y had been adopted when she was 10 weeks old. She had, at least as she understood it, been looked after very lovingly by the couple she had thought of as her parents. However, when she was 12, they informed her of her adoption. She felt furiously betrayed about "having been lied to" about her parentage until that moment, whereas, in marked contrast, she was inclined to be forgiving regarding the original adoption itself, claiming that no child could have felt very much at such an early age—this despite her often acute observations of her own young children's emotional development.

She came across as very forthright and excessively sure of herself, restrained by no inhibitions in aggressively criticizing her husband or, from time to time, her therapist. It seems that, for this couple, a strongly moralistic, rather self-righteous ideal was very attractive, constituting a joint defence of their shared, fragile base: Mrs Y its active protagonist and enforcer, Mr Y as its potential traitor. But fairly soon Mrs Y revealed that this over-assertive self-presentation masked extreme uncertainty and anxiety. A possible understanding emerged that her experience of being handed over as a 10-week-old baby might have had deep unconscious repercussions, pushing her to reorder and create a defensive internal world where any apparently "good" objects were absolutely not to be relied on; instead, she had to exert the tightest control over them. Betrayal was always to be expected. The intensity of her feelings about the "betrayal" when she was 12 appeared to be over-determined, *unconsciously* invested with the terrible significance of the earlier betrayal. As a result of my cancellation, Mrs Y had experienced a panic attack and had nearly broken down. When we met again, she was depressed and very hostile. It took some weeks before she felt she could trust me again. It was clearly of the utmost importance to bear the negativity rather than attempting to reassure her of my "goodness", which she had expected, or, rather, dreaded. She appeared to have been, for a time, in the grip of an inner-world scenario of catastrophic betrayal—she could hardly envisage any alternative explanation for my cancellation.

Mrs Y lived in constant anxiety that her husband would let her down and betray her, particularly if she allowed herself to be persuaded into the "weak" position of depending on him. She had managed in the main to stave off this danger until her pregnancy and delivery, when, as if on cue, Mr Y had apparently found the whole situation of the arrival of the twins emotionally overwhelming. Like his father, he fled, if not literally, nevertheless psychologically. The couple, then, found themselves in a jointly created impasse: they seemed timelessly fixed in the roles either of nagging mother and guilty, resentful boy, or betraying father and abandoned wife/daughter.

Like Mr and Mrs X, the Ys had created and were now living in a closed, mutually projective system that external reality, instead of providing the oxygen of difference, seemed only to confirm. Mrs Y was, for Mr Y, a carbon copy of his internal mother. In his fecklessness, his dislike of his wife, and his defensive but shallow jovial manner, Mr Y created himself in an almost exact identification with an internal father. For Mrs Y, therefore, her husband was a perfect fit for her projection of an unreliable object, one who promised well but delivered badly, finally committing the ultimate act of betrayal and rejection. For each of them, their spouse represented too closely their opposite-sex parent, and, in addition, they unconsciously viewed and structured their marriage as an almost literal repetition and representation of these unconscious, internal versions of their parents' marriages. Mr Y had not experienced ordinary oedipal defeat in his childhood, whereas Mrs Y had experienced the news of her adoption as tantamount to annihilatory oedipal defeat. The result was, as with the Xs, that Mr and Mrs Y were living in a virtually undifferentiated domestic universe, their relationship structured like an agglomeration rather than allowing freedom of psychological movement between two separate persons. Their self-righteous ideal held them together not so much through genuine moral uplift as through a tormenting, mutual purgatory.

Mr and Mrs Y had each been whipped relentlessly by their superegos for not managing to create an ideal, happy family. Each was unconsciously expecting their therapist to become the embodiment of these intensely critical figures, much as each of them had expected of the other. They were surprised and, on the whole, responsive to a different, non-judgemental approach. They initially responded by taking some risk in moving away from these fixed positions. Both in his professional situation and at home, Mr Y appeared to grow in stature. Mrs Y relaxed her moralizing ascendancy, and she took the risk of trying once more to trust and regard her husband afresh, noticing his better points. They began to find a more satisfactory sexual life, in which Mr Y's tendency to impotence righted itself and his wife could for the first time begin to enjoy being penetrated.

But maintaining these achievements proved difficult: they were regularly hauled back by the previous, powerful identifications and styles of relating. They had more to tell: what Mr Y had formerly described as a minor problem with alcohol now emerged as a serious addiction; on her part, Mrs Y revealed that she was bulimic. Each of them had felt for a long time that alcohol and food were more dependable than human partners, particularly each other. Instead, they relied on an unconscious agreement, almost a contract, that each would let the other down just when it mattered most, so proving that their closest objects were absolutely *not* to be depended on, or, more accurately, could be trusted to betray them. It emerged that Mrs Y often binged and then made herself vomit directly after therapy sessions, especially after sessions that she had experienced as unusually helpful.

The couple themselves quickly perceived that Mr Y's addictive behaviour was similar. He, too, drank secretly; his alcoholic indulgence made him, too, vomit. Just as his wife's bulimic activity could be provoked by a "good", nourishing session, Mr Y told how, during his secret drinking, he would excitedly imagine getting on particularly well with me, in sessions or in imagined coincidental encounters outside the therapy. These quasi-daydreams were characteristically followed by vomiting. His feeling of triumphant well-being was invariably short-lived, followed quickly by guilt, depression, and resentment.

Thus, after the opening weeks of therapy, the Ys were able to expose a much more disturbed, perverse, and paranoid realm, in which, as the rigidity of their defensive and accusatory ideals relaxed (or, rather, crumbled), each alternately played the role of the cruel, rejecting object, or the one who was cruelly betrayed. The couple had surrendered to the grip of this very disturbed relationship. They felt excited by these destructive activities and, when "enjoying" them, felt superior to me and my "boring therapy" and to their own "boring" lives as parents, workers, money-earners, and so forth. Nevertheless, before matters had gone too far in a mutually destructive direction, they had been able to turn to a third party, a therapist, for external help. Like Mrs X, and unlike Mr X, they were each able, slowly, to develop a capacity to step outside their mad world and begin to observe their dangerous predicament more accurately.

They began to worry about how they were affecting their children, describing how each would start to "slag off" the other spouse to the children. I suggested that these "developments" were aimed to make me feel defeated and slagged off myself, and I also spoke of my impotence to stop them carrying out this abusive practice. The couple responded by becoming more aware of their anxiety about their own relative impotence to inhibit their growing addiction to this sadomasochistic behaviour. They began to struggle to move the central marital relationship towards a more complementary collaboration of valuing and depending on each other and working on creating a constructive, rather than destructive, family life. Many times each would report in tones of fairly undisguised triumph that the other had let them down, had betrayed them yet again—and the victory was, of course, over the therapist as well as over the spouse. But, unlike Mr and Mrs X, the Ys showed signs of being quite determined to persevere in their joint attempt to move away from the aggressive and perverse sadomasochistic dynamics of their marital relationship to a predominantly collaborative, developmental, and loving partnership.

Mr and Mrs Y provided the therapist with the genuine satisfaction of working with a couple who, over time, developed their shared capacity for insight. The work was aided by the couple's appropriate anxiety about the damaging effect they were having on each other and on their young family. The presence of children can sometimes help to alert a couple who are stuck and submerged in an undifferentiated swamp, to become aware of the passage of time, its developmental demands, and the terrible consequences if this is ignored. Mr and Mrs Y began to set up more humane and realistic ideals. Forgiveness no longer felt like an impossible, persecutory ideal, but attained a more gritty, everyday quality. Real development was now possible. One had a sense, with this couple, that, broadly speaking, they had managed to move out of their threatened, shared enclave and were now claiming their rightful modes of functioning in "developmental time". Their ideals became more oriented towards reality, accompanied by ordinary oscillations between the paranoid-schizoid and depressive mode of functioning, with a general sense of forward movement.

Conclusion

Both couples initially presented as if they were ordinarily rational. However, at a deeper level they were living in a very disturbed universe, their joint couple psyche consisting of an agglomeration of two people stripped of their differences, individuality, and separateness, functioning virtually entirely on massive joint projection. Time effectively stood still or was meaningless: the couple were living a continuous re-enactment of a phantasized past in the present. This usurping of the potential of the developmental present expressed a hatred of developmental reality, a hatred that had the couple in its grip (see Bion, 1957; Freud, 1911b).

In work with couples where betrayal is a major factor, the quality of each of the partners' superego, and therefore of their joint superego, is one of the most crucial factors. Mr and Mrs X's superegos were excessively moralistic and punitive. They would join in a virtual orgy of self-righteous, mutual condemnation. For Mr X, this never changed. For Mrs X, there was a sea-change when she became able to perceive the fundamentals of their relationship differently. Mr and Mrs Y had to negotiate a similar move. It rocked Mrs Y to perceive that the superior certainty she had cultivated delivered only superficial conviction and, ironically, was more likely to lead to the very betrayal she feared. It required courage for her to risk searching for a different kind of moral compass with far fewer absolutes and where she had to renounce her superior position in order to join her husband on an equal level.

Both couples struggled with betrayal of their unconscious ideals. Definitions of betrayal came to differ substantially, as did their sense of what might be forgivable. The paranoid-schizoid kind of forgiveness (exemplified by what Mr X was prepared to offer his wife) seemed absolute, manifesting a dogmatic certainty as to what constituted an offence; whereas depressive forgiveness (exemplified by what Mr and Mrs Y were eventually able to offer each other) seemed deeper, though, of course, never offering the same quality of absolute assurance. Ideals, similarly, either remained intransigently triumphantly idealized, or they became partially dismantled, more relative and more flexible for the therapist as well as for the couple.

One might envision many a couple's developmental journey as consisting in the transition from a primarily projective system (often involving mania and denial) to a more mature state of mind in which each partner projects less, so that the self becomes less confused with a partner. Here the boundary between self and partner becomes more conscious, as does that between the couple and others (e.g., children). In line with this process, the couple's overall ideals need to become more humane and tolerant; simultaneously, the couple will experience the quality of their relationship less as unchanging, eternal, as they move to become much more aware of shifts and changes in their feelings towards each other over time. If the couple are able to be realistic enough to accept this process as inevitable, and in itself dynamic and interesting, they are far more likely to reap the fruits of an, in the main, developmentally benign atmosphere within the totality of their relationship.

Note

The author is indebted to Richard Rusbridger, Anjali Grier, and Betty Joseph as well as to the editors for their help and constructive criticism in the writing of this chapter.

CHAPTER SIX

The Frozen Man:
further reflections on glacial times

Salomon Resnik

This chapter is a contribution based on my experience as a psychiatrist and psychoanalyst working with psychotic patients in different contexts, in both institutions and private practice. The patients I write of here have been treated in individual, group, or institutional settings. I have chosen the "Frozen Man", whom I mention in my book *Glacial Times* (Resnik, 1999), because that case impressed me a great deal and I was able to follow the patient institutionally, individually, and then in a group. I shall try to express my personal approach to psychoanalytic psychotherapy with such a severely psychotic patient.

The Frozen Man

Mr V was referred to me by Dr R, a psychiatrist colleague who worked in the mental hospital where I was a consultant supervisor. My colleague had already started to treat him, but he found it very difficult to deal with such a complex case. I agreed to see Mr V for an extended assessment with a view to either seeing him on an individual basis or offering him a place in my group for psychotic patients. Here I will discuss my initial meetings with Mr V and his subsequent experience in a group. He participated in this group for two years. I shall try to describe my impressions of the patient and of the transference situation.

Mr V was someone who was cut off from the warmth of the world around him and seemed to exist far away from life. At a particular moment in his life, Mr V was compelled to stop feeling anything at all and to exclude from relationships anything vital to the nature of man. His frozen state highlights what is, in effect, an ontological dilemma: can we live without feelings, without pain, and without pleasure? A case like his raises the question of what it is that is so upsetting and anxiety-arousing for some people to relate warmly to others in the world. Why can an emotional engagement be so traumatic to a fragile and sensitive mind like Mr V's?

He was aesthetically and metaphysically attached to Nature and admired certain magnificent mountainous landscapes. Their majesty and their message had an impact on him: grandeur in nature reflected his own grandiose ideas. Looking at such giants of nature—mountains, rivers, and open landscapes—made him very excited: the whole of the surrounding world became the living field of his erotic transference.

After some work together, Mr V became aware of his suffering and fragility and of the susceptibility that lay hidden behind his frozen mask. Since he felt so vulnerable underneath, he needed to stop living within the confines of his own body in order to "survive". This was an enormous contradiction: trying to exist without feelings, without a real state of "being", without mortality, without the passage of time, a sort of immortality.

Mr V needed to block off any feelings, to refrigerate his humanity. This meant that he had to stop thinking, feeling, and being a "real" person, someone who was alive. In his delusional world, in order to avoid feelings and pain, he turned himself into a sort of mechanical being or robot without any emotion. I call this an *a-motional* state, meaning that there are still some affects but they are in a de-vitalized condition. His feelings were in a state of suspension and without "motion", without life. His affects and anxieties nevertheless still remained in his frozen body. His a-motional state "affected" other people unconsciously, as he was able to create a climate [*Stimmung*] of emptiness and increasing disturbance in those around him.

My first encounter with the Frozen Man

A passion for mountains

Mr V was a young man, somewhat ceremonial in his manner. His presence gave me the impression of someone extremely inflexible and cold. Something mechanical emanated from his body, reminding me of Dr Frankenstein's *doppelgänger*.

He was carrying a large package, and at one particular moment he handed it to me in a forceful way. I could not refuse it because it was suddenly thrust upon me. It was a very heavy object.

Mr V said: "This is a gift for you. Please take it and open it very carefully."

"Can I open it now?" I asked.

"Yes, but be careful because I have wrapped it up in a very special way in order to protect the gift."

"Why?" I said. "Is it both heavy and fragile?"

I began to open it. It was a big, heavy book of magnificent photos of the Dolomite mountains to the north of Venice. I looked at them with him; they were desolate, cold images, with much snow, the eternal snows, and apparently with no human beings.

The book bore the title *Dolomites: 360 Degrees*. I was torn between looking at the book and looking at Mr V. He stood before me as though paralysed, imperturbable, immobile, until I asked him to sit down.

He took a deep breath, and said: "I love mountains, I love solitude . . . ". I was surprised by the contrast between his passion for the mountains and his apparent coldness. When I said to him, as I looked at the photos, that the snow and ice seemed to be eternal, he touched his head. "Are you cold in the 'summit' of your body, as though it were a heavy rocky mountain?" I asked.

After a pause, he took another breath and said: "I'm not here for myself". He spoke then in a flat and inexpressive voice, with no apparent passion.

"I came for my sister. Perhaps I will tell you why later." He added that the book he had given me was to do with his philosophy of life.

Then he said: "Dr R, from the G clinic in Verona, sent me to you because he wanted your opinion as a known specialist."

There was a split in Mr V between his coldness with regard to his sister and his passion for the mountains.

Another pause, then, as inflexible and formal as always, he told me that he worked as a solicitor, that he was 32, and that he found it hard to think and to concentrate.

"And perhaps to feel what you say?" I asked.

"Yes, perhaps", he agreed. At that point, I saw him make a face, as though in pain, as if he were trying desperately to put feelings and thoughts together.

After a few moments, he said: "I find it very difficult to make contact with other people. You are the third psychoanalyst I have seen. Now I will tell you that the reason I am looking for a psychoanalyst has to do with my sister. It all happened when she became pregnant by a man who was not her boyfriend; I became her confidante and support for such a heavy event."

"A heavy package for you?" I suggested.

"It was a real tragedy, because at that time her boyfriend, Maurice, who later became an important law professor, had a terrible car accident, which left him almost completely paralysed and impotent."

Later I learnt that when this terrible accident occurred, some parts of Mr V started to die. Later on, when he was visiting his sister's boyfriend, he saw a book on law, and when he opened it he became interested in the word "*commorienza*": in Roman Law, one or more people dying at the same time. "To die", in Old Gothic, was akin to "kill", to "cause to die". Mr V's phantasy was that Maurice, his sister's boyfriend, was killed in an accident, and by identification he felt that something was "killed" (murdered?) inside himself. Somewhere inside, the Frozen Man became a living corpse, like Frankenstein's creature.

The marine calendar

After a "pregnant" silence, Mr V moved his head and looked at my desk, particularly at a small metallic object. He asked if he could take it in his hand. He noticed that it was a marine calendar and asked me how to use it.

I replied that I had bought it because the object itself pleased me, though I did not know how to use it. Looking at him, I was interested in following up his investigation.

He then read the small print on the calendar, which said, "This calendar goes from 1991 to 2040". I was surprised, since I had not read it myself as my vision is not so good and the print was very small; I found it almost illegible. I had bought it in Paris near my consulting room, in Saint-Germain-des-Prés, in a specialist shop for people who are nostalgic for objects connected with the sea.

I was more concerned about the aesthetic and playful side of this object, which took me back in fantasy to my imaginary trips to the North and South Poles, my own private frozen penguin world.[1] I had bought the small calendar because, in my imaginary world, I was very attached to the fantastic adventures of Jules Verne. Perhaps such an instrument could have belonged to Captain Nemo or his submarine.

For Mr V, this calendar was a great discovery. I said to him, "You seem curious and enthusiastic about this calendar."

He replied in a scholarly tone: "Yes. I am very concerned about problems of time, especially about my present and my future." He said this with a pathetic smile on his face, a painful grimace.

Mr V always had a fixed look on his face and an inflexible expression. After a while, he became more "human", seeming almost moved. This attitude awoke in me feelings of empathy and of sympathy.

I could therefore contrast the heavy package of his gift with lighter, more emotional kinds of bodily feelings, though these were still partially enveloped in a cold wrapping.

With his heavy, painful body-package, one could think that Mr V himself was pregnant like his sister; he carried a heavy load inside him and required my help to bring it to life. Would I be the right midwife for Mr V? Could I help him come out into the open, to be born again? Would the two of us, in time, be able to create a climate in which delivery could go well? Or would he remain covered up, wrapped up in a package like his gift: to be contained and recovered in a proper package-hospital?

My impression was that in leaving the heavy package with me, he was trying to find a cover-wrapping inside me as an analyst-hospital. Was I to be a containing mother, available to the patient, taking care of him and restoring some degree of affection and comprehension?

Mr V's sister's pregnant body was the living metaphor for his unconscious fantasy of being reborn. In that transference, which was both moving and theatrical, he was trying to be helped to be free of his frozen container and to be re-born and "re-warmed" somewhere.

In my book *The Delusional Person* (Resnik, 2001), I speak of "metempsychotic" phenomena in schizophrenic patients who try unconsciously to find a place in Nature for their transmigrating fantasy of being brought back to life in a different and more promising way.

Herbert Rosenfeld (1965) describes an autistic, psychotic ideology, in which the individual always lives inside an object felt to be outside him/herself (achieved through projective identification) or inside organs in him/herself or in others (perhaps recalling Frankenstein's Creature).

One could think of the whole delusional system as a sort of "package" in which the psychotic patient feels himself to be a prisoner (or to omnipotently control, like a god). In the case of Mr V, his realistic anxiety [*Realangst*], his disturbance as regards living itself, made him feel very small and hopelessly defenceless; he was looking for a big, solid body like a giant mountain or giant package able to keep him in a petrified, solid "womb", a temporarily painless, frozen, anaesthetized state.

The Dolomites seemed to represent an idealized "hospital". He then became very passionate about an even more important possible "hospital"—the powerful Himalayas. In fact, he had been there on an adventurous visit, alone, for two weeks. On this trip, he had hoped to find out the truth about life, time, and destiny, for life "down below" was Hell, or at least a kind of purgatory.

This Dantesque image sent me back to a bookshop near Hampstead in London where I used to live in the 1960s; I had found there a very exclusive, old, bilingual edition of Dante's *Divine Comedy*. I remembered an illustration at the beginning of the book, where the poet says: "In the middle of the journey of our life, I found myself in a dark wood, the straight way was lost." It was not until he reached the foot of a hill, where a valley ended, that the poet saw the rays of the planet that "leads men straight on every road". The illustration for this section is a section of the earth showing Hell, Purgatory, and the passage by which the poets ascend.

Mr V's Dantesque journey inspired him to seek a psychoanalytic encounter, a place in which he could perhaps find some answers to his philosophical questions and help with his ontological problems.

A surrealistic evocation

Looking at Mr V, my feelings and thoughts led me through ascents and descents in the history and geographical spaces of my psychoanalytic field and life. It was as if I were following his Dantesque surrealistic travels with my own fantasies.

It made me think of a paper by Leonora Carrington, "Down Below" (1944). Her husband, Max Ernst, was a prisoner in a concentration camp and she tried to escape from the Nazis by crossing the Pyrenees. She described the feeling of mental paralysis that coincided with her paralysed car. I realized that the state of mind so well described here was very much like that of my patient. :

> Suddenly, (my) car came to a halt; the brakes had jammed. I heard Catherine (her companion in the trip) say: "The brakes have jammed". Jammed! I, too, was jammed inside myself by forces that were foreign to my conscious will, which I was sure was paralysed by the pressure of my anxiety acting upon the mechanism of the car. . . . I was the car. The car had jammed on account of me, because I, too, was jammed between Saint Martin (in the South of France) and Spain. I was horrified by my own power. [Carrington, 1944, p. 70]

Coming back to the transference situation and to my countertransference and free "dissociations", I woke up from my dreaming state. Mr V was saying: "I would very much like you to be with me all the time, so as to give me all the answers."

He was asking me to come back from my identification and distractions (my own travelling), while at the same time he was making me dream and escape or perhaps asking me to meet him somewhere in our common dreaming illusory and delusional world.[2]

Attempts to de-freeze

Mr V was silent, but present nonetheless. I too was present, and looking at him.

His face wore its usual, painful expression; I could see this in the wrinkles on his forehead and in his eyes: he seemed about to cry.

Then he said: "I want a reply from you."

I asked him what he thought about myths. "Why are you asking that?" he said. Then he went on: "Myths are fantastic beliefs, visions of life, perhaps a philosophy of existence—a fantastic one".

I asked him then about his own personal mythology and beliefs.

The book *Dolomite 360 Degrees* made me think about *dolus* (pain) and myths, something to do with a painful myth, perhaps a need for a less painful one, a gentle one. In Italian, *mite* also means "gentle". Mr V's phantastic mythology and philosophy interested me. I felt that his body was pregnant with his world.

Distressing myths

I think Mr V's unconscious "mythological" preoccupations were implicit in the message of his gift. I was supposed to understand his demands, help him with his personal "package" and go with him into his own woods; the forests of Purgatory and Hell.

He felt constantly guilty about his sister's pregnancy. He was identified both with her and with the helpless and paralysing world of her handicapped boyfriend.

In the transference situation, I was to travel with him, in our intimate and complex topography, from the hills and mountains to the valleys of our unconscious.

After a pause, Mr V said to me: "I am afraid to let you know about my emotions."

"I can see that in your eyes and in your voice", I replied, witnessing from time to time certain moments of de-freezing.

At the end of the session, he expressed the wish to see me again: "Will I have to wait long?"

I looked in my personal calendar, not the toy one, and said: "Yes, you will have to wait for some time—but not until the year 2040."

Time and destiny

Some days later, I met Dr R, who had sent the patient to me. He showed me a strange letter from Mr V. "We didn't know if we should open it or not, you will see."

"*Do not open this envelope, if possible, before 13 February 2004*" (a variation on 2040), said the attached message. In fact Dr R and myself, for reasons to do with my age, felt we should not wait, so we opened the letter.

The letter concerned the destiny of human pain: Mr V said he would like to solve the problem, perhaps with the help of other scientific minds. He added that he would like to be useful to mankind, especially to all those who were suffering like him. He mentioned the philosopher Karl Popper, who said (according to Mr V) that psychoanalysis was interesting but not entirely scientific. So Mr V was identified with Karl Popper—who was very critical of psychoanalysis—but wanted help all the same.

Karl Popper, whom I met at the London School of Economics where I used to teach, was not so cold towards me. His name evokes that of Josef Popper-Lynkeus, mentioned by Freud, who wrote a very interesting book (Freud, 1923f; Popper-Lynkeus, 1899). That author was also a dreamer with his eyes open in a way that reminded me of Mr V with his magic-realistic outlook.

Mr V remained very present in my mind for several days. He managed to communicate a deep ontological feeling about history.

With his cold passion for the mountains and their eternity, Mr V impressed me as a mysterious being, like a character from Gothic literature. The term *"Gothic"* suggests the sinister corner of the modern, Western imagination. Freud in his paper *"Das Unheimliche"* ("The Uncanny"; Freud, 1919h) discusses dread, horror, and fear of the unknown, the unknown side of life. The French translation, *"L'inquiétante étrangeté"*, gives us a clear sense of an adventurous feeling that can rise up in anyone who wants to find out what lies beyond. Between life and death, I imagined a potential space where fantasies exist in a state of immobility and frozenness, waiting to be awakened at the right time and in the right place. How could I help wake up Mr V into our present time?

Fetishism of the sacred

Mr V had mythical and religious beliefs about the mountains, a fetishism of Nature and of all cultures that were concerned with the magical side of Nature.

In the Sumerian civilization, in the era of polytheistic Semitic culture, all elements of Nature were personified by a *baal*, the spirit of the mountains, of the rivers, of vegetation, of storms, and so forth. I also learned that the cult of baals involved human sacrifice. I was curious to investigate Mr V's religious and romantic, delusional and cold world. But what were his intimate religious beliefs? What was the relationship between religious beliefs, dreaming, and living in his delusional world?

Reminiscence of a living dead: the faceless man

Two years after our first meeting, Mr V said: "I'm coming back to life, and life is not completely dark—there is some grey. At times, I can even see the colours of Nature, but at others I feel I am alone in a red desert."

The red desert was the landscape of a dream. In fact, he was able to wake up and therefore to tell me a real dream: *he saw heavy tanks completely empty of any crew and immobile.*

The dream had the atmosphere of a battleground where all fighting had been suspended, as though petrified. He added: *"I see now a dark wall, with breaks in it like scars . . . Then a corridor, with some light. I feel I'm entering that corridor."*

I thought Mr V was telling me of his Dantesque travels into the unconscious, with me as his Virgil. We were therefore travelling together in a dreaming delusional climate beyond his cold, autistic labyrinthine fortress.

At a particular moment he described a character that he called "the man without a face"—that is, without a personal mask. This distressing character (or ghost) appeared in another dream in which *Mr V was inviting some friends to his lonely country house. But no one came—with the exception of the faceless, ghostly man, who told him that somebody had died.* Mr V understood that the faceless man was himself.

After a pause, he told me that he once went to Athens, where something strange and curious had happened. Looking though a shop window, he saw a beautiful silver brooch, representing half a face or half a mask; as he was admiring it, two boys nearby looked at him rather than at the shop window. They were looking at a diving-mask he had in his bag and asked him if he wanted to sell it. He asked a price equivalent to the cost of the brooch, which meant that he was then able to buy his ideal jewel-object.

Mr V told me about a strange transformation of his head: at one point it had changed into a prismatic mirror that reflected everything. His mind was like a mirroring crystal that reflected back every intruding image.

After a silence, he touched the back of his head and said: "I have a hole there, and I feel that the wind of the Red Desert is getting into my head." He was afraid that past time and a desert-like open world would suddenly force its way back into his mind: re-introjection became unbearable.

At another moment, he spoke about his adventures in the Himalayas. In fact, I didn't believe it at first, but he really did go there all alone. "Time is concrete, grandiose, and immobile there", he said. Then he added: "It was like a solid wall of green crystals able to stand any impact of passing time."

In describing his fantastic trip to the Himalayas, he said: "I was crossing the Brahmaputra river." (Brahmaputra means "son of Brahma"). He was going towards Tibet, approaching a place of danger where the Monsoon winds raged wildly.

He said: "As I was walking through the heavy rain, there were many movements and colours in front of me. Then I arrived at a dry part of the landscape, where no rain had fallen—it was without life. I felt afraid, and decided to turn back."

I thought the presence of winds and colours created a living landscape; the vital humidity of the earth made him feel alive, without dryness and coldness. This was both disturbing and pleasing at the same time. He felt he was coming back to life.

At another point, Mr V said: "I know that my life defies time; it is a challenge to grandiose and monumental spaces. . . ."

"Because of fear?" I added.

After a thoughtful pause, he looked at a CD on the table entitled *Gothic Music from 1160 to 1300*. This discovery in my own intimate working space brought to mind the "oracle-like" calendar of the first session.

I would like now to say a word about the fate of this lovely little magic calendar-toy of mine. For many months, I thought it was lost. I almost felt persecuted, thinking that the patient had taken it away, as a kind of fetish. I was, of course, wrong—and I felt guilty. In fact, the calendar was in my library. It was metallic, but it was inside a kind of wooden container—that is, it was also warm. I couldn't see it because it was hidden: I had hidden it myself among my books.

I will end this story of my therapeutic journey with Mr V by introducing more detailed material from a session in a group that he was able to attend for about two years.

A dream in a group of psychotic patients

In 1997, I began a group in Venice for chronic psychotic patients. In becoming part of the group with his "big frozen mountains", Mr V was able to reveal other aspects of his personality and of his illness. The group setting provides a multidimensional context as well as the possibility of mirroring: the patient learning from the responses of others in the group.

Sometimes, the atmosphere of his desolation and inner loneliness in a frozen world came out in other forms as he began to be able to introduce his "inner climate" into the group landscape. However, this had its more grandiose aspect, as he tried to impose himself on the other members' personal landscapes.

Why in a group? I am convinced that schizophrenic patients share a common language, as they have a direct understanding of the language of the unconscious. Other patients in the group included Richard, a music composer with a history of depression and suicide attempts, whose disturbance manifested itself in splitting processes with paranoid feelings, and Eleanor, a young schizophrenic girl who was pretty and markedly inflexible. On several occasions, she had thrown herself from a second-floor window.

In the session, Eleanor sat exploring her hands and said, "I have the same hands as my mother, who suffered from rheumatics. My mother feels useless—she is a painter, but she cannot work any more." She added, "I think there is something distorted in my anatomy." Then Mr V put his hand on his heart and said, "My heart is beating. I feel myself moved." Richard, the musician, said the same, touching his own heart. I felt that very warm but distorted feelings were emerging within the group. Laura, another member, a university professor who suffered from a relapsing psychosis, spoke about her self-destructiveness—for instance, how she used to burn her hand (and sometimes her face or her genitals) with cigarettes—the places that, according to her, her father used to examine when she was a little girl. She said: "Eleanor is looking at how her blood circulates. It is distorted and not flowing properly." She went on: "My mother died of a tumour somewhere between her heart and lungs, with a lot of bleeding."

I took up the common theme concerning coldness, lack of life, paralysis of the "circulation" of life, and the fear that suddenly the frozen feelings might thaw; an uncontrollable circulation of feelings that might then emerge, a kind of mental bleeding experience, a psychological haemorrhage. At that point Mr V said, "My time was immobilized for a long while, like a grey concrete wall made out of crystals." "Maybe the wall can break?" I wondered. He responded by saying that he admired the Himalayas because they resisted the passage of time, but he was afraid to go on exploring by himself, so he decided to come back down to earth.

Eleanor spoke of the fear she experienced when she saw the film *Mississippi Burning*; she became the spokesperson for the group; when feelings begin to circulate after a long time of hibernation, the danger is either a flood or the emergence of burning sensations.

In the following session, Mr V reported a dream in which *there were different musical instruments. He wanted to set up an orchestra with a broken cello, a violin with no strings, and a harmonium.* When he recounted this dream, the other members were delighted as they imagined themselves trying to create an orchestra. Richard, the composer, spoke about Schoenberg and Berg. These are among the composers I prefer, particularly for their capacity to use ostensibly discordant tones in order to discover new harmonies. Richard was, of course, talking about the discordant notes in the group, perhaps also about the fact that Mr V was taking into his dream-mind the broken elements deriving from different catastrophic experiences, leaving a mind very much in need of repair.

Mr V's dream suggests the antithetical sounds within his inner orchestra, his need, perhaps, to discover a new form of harmony. At the same time, the dream provides a perspective on the psychotic dilemma of the group itself as a broken instrument, the attempt to find new tones, a new structure, or, perhaps, even to understand other rules of the unconscious. As we have seen, one of the patients was afraid that a wrong connection between different chords and instruments could provoke a catastrophe: the burning fire (*Mississippi Burning*).

As he was speaking of his harmonium, Mr V began to move his hands as if he were actually playing the instrument. He then appeared to be paralysed and frightened; with his right hand, he pointed to his ear and said, "A very disturbing, disconnected sound has come from the harmonium into my head. It is driving me crazy." After a pause, Eleanor looked at the window and said that from time to time she can hear sounds of explosions. She added: "I became ill after my mind began having blackouts. I remember when, with an explosion, the colour of the sky changed. I was walking with my father, and I told him that all the people around us were actors, not real people." I thought that Eleanor's reference to the fear she experienced in watching the film *Mississippi Burning* was an anticipation of the disturbing explosion in Mr V's hallucinating mind. But Eleanor was worried about her alienated life and the alienated world in which the psychotic mind experiences reality—that is, reality experienced as something artificial, something unreal but repetitive. There was another film that had made a deep impression on Eleanor which was related to the pervasive feeling of unreality, *The Truman Show*. I recognized her description of the atmosphere of the film, which I had seen myself.

Mr Truman, the protagonist of the film, was used as a narcissistic object of the television audience. His life is shown as a sort of "sit-com" or "reality TV", from birth (perhaps even before, if the pregnant mother was also shown) into adulthood. There is an unforgettable moment in the film when Mr Truman becomes aware that everything in his life is fake and that the people are actors, the city mere props.

This recalled Eleanor's feeling when she began to fall ill. She felt that everything was "theatre" and all those around her were "actors". This disharmony between inner and outer realities was revealed as a common dilemma for the members of this group. How could they recover a feeling of reality and some harmony between inner and outer worlds? The harmonium in Mr V's dream was, I thought, related to the group's need for harmony between different realities, in order to be able to work together, be more "in tune", and so "orchestrate" their disjointed minds. The group itself, and also, of course, the individual minds of the members, were experienced as discordant entities.[3] Through Mr V's dream-hallucination, the group was trying to discover the inner logic of their disharmonious (broken) mental world.

Discussion

Schizophrenia has been understood in terms of splitting in the structure of the personality (Bleuler, 1911) or dissonance in the mind (*folie discordante*; Chaslin, 1912).[4] Bleuler also referred to "autistic" phenomena. Perhaps the therapeutic task of the group is to manage and contain the meaningful dissonances and give meaning to delusional ideas. I felt that Mr V's dream and his alarming hallucinations in the group placed a demand and heavy responsibility on me and on all the group members, including the observers. In the "logic" of madness, there are contrasting positions, but a central issue is the extent to which individual patients can accept the opportunity to think more about their inner world, repair some of the links, and restore some relation between inner and outer experience.

Helping Mr V in a group context, in a multiple mirroring experience, made public his delusional and hallucinating world for me, for him, and for the other members. It was a way of experiencing, intensely and in a living manner, a contained psychotic breakdown within his de-frozen world.

I would say that, in my experience, the group completes the individual setting through a complex and multiple structure (the group matrix). This allows the schizoid members to become more aware, in a social setting, of their own delusional principles, which are in marked contrast to (and perhaps even in a state of war with) the reality principle.

It is important also to emphasize that a group of psychotic patients can speak the schizophrenic "language" (Senatspräsident Schreber often used the expression "basic" or "common" tongue; Freud, 1911c [1910]) with great fluency. As well as putting them in touch with the more disturbed aspects of themselves as individuals, this helps them to feel less isolated—they are part of a social setting.

Mr V and the group had an interesting and eventful development over three years, and he and some of the other patients benefited greatly. Mr V began working at the university in a very responsible position. He was still seeing Dr R from time to time, and also myself when he had dreams that he wanted to discuss with me. As he became more and more de-frozen, he became more able to dream. Inevitably, this was accompanied by intense feelings of anxiety and depression that were barely tolerable. In the course of his professional career, he was sent to a far corner of Italy but would still phone me from time to time, and our contact overall lasted for about eight years. Sometimes he would send me news via Dr R, whom he phoned regularly. Although there are dangers of splitting in this kind of situation, and these of course have been well described, my sense of it was that the patient benefitted greatly from our capacity to understand this and to continue to work together as a team. It is sometimes said that analysts believe that psychotic patients cannot dream. In my view, and here I follow Bion, it is not so much that patients cannot dream, but more that they live in a kind of "waking dream" and it is only when they wake up that they can realize that it was indeed a dream.

Over the years, Mr V's persecutory feelings began to diminish, and powerful depressive feelings came to the fore. He never married, but he was attracted to girls on several occasions, although nothing more came of these attachments. Latterly, he became involved with a colleague, who became very attached to him and wanted to live with him. However, he was still afraid of letting himself become formally attached to someone else. His loving feelings stirred up a deep sense of insecurity and doubt.

The Frozen Man and the Gothic novel

While writing about Mr V, I re-read the story of Dr Victor Franken-stein and his double, and this proved very helpful, enabling me to deepen my understanding of severe levels of disturbance.

My "creature", Mr V, was preoccupied and fascinated with the idea of bringing back to life something that he felt was dead and disarticulated inside himself, and so he experienced Nature in this way. As I have said, he became a metaphysical thinker contem-plating monumental, frozen landscapes and asking fundamental questions about human existence; he often spoke of "man search-ing for himself as a whole being throughout the universe". It was as if he were living in different spaces and times. Saying that his problem was his pregnant sister could be understood as a way of saying that he himself had to give birth to his own disturbed and frightening world.

As with Mary Shelley's *Frankenstein*, the mourning process played a very important role in my "creature's" life. Years after the accident, Maurice (his sister's boyfriend), being from the same profession, bequeathed to Mr V his library. Maurice's death revived an ancient grieving and mourning process. The idea of living death plays a very important role in other Gothic novels, such as Horace Walpole's *The Castle of Otranto*.

In Mary Shelley's drama, Victor Frankenstein and his "creature" were very much attached to each other—but at the same time there were many misunderstandings and misperceptions between them. In a similar way, there were two parts of human nature in conflict in the case of Mr V; however, when I met him for the first time the freezing of his feelings was able to contain, to paralyse and so block off, this inner state of war.

If war and fire implied life for Heraclitus, Mr V's anesthetized feelings allowed him to be partly, but not entirely, at peace. However, beyond his cold mask, he was very afraid of his own violent demands and criticisms of people in general, as well as critical of psychoanalysis as a "false science".

Frankenstein, or the Modern Prometheus was written when Mary Shelley was only 18 years old. Victor Frankenstein, the main character in the book, was able to create or re-create a creature—a sort of mechanical or dead "mirror-image" of a part of himself. He was also the "father", the "creator", of a concrete, hallucinated, and real pathetic subject. He often called it his "creature". There was apparently no "mother", just a mechanical matrix. In a similar way, Mr V felt that a machine gave birth to him. He felt he was an unconnected collection of organs, fragments, and limbs. He strove, unconsciously, to "compose" a "good body-orchestra", in this way transforming himself from the dismembered creature he felt himself to be. He also projected aspects of himself, like a kind of spread-out body, into different parts of a cold landscape, the snow-capped mountains. The disjointed Frankenstein "corpse" part was projected into different elements of Nature. He sought a resolution through the use of a psychoanalyst, viewed as omnipotent, and during our work there was a continuous struggle with these delusional idealizations of me as a kind of shamanic figure endowed with magical properties.

Dr Victor Frankenstein, the protagonist of the novel, appears as a man of science, greatly inspired by the ideas of Erasmus Darwin. Erasmus Darwin, the grandfather of Charles Darwin, was fascinated by the problem of death and the question of how new energies and discoveries such as galvanism might "re-awaken" a corpse. The idea of the monster was closely related to mixing together and making sense of an artificial aggregate of different natures of dead beings, gathering together their forces through scientific mediation.

"Farewell! I leave you Frankenstein" says the suffering creature in the glacial landscape of the North Pole. With a solemn, sad enthusiasm, the creature says, "I shall ascend my funeral pyre triumphantly and exult in the agony of the torturing flames" (Shelley, 1818, pp. 214–215), floating on an ice-raft that lay close to the vessel where Dr Frankenstein was suffering an unbearable grief. Like Frankenstein's monster, Mr V had to ice up his raging feelings and isolate himself from all human contact.

Conclusion

While carrying out this work, I recalled an earlier publication of mine (Resnik, 1986) where I tried to transmit my experience not only of the mind of the patient but also of what was occurring spontaneously in my own mind, split between the present patient and an old story (as here with Frankenstein) or with other patients in a juxtaposition of experiences.

There I tried to find links and transform them into useful observations or interpretations. In the present chapter, I try to transmit my own feelings when confronting schizophrenic patients who find it difficult to come back from their frozen world into life.

With Mr V, as with others who suffer from psychosis, I was able to learn a lot about the philosophy of life of a delusional person—born of a great disillusion, creating the construction of a new illusion or, rather, delusion.

How are we to bring a deluded mind back to reality so that it can deal with fear, unconscious guilt, and loss of the ego-ideal and ideal ego?

As in everyday life, the analytic field of the transference situation, individual or group, demands spontaneity and an adventurous curiosity towards the unknown. The analyst has also to be able to deal with his or her own basic multiplicity and to stand (and understand) his own psychotic anxieties.

I feel that my work with psychotic patients, who always preserve a healthy part of themselves, has been always a very enriching but often painful experience.

My writings in the field of art and the aesthetic experience are inwardly related to my daily work. For me, psychoanalysis is a craft, and it can become an artistic adventure.

Notes

1 In my book *Glacial Times* (Resnik, 1999), I speak of a chronic psychotic patient who did not speak until, in a cold atmosphere in a group with other chronic psychotic patients, he said, "I am a penguin."

2. See my *Delusional Person* (2001), chapter 7: "The Experience of Space in the Analytical Situation".

3. Philippe Chaslin (1912) coined the term "discordant madness" (*folie discordante*) to describe what E. Bleuler, at around the same time, called "schizophrenia".

4. Eugen Bleuler (1911) states that Philippe Chaslin, with his contemporary Séglas, was particularly concerned with catatonia and other related processes. In his 1912 book, Chaslin mentions the fact that he was already using the term "*folie discordante*" and dissonant mimicry before the term schizophrenia began to be used (the current term up until that point was *dementia praecox*). Bleuler seems to have been helped by Chaslin's concepts of discordance or dissonance and disharmony. These concepts complete Bleuler's concept of *Spaltung* (splitting). In my book *L'esperienza psicotica* (Resnik, 1986), I mention E. Stransky, who spoke of intrapsychic ataxia.

CHAPTER SEVEN

Psychotic processes:
a group perspective

Aleksandra Novakovic

In this chapter, I present some complex situations that arose when patients from a psychiatric rehabilitation inpatient unit went on outings in the community. In the incidents I describe, acting out by certain patients created upheavals in a transitory group composed of patients, nurses, and members of the public.

The chapter is divided into two sections. In the first section, "Disarray on patient outings", I describe the incidents on the outings, as recounted by the nurses during the course of a staff group, and discuss the implications of the patients' acting out in psychiatric rehabilitation work with these patients. In the second part of the chapter, "Dynamics of psychotic experience", I look at the parallels between the psychotic patients' experiences and experiences in the group and consider the impact of patients' acting out on others in the group, specifically the nurses. As I understand it, the nurses were forced to endure irreconcilable feelings, and this culminated in an experience akin to a kind of breakdown, characterized by the inability to think. This observation led me to think of the psychotic patients as concurrently experiencing and enacting different feeling states.

I refer to a *group* or a *group situation* when a number of individuals (patients, nurses, and members of the public) participate in the event precipitated by patients' acting out and are involved, in one way or another, in jointly creating or sharing experiences in the given situation. Such a group is highly specific: it is very short-lived, and some participants will not have met before and will never meet again.

Disarray on patient outings

The context of the work I wish to describe is as follows:

I was facilitator for a staff group for nurses on a psychiatric inpatient rehabilitation unit. The group aimed to enable staff to think together about rehabilitation work and about their own experiences and the feelings stirred up in them in their work with the patients. The staff group met fortnightly for a period of one year, with sessions lasting an hour and a quarter. During the course of this work, the nurses discussed the difficulties they encountered when patients acted out on the outings in the community, creating very disturbing situations.

The unit consisted of 12 patients and 16 full-time nurses and nursing assistants who worked in shifts; the occupational therapist, the clinical psychologist, and a psychiatrist were involved part-time. All patients suffered from a chronic psychotic illness, most with a diagnosis of schizophrenia, and most were between 30 and 50 years old. The patients had "challenging behaviour"—that is, they were more difficult to work with and had a greater propensity to become violent. These were important factors that contributed to the problems around their discharge. Some patients had been referred from other rehabilitation units as they were considered at risk and too difficult to manage, while others were referred directly from the acute wards. The patients usually stayed on the unit for at least a few years before they could be referred on to appropriate supported-living accommodation in the community.

The aim of the unit was to engage the patients in rehabilitation, to support the development of the skills they would need to lead a more independent life, and to facilitate their move into the community. Outings were therefore an important part of the work. Patients and nurses would go on outings to different places, such as restaurants, shops, and the cinema, as part of the programme. Usually, outings were either in small groups (up to approximately six patients accompanied by four to six nurses) or were organized on an individual basis (one patient accompanied by one nurse).

Disappearance of two patients

The nurses were faced with a highly complex task on these outings. They had to be aware at all times of what the patients were doing, without appearing to be supervising them continuously, for if the patients believed that they were being closely monitored, they could become angry and defiant. As the nurses put it, they had to watch the patients all the time, but at the same time they had to keep their distance. They gave two examples of situations that might have led to disastrous consequences when, for a very short period of time, they did not focus on the patients.

> The first example involved a group outing to a cinema, during which one of the patients disappeared. The nurses became very alarmed and looked for him everywhere, including the toilets. This caused considerable commotion in the cinema and inter-rupted the film projection. The nurses were anxious about the patient's disappearance, but they were also annoyed and embar-rassed about the upheaval this created in the cinema. The patient reappeared a little later, saying that he had been to the toilet, and he behaved as if nothing of note had happened. The nurses suspected that he had deliberately hidden himself to cause the turmoil, particularly as he could not come up with a credible account of his absence.

> On another occasion, on a street, a patient suddenly ran away from the group. Some of the nurses ran after him, but they failed to catch him. Later, he returned to the unit of his own accord. Meanwhile, the nurses had been terribly anxious and angry; they had searched for him everywhere and had enlisted the help of the police.

In the first example, at the cinema, it might have been the fact that the nurses were watching the film (and therefore were less engaged directly with the patients) that caused the difficulty, possibly pro-voking the acting out that probably spoiled the nurses' and other people's enjoyment of the film. Nurses have to keep the patients in physical view but also have to keep them in their minds in a particular way, and they are under great strain to get this distance just right. Furthermore, the patients are not only big and dextrous, but they have been capable of violence. Finding and sustaining a "perfect distance" and simultaneously a "perfect closeness" in such a situation is clearly an impossible task.

It seemed to me that the patients themselves were very active in controlling the nurses, while the nurses had to be mindful of any minute change in the patients. Such a situation can easily become intensely claustrophobic, and the patient in the second example perhaps dealt with this by running away. On outings it is, of course, difficult to physically restrain a patient, or to catch a patient who runs away, as team support is limited or unavailable. Nurses and patients alike are aware that there is greater scope for patients' acting out in this situation, and this impacts on the nurses' anxieties concerning risk to the patient and to others.[1] Furthermore, in this context the nurses are inevitably more concerned about their professional responsibility and legal liability, and this in turn must impact further on the patients.

Going on outings is also experienced as a kind of test of how the patients might later manage being in the outside world and living in the community. Patients are reminded of how uncontrollable life is outside the unit, how small and estranged, unwanted, and even hated they can feel "out there", as the following example illustrates.

Responses from the public

The nurses thought that, apart from the patients' propensity to engage in potentially disturbing interactions with the members of the public, members of the public also sometimes related to the patients in a disturbing way. On outings, responses from members of the public to the patients could vary from fear and anger to ridicule and denigration. The nurses found it particularly frustrating when people related to the patients in a negative way "for no apparent reason".

One nurse remembered a group outing to the large department store, Harrods. On this occasion, the shoppers' attitude to the patients affected all the patients, provoking one of them to make an offensive remark. The patients did not engage in any particular behaviour that was disturbing, yet the people in the store behaved in a strange way; eyes were cast downwards or averted, as if people did not want to know about the patients' existence in the store or were pretending that they were not there. They seemed to move away from the patients, and the nurses thought that they feared being "infected". One nurse said that as she walked through the store, she experienced rising anger towards the public; she also noted that the patients seemed quite uncomfortable, walking in silence and keeping unusually close to each other and to the nurses. Suddenly a female patient raised her arm and announced loudly that she wanted to go to the toilet. What felt like a terrible silence fell, and although it seemed as though no one paid any attention to her, the situation felt extremely humiliating. When they found out that they had to pay a pound to use the toilet, the patient proclaimed very loudly, "A pound for a shit!", and the words seemed to reverberate through the store.

The nurse said she perceived in the public an anxiety about some kind of contamination or intrusion of something noxious from the patients, and this perhaps contributed to the patient's need to go to the toilet. The patient might have been additionally stirred up by the discomfort and embarrassment the staff felt. All the patients seemed to feel quite intimidated and were unusually silent.

The other shoppers in the store ignored the patients and the patients must have seen that nobody wanted to look at them and so were affected and provoked by the disturbing impact they appeared to have on others. They probably felt both humiliated and angry. It is very likely that in addition to the manner in which the patients walked, their peculiar expressions and their odd attire combined to make them particularly conspicuous. Perhaps the patient's sudden mentioning of her need to defecate was an attempt to soil this pristine and enviable place, with its seemingly infinite plenitude. In different circumstances, her comment, "a pound for a shit", might have been thought of as ridiculing the toilet-money and wealth connection, a parody on the extravagant and "filthy" prices in the store, a mockery and denigration of consumerism, and so on. However, in this particular context I think that the patient felt compelled to attack the customers and shopkeepers in order to manage the experience of being made to feel like "shit", dirty or worthless.

The nurses argued that the patients were well behaved prior to the incident and that the people in the store were hostile towards the patients "for no apparent reason". This situation recalls what Hedges (1994) points out: "Throughout all time and in all cultures people have developed a variety of ideas and prejudices about madness" and there is a general tendency "to externalize and then to persecute our own sense of fear and uncertainty—our own private madness" (p. 12). Looking at it in this way, the customers projected something intolerable (their own fears of madness in themselves) onto the patients and the nurses, and so the nurse's experience in the store mirrored the general fear and hatred of madness. In any case, being in the vicinity of people who could become uncontrollable, violent, or unpredictably provocative is understandably in itself very unsettling. The concerns about making eye contact may also have arisen from the realistic fear of provoking the patients and so making them more disturbed and possibly violent.

Apart from the ordinary universal fear of madness, class and racial differences contribute towards understanding this incident. There was a tension between the affluence of Harrods' customers and the patients: the customers and shop assistants were mostly white, the patients and nurses were mostly black. The all too apparent social and financial superiority of the customers and shop assistants may have brought the nurses and patients closer together.[2]

A patient's seizure

A female nurse went on an outing with a male patient who was known to be able to produce pseudo-fits that had all the appearance of dangerously uncontrollable behaviour. The patient would start to shake violently and would then lose coordination and throw himself onto the floor. When this happened in the unit, if he was ignored, he would eventually stop. However, on outings this behaviour was much more difficult to manage. The patient started trembling in a shop and falling all over the place. The nurse said that there were many customers and shop assistants around, but she felt quite alone with him. Although she was familiar with this behaviour, in this particular context it nevertheless made her very anxious. She did not know when he would stop, how far the fit would escalate, and to what extent he might become uninhibited and unrestrainable. At the same time, she felt that he was doing it on purpose, to gain control of the situation. People in the shop were disturbed and quickly moved away, forming a circle at a safe distance. The nurse felt very uncomfortable, thinking that she must appear uncaring or cruel, even allowing the patient to terrorize other people.

She could not restrain the patient and take him back to the unit, so she was forced to wait as it seemed indefinitely, her anxiety escalating. As her repeated attempts to make contact with the patient failed, she was finding it almost unbearable to be so helpless. She felt more and more trapped, and this in turn made her feel increasingly angry with the patient and also quite resentful towards the onlookers. At the same time, she thought that the others were watching her from a distance to see how she treated the patient. She thought that they were angry with her for not "doing" something.

The patient's behaviour stirred uncomfortable feelings in all the participants. By creating this upheaval, according to the nurse, the patient was able to evoke fear and resentment in the group. This turmoil, in all likelihood, confirmed to the patient that the world was a frightening and hateful place, where attacks could come from all sides, persecuting everything and everyone. In the midst of all the disarray provoked by the patient, it was impossible for the nurse to contain him; she felt trapped and paralysed. It seems that all the participants shared the same experience—"no one to turn to", no one who could help. The onlookers could not, or would not, step in to help the nurse, and the nurse did not, or could not, alleviate the tension in the group by doing something. In many ways, the group's experience reflected a state of mind that was very familiar to the patient—that is, feeling in the grip of an overwhelming experience, without any containment, without any support internally or externally.

Furthermore, there was a sense of confusion with mixed, if not conflicting, feelings. The nurse thought that the patient's behaviour was experienced by other people as increasingly persecuting. Simultaneously, the patient also appeared to feel increasingly persecuted. By becoming more uncontrollable, the patient was also forcing others to experience something that was out of control. So all participants were caught up in a mutually reinforcing cycle of persecution, which in turn made the patient become increasingly disturbed.

The nurse felt angry with the patient for making her feel so anxious and helpless. She was also angry with the other people in the shop because she thought that they blamed her for allowing the patient to "fall all over the place". Or even worse, she felt harshly scrutinized and imagined that the bystanders thought that she had provoked the patient into a fit of uninhibited rage by maltreating him.[3]

She also thought that the patient had deliberately tormented her, that he was triumphing in the chaos he created and even in her suffering. The nurse was unable to make contact with the patient; she felt anxious and uncontained herself, and this may have further fuelled his acting out. Although the patient forcefully seized control, he ended up feeling quite uncontained and uncontrollable. When the patient became unreachable while fear and hostility were circulating throughout the group, everyone, including the patient, could believe that this confirmed that he was, after all, dangerously insane.[4] The more painful feelings arising from witnessing an unstoppable regression towards disintegration were denied. There was fear, resentment, and anger in the group, but all participants seemed to manage the turmoil by locating the blame elsewhere, in the patient, the nurse, or the bystanders in the shop.

Outings represent contact with a larger social reality than life inside the unit; this is always a difficult situation to manage because being "outside" brings feelings of being out of control, both internally and externally. Moreover, patients facing the prospect of discharge into the community clearly have mixed feelings about this challenging transition. Outings give them an opportunity to show how disturbed they are and, so, to influence the prospect of discharge.

A patient's verbal abuse

A female nurse recounted an incident where she had felt utterly humiliated by a male patient. She was walking down a busy street with the patient, who became very angry and began to shout and insult her. The nurse felt trapped: she could not help him, because she knew he would become more enraged if she talked to him, but neither could she walk away and leave him. She also thought that the people in the street could see that she was maltreated and debased. The nurse said that people did not know that he was her patient, and so they might think that she was in some kind of intimate relationship with him and responsible for having provoked him. She felt very ashamed, anxious, and angry, but she kept quiet in order not to arouse the patient further.

The considerable disturbance the nurse experienced reflects the violence of the patient's attack. The nature of the relation established here is between sadistic perpetrator and helpless victim. The patient's attack angered the nurse, but she also felt anxious and embarrassed about how other people would perceive her. The cruelty in the patient's treatment of the nurse is apparent, but in considering this aspect of the patient's relationship, the connection between merciless control and the experience of humiliating helplessness also needs to be noted. Through this enactment, the patient became identified with a cruel tormenting object, his own helplessness denied, projected into the nurse and then attacked.

This brings to attention a further consideration in understanding the enactments on these trips. Outside the hospital, the nurses lose the ordinary protection of their professional identity, and they know that they may mistakenly be perceived as a member of the patient's family, a partner, and so forth. This makes the nurses embarrassed, and potentially resentful, something that the patients may well pick up. When patients sense the nurses' discomfort about being associated with them, they then feel rejected and angry. The nurses, in turn, have their own ideas about how their patients come across to others and what people make of their relationships with the patients. At times, the nurses can be made to feel more or less identified with the patients under their care. In this way, the nurse comes to feel debased, not just because she sees herself perceived as being related to the patient, but because she feels anxious that she is seen to be in a *despicable* relationship with the patient.

On outings, the nurses have to remain in continuous and close contact with the patient. If the patients are "misbehaving" on the unit they can be left alone until they calm down, but on outings it is not possible to manage the situation in this way. So an outing can give patients an opportunity to force the nurses to attend to them, to give them their absolute attention, or, alternatively, to make the nurses feel trapped in the intolerable experience of being at the mercy of a ruthless or unpredictable object.

A patient's exposure

A female nurse and a female patient went on an outing. In a queue for the bus, the patient started struggling—she did not want to get on the bus, but the nurse insisted. This made matters worse. The patient became more restless and quite suddenly she pulled up her blouse and exposed her bare breasts. There were a lot of people in the immediate vicinity, and at first the nurse was stunned. She reported that the patient had done this with considerable pride yet also with a shocking mockery. The patient then started running down the street, exposing herself to a person who happened to be near her. She then ran towards other people, repeating this sequence.

The nurse felt profound shame and humiliation as she followed the patient helplessly. She explained that it was not only humiliating that the patient was partly naked; the patient was sexually provocative to bystanders, looking directly at each person and offering them her breasts, and they, in turn, watched the display with awe, turning their heads as if to follow with interest what might happen next, and an element of excitement was unmistakeable. The nurse was very worried about what these onlookers would think of the patient, but, over and above this, very concerned about what they might think of her, imagining that it was apparent to all that it was she who was responsible for allowing this disorder to occur.

It is hard to say why the patient decided that she did not want to get on the bus, but her manner conveyed some sense that she was driven to this act. She was ecstatic and uncontrollable, and the nurse, until she recovered, felt trapped and helpless, but also ashamed and angry. The patient seemingly ignored the nurse, but, while she engaged with the members of public in this unpredictable and arousing manner, she was making the nurse a witness to what looked like a bizarre mixture of seductive teasing, triumphant denigration, and some kind of insatiable and greedy pursuit. It was as if the nurse was forced to be an accomplice in these different scenarios, and she felt that she was silently blamed by onlookers for allowing this outrage to happen. And so the patient felt increasingly powerful and exalted, while the nurse felt increasingly helpless and ended up feeling, as she put it, "destroyed".

This episode seems thus to condense a number of different inner scenarios. The profound embarrassment and humiliation felt by the nurse may well have been in part a projection of the patient's own experience of herself: as being bad, wishing she could disappear from reproachful and accusing eyes (as the nurse had described her own experience). On the other hand, the patient expressed other aspects of her object relationships, for she also subjected the public to this exposure, which on some level both violated those around her and swept them up in uncontrollable and reckless excitement. One important source of this enactment derives from the fact that the patient was now "outside", no longer in the more secure space provided by the ward, and so she, in her turn, may have felt enticed or even forced into a confrontation with this different, exciting, and dangerous world outside. The manner of the patient's exposure, as if she were offering those around a glimpse of a boundless sensuous experience, might express a denigration of the poor provisions that were offered her by the nurse/mother/breast. The patient could be seen as showing that *she* did not need the nurse, that *she* was not dependent on her for *she* "had it all" and was "totally free". Furthermore, it was now the nurse who depended on her (for relief from this disturbance).

Dynamics of psychotic experience

In the situations of disarray on the outings, the nurses experienced a transient breakdown in their ability to think; they referred to feeling crushed, shattered, or destroyed. There are important parallels between the patients' experiences of being confused, split, and fragmented and the blurring of the individual boundaries that can arise between self and others in the group, as I will show.

All the vignettes in this chapter describe episodes of acting out that occurred in transitory groups composed of patient(s), nurse(s), and the onlookers in shops, a cinema, or on the street. A group perspective provided a framework for considering the patients' relationships in terms of the *effects* that they had on other individuals, specifically the nurses. This was manifest, for example, in the nurses' dismay, which seemed to arise from having to bear a combination of very different feelings, all felt intensely—not only the feelings stirred up by the patients, but also the very divided feelings as regards the members of the public.

It needs to be noted here that, although it was the patients who acted out in disturbing ways, the nurses and members of the public all made their contributions to the experiences felt in the group. Foulkes's concept of "transpersonal processes", though referring to a different context, is helpful here:

> To do justice to the fact that this mental field of operation very much includes the individual but also transgresses him, I have used the term "transpersonal processes". These processes pass through the individual, though each individual elaborates them and contributes to them and modifies them in his own way. Nevertheless, they go through all the individuals—similar to X-rays in the physical sphere. [Foulkes, 1973, p. 229]

The upheavals that occurred on the outings created a sense of confusion as to who was the victim, who was being humiliated, hurt, controlled, or terrorized, and who was responsible and thus guilty of stirring up these feelings. This recalls the experiences described by Coleridge (1816) in the poem *The Pains of Sleep*:

> . . . A lurid light, a trampling throng
> Sense of intolerable wrong,
> And whom I scorned, those only strong!
> Thirst of revenge, the powerless will
> Still baffled, and yet burning still!
> Desire with loathing strangely mixed
> On wild or hateful objects fixed.
> Fantastic passions! maddening brawl!
> And shame and terror over all!
> Deeds to be hid which were not hid,
> Which all confused I could not know,
> Whether I suffered, or I did:
> For all seemed guilt, remorse or woe,
> My own or others still the same
> Life-stifling fear, soul-stifling shame . . .

What is so vividly conveyed here is the tormenting persecution, "thirst of revenge", "sense of intolerable wrong", and "life-stifling fear", but also "desire with loathing strangely mixed", disconcerting and "fantastic passions". Most of us can identify to some extent with the unsettling experience that Coleridge describes, can understand the madness conveyed in the poem, the fleeting experience of non-differentiation between self and other: "Deeds . . . Which all confused I could not know, Whether I suffered, or I did." Yet there is also something quite unthinkable about the experience of madness. What I want to suggest here is that the difficulties we face in work with these patients arise not only from the difficulty of being in touch with such intense or unbearable feelings and the disturbances in thinking they cause, but also from the fact that, when psychotic processes predominate, they produce *simultaneously* bizarre internal and external relationships that are in conflict with each other. It is the (inevitably failed) attempt to hold such ambiguous or opposing ideas together in the mind at the same time that, I think, evokes the profound difficulty in thinking and the sense of frustrating limitation and disorientation.

Bion (1967a) in his "Commentary" at the end of *Second Thoughts*, describes a disturbing experience that can arise in work with psychotic patients. He refers to a "complex situation" in the "field of emotional force" where individuals lose their "boundaries as individuals":

> The psychotic patient is subject to powerful emotions and is able to arouse them in others; so at least it appears until the situation is examined more closely. The psycho-analysis of such a patient soon reveals a complex "situation" rather than a complex patient. There is a field of emotional force in which the individuals seem to lose their boundaries as individuals and become "areas" around and through which emotions play at will. Psycho-analyst and patient cannot exempt themselves from the emotional field. The psycho-analyst must be capable of more detachment than others because he cannot be a psycho-analyst and dissociate himself from the state of mind he is supposed to analyse. The analysand cannot dissociate himself from the state of mind he needs to have analysed. That state of mind is easier to understand if it is regarded as *the state of mind of a group* rather than of an individual, but transcending the boundaries we usually regard as proper to groups or individuals. [p. 146; emphasis added].

Bion suggests here that within the "emotional field" that surrounds a psychotic patient, individuals are compelled to share intense and extreme experiences in a particular manner, and that in doing so they transcend their individual boundaries. In the situations of disarray I have described, the nurses were in "the state of mind of a group". The nurses were profoundly affected through the patients' particular use of projective identification, and they were "forced to partake" in patients' experience. O'Shaughnessy (1992) describes the characteristics of projective identification in such very disturbed states:

> Once the psyche is no longer a thinking, perceiving mind, it uses projective identification not only excessively, which it does, but also differently. Instead of being used for normal communications with objects, as when a normal infant cries to and for his mother, projections are used to evacuate and to eradicate the awareness of the self and the object. They are loaded with enormous hostility; they are weapons—boomerangs which destroy the foundations for intuitive knowledge of the self and object. [O'Shaughnessy, 1992, pp. 92–93]

O'Shaughnessy describes both the quantitative and the qualitative factors—that is, massive or excessive projective identification and projective identification that evacuates the awareness of reality. These factors account for some of the disturbing experiences on the outings: the nurses' feeling caught in "something" that was overwhelming, confusing, and uncontrollable. However, introjective identification also plays a key role in generating the experience of loss of the individual's boundaries, and I suggest here that the confusion between self and others within the "emotional field" around the psychotic patient thus results from:

» projective *and* introjective identificatory processes that move, so to speak, in opposite directions through *space*

» concurrent relations—that is, processes that occur *at the same time.*

In the following two sections, I consider the projective and introjective processes and concurrent relations in the "state of mind of a group" experience.

Confusion between self and others: projective and introjective identification processes

Central to Klein's theoretical model (see, for example, Klein, 1946, 1952) is the dynamic interplay of introjective and projective identificatory processes. For her, these processes interact from the beginning of life. They are complementary but also interdependent processes, which continually shape and transform each other:

> Even if the balance is disturbed and one or the other of these
> processes is excessive, there is some interaction between intro-
> jection and projection. For instance the projection of a predomi-
> nantly hostile inner world which is ruled by persecutory fears
> leads to the introjection—a taking-back—of a hostile external
> world; and *vice versa*, the introjection of a distorted and hostile
> external world reinforces the projection of a hostile inner world.
> [Klein, 1946, p. 11]

Klein argues that introjection, in dynamic interaction with projection, is central in reinforcing the experience of persecution. Furthermore, she links greed with the aggressive aspect of introjection and
envy with projection (Klein, 1957). The unconscious aim of greed
is to scoop out, suck dry, and devour the breast: "that is to say, its
aim is destructive introjection" (p. 181). Rosenfeld (1987c) similarly describes destructive introjection in narcissistic states and finds
that psychotic patients omnipotently and greedily incorporate their
objects and appear to "make insatiable demands on their objects, to
confuse self and others, to take others into themselves, and to put
themselves into others" (p. 20).

Bion (1956) suggests that, because of excessive projective identification, psychotic patients are unable to introject. Rosenfeld (1952)
seems to agree when he states that "in schizophrenic patients the
capacity to introject and maintain good objects inside is severely
disturbed" (p. 70). However, Rosenfeld (1964) also suggests that
psychotic patients do introject but do so in a particular manner—
that is, they "omnipotently incorporate" their objects:

> When the object is *omnipotently incorporated*, the self becomes so
> identified with the incorporated object that all separate identity
> or any boundary between self and object is denied. In projective
> identification parts of the self *omnipotently enter* an object, for
> example the mother, to take over certain qualities which would
> be experienced as desirable, and therefore claim to be the object
> or part-object. [Rosenfeld, 1964, pp. 170–171; emphasis added]

Bion and Rosenfeld thus consider introjective identificatory processes on different levels of development.[5] Rosenfeld refers to
omnipotent incorporation, which he regards to be the most primitive, earliest form of introjective identification in infancy, and, like
Klein, he places some emphasis on the aggressive, destructive
aspects of introjection. From this perspective, the disturbances that

the nurses experienced in the group do not result solely from the patients' particular use of projective identification. Projection *and* introjection, primitive phantasies such as entering into the object *and* engulfment or omnipotent incorporation of the object, were all generated in the group and impacted on the nurses (and probably all participants), creating confusion about *who was feeling what, who was doing what to whom.*

Confusion between self and others: concurrent relations

Rosenfeld (1964) finds that "identification by introjection and by projection usually occur simultaneously", and Bion also indicates processes that occur simultaneously when he states that "the psychotic splits his objects, and contemporaneously all that part of his personality, which would make him aware of the reality he hates" (Bion, 1957, p. 47).

When these very disturbed patients acted out, they were engaged simultaneously with different objects, or, rather, part-objects. Because these are simultaneous occurrences, they are not easy to imagine in an individual. Bion (1954) captures something of the state that I am trying to describe, although here the emphasis is on the experience of greed:

> This greed was ministered to by his splitting himself into so many people that he could be in many different places at once to hear the many different interpretations which I, also split into "lots of people", was now able to give simultaneously instead of one by one. [p. 31]

Rosenfeld (1952, 1987c) states unambiguously[6] that the confusion in psychotic patients can result from patients having phantasies of being inside the object *and* phantasies of having the object inside the self at the same time:

> This confusion seems to be due not only to fantasies of oral incorporation leading to *introjective* identification, but at the same time to impulses and fantasies in the patient of entering inside the object with the whole or parts of his self, leading to *"projective* identification". This situation may be regarded as the most primitive object relationship, starting from birth. [Rosenfeld, 1952, p. 72]

> I took the view that identification by introjection and by pro-
> jection usually occurs simultaneously and emphasized that
> narcissistic omnipotent object relations are partly defensive
> against the recognition of the separateness of self and object.
> [Rosenfeld, 1987c, p. 21]

Psychotic patients have difficulty in bringing together and integrat-
ing different and split experiences of their objects and part-objects.
This creates a paradoxical situation of having two irreconcilable
experiences at the same time, being in two mutually exclusive "locations" in relation to the object, so that in phantasy patients can experience entering/being inside the object *and* engulfing/incorporating
the object inside the self. Thus, these patients feel both invaded and
invading, controlled and controlling, and so forth. Their capacity
to provoke others into enacting different facets of their own experiences is observed in the group context, and hence some members of
staff feel that they are controlled by the patient, whereas others feel
that they are controlling the patient.

What was striking on the outings was that, at one level, all the
nurses had a very similar experience. They felt they were subjected
to merciless control, but also, simultaneously, they felt that they
themselves were cruelly controlling in subjecting "someone" to
endure "something" that was unbearable. These experiences in the
group, centring upon the patients' acting out, mirror the patients'
psychotic experiences.

Furthermore, in the group situation the feelings *changed
locations*. In Harrods, the nurse experienced the customers' averted
gaze and fears about being contaminated by the patients as attack-
ing/intimidating/hateful; the nurse thought that patients felt
attacked/intimidated/hated; the patient made the attacking/
intimidating/hateful statement, leaving the nurses (and probably
the public) feeling attacked/intimidated/hated.

In addition to feelings moving around (circulating in the group
between different individuals), different feelings simultaneously
occurred in *the same location* (in a single individual). All the nurses
agreed that at some point on the outings they felt crushed or in
some way disabled. I think that the nurses felt profoundly disturbed because they were "forced" to endure irreconcilable, *concurrently diverse* (even opposing) feelings that were impossible to
contain.

In the example of the patient who had a fit, the nurse simultaneously felt anxious (about what the patient might do and about how

onlookers might perceive her), angry (with the patient and with onlookers), punished (by the patient), punishing (to the patient and onlookers), trapped (by the patient), as though she was entrapping (the onlookers), and guilty (*vis-à-vis* the onlookers and the patient). And so it is clear that the nurse felt divided, experiencing different aspects of herself in relation to the patient and the onlookers.

Similarly, in the example of the patient who exposed herself, it seemed that while the patient was acting out her phantasies, perhaps pertaining to an early oedipal scenario or an infantile feeding situation, the nurse struggled with feelings she could not reconcile; she felt simultaneously anxious, angry, humiliated, persecuted, and guilty towards the patient. As well as being "fragmented" in her experience of the patient, the nurse was "fragmented" in her experience of other people. She was fearful that members of the public would accuse her of allowing them to be violated; she was angry with them for looking at the patient in such a way that it fuelled the patient's excitement, and she felt guilty that she had been unable to prevent the disaster.

Psychotic patients split coexisting parts of personality

The fact that some patients are able to go on perpetuating destructive attacks on their own minds over many years without becoming so depleted that they end up in a chronically psychotic "burnt-out" state suggests that some other factors are active in maintaining their connections with themselves and with the world around them. At times, their acting out seems to have an additional aim of maintaining some communication and contact, however tenuous or bizarre, with others around them.[7] In the case of the patient who exposed herself, the patient's attacks and her intent to humiliate, intrude, and destroy were manifest. On the other hand, the patient seemed to express a need, for something that she felt was precious, magically potent, that she wished to possess or control. This can be thought of in object—or, rather, part-object—terms such as "breast", "penis" or, alternatively, in terms of a particular relation/function, such as "feeding" or "intercourse". The patient moved from one person to another, as if attempting to appropriate all that she could without any interruption in her experience. From this perspective, the patient can be thought of as seeking to re-establish a connection with her object(s), albeit in a manic way.

The nurse felt bruising shame, but she also felt vulnerable and was painfully persecuted by her inability to prevent the disaster. She felt anxious that she would be blamed for allowing something to happen that should not have happened, but also concerned and guilty for not protecting the patient. These feelings can be thought of as representing different aspects of the patient's internal and external relations. The patient's ability to experience some form of affection, although lacking consistency and integration with other aspects of her personality, was in this sense confirmed by the nurse, who thought that the patient was able to experience a warm attachment to the nurse, reciprocated by the nurse's fondness for the patient. However, these aspects are widely split from each other. "This splitting of the self, drives the patient to behave both in his external life and in analysis as if he were two or more different people" (Rosenfeld, 1960, p. 131).

It seems to me that the very difficulties we have in conceptualizing psychotic experiences, which require the holding together of different parts of the patient's personality, mirror something of the splitting, dispersal, and coexisting phantasies characteristic of the psychotic states themselves.

The group perspective: some further theoretical implications

Examining the processes described here from a "group perspective" brings several considerations to the fore. First, there are the experiences that occurred in the group; second, there is the nurses' experience of being in "the state of mind of a group"; third, as I will present below, there is a further dimension, what one might call the individual's "internal group relations"—that is, the relations between the patient and his or her various internal figures.

(1) *Context of the observation: observation of psychotic processes in a group.* Patients (and people in general) can project different aspects of themselves into different individuals in a group. However, what was particularly highlighted here was the impact of a patient's acting out on one individual within a group. This provided an unusual vantage point for examining how an individual—in this instance, a nurse—can become "split" by having irreconcilable but contemporaneous feelings concerning different participants in the group.

(2) *"The state of mind of a group" experience.*   The nurses' confusion in the situations of disarray on the outings can also be understood as arising from being in "the state of mind of a group" (Bion, 1967a, p. 146). That is, the nurses were compelled to share intense feelings within the "emotional field" that surrounds a psychotic patient, resulting in their confusion as to who did what to whom, aptly described by Coleridge (1816) as: "Deeds . . . Which all confused I could not know, Whether I suffered, or I did."

(3) *The individual's "internal" group relations.*   Bion (1975), in his trilogy *A Memoir of the Future*, makes use of a group "perspective" or group "vertex" to express complex relationships between parts of the self. In this work, different protagonists are in communication with each other, such as "Bion", "Myself", "Twenty Years", "Mind", "Body", "Girl", "Boy", and so forth. Meltzer (1994) makes a similar point, seeing the trilogy as "the dismembering of the universal preconception of the unity of the mind . . ." (p. 521), and an investigation of "the individual as a 'group' with only the tools of analogy, reversible perspectives, multiplication of vertices, and negative capability as our equipment" (pp. 532–533). Earlier on, he suggests that "The group, however, is not only external, but internal as well . . . [with] different parts of the personality separated from one another, incommunicado" (p. 529)—that is, an internal group composed of different internal figures.

However, an important further feature of the trilogy is the *dynamic* aspect—that is, the nature of relationships *between* different internal figures or objects and the overall *emotional tone* of the "internal" group constellation as a whole. This focus on the *dynamic between* the internal objects corresponds to the distinction Bion (1959) draws concerning part-objects (structures), and part-object relationships (functions):

> The conception of the part-object as analogous to an anatomical structure, encouraged by the patient's employment of concrete images as units of thought, is misleading because the part-object relationship is not with the anatomical structures only but with function, not with anatomy but with physiology, not with the breast but with feeding, poisoning, loving, hating. This contributes to the impression of a disaster that is dynamic and not static. [Bion, 1959, p. 102]

Consideration of the relationships between different participants in a group can be compared to the simultaneously occurring relationships in dreams—what can be thought of as a "dream group". Resnik (1995) asks how it is possible that the different characters in a dream can reflect and contain the dreamer. He makes use of Matte-Blanco's concept of "multiple dimensions" to provide a structure for understanding these otherwise chaotic and incomprehensible phenomena (the coexistence of part- and whole-object relations, the potential in dreams for thoughts or feelings to occupy simultaneously the whole ego *and* only a part of the ego). Resnik points out that:

> When we dream, we become multiple personalities, experiencing our adventures in time and space simultaneously through each of the protagonists. [Resnik, 1995, p. 10]

The relationships depicted in dreams reveal the relationships between the *parts* and the *whole*, the interplay between the part-object relations, whole-object relations, and also the dynamics of the *dream group* as a whole. A common feature of all group constellations, whether a group composed of different individuals, a *dream group*, or an *internal group*, is the existence of concurrent relations between different *parts* within a *whole*. It is inevitable that, in any group, *a lot goes on* at the same time. The universal phenomenon of a dream group and the particular phenomenon described here, where very disturbed patients both suffer and evoke in others concurrent experiences and phantasies, can be understood as all deriving, at some fundamental level, from internal group relations.

Conclusion

In the first part of this chapter, the focus was on the patients' acting out in the community and on the way this impacts upon their rehabilitation into the community. These outings are an important part of rehabilitation work and are experienced by patients and staff alike as a test of how the patients might manage living in the community. The patients feel anxious about this transition and so may create upheaval in order to postpone the prospect of their discharge. Nurses need to find the optimal "distance" and be able to contain their patients' feelings, as well as their own feelings, while also managing disturbing projections from members of the public.

It is beyond the remit of this chapter to discuss the staff group input in any detail, but what was notable was that the staff in this team were able to be curious about the patients' acting out—they wanted to understand what it meant. The staff's openness to their own experiences and those of their patients in the "situations of disarray" was vital in helping them gain a greater understanding both of their patients and of the whole process of rehabilitation, particularly the dynamic meanings that underlie rehabilitation work.

In the second part of the chapter, "Dynamics of psychotic experience", I suggest that the disturbing experience suffered by the nurses in the group mirrored the patients' very disturbed experience of this paradoxical situation—that is, of being in different "locations" at one and the same time. I have suggested that this external situation supported the patient in feeling that she or he could simultaneously enter the object and engulf or incorporate the object, feel both invaded and invading, controlled and controlling, and so on. I have also suggested that it was these disintegrated and disintegrating experiences that underlay the transient breakdown in the nurses' capacity to think. The very primitive processes generated or unleashed in the group when patients act out create a bizarre shared experience of persecution and excitement, a blurring of the boundaries between the individuals and confusion about *what belongs to whom*.

The nurses' discussion of their experiences suggested a parallel between "the state of mind of a group" experience and the patients' psychotic states. This observation of the different and multiple effects that these patients have on one participant in the group (a nurse) provided a particularly useful context for understanding the concurrent relations that, I have suggested, are characteristic of psychotic states of mind.

A parallel has also been drawn here between the concurrent relations of the psychotic experience and the more ordinary "dream group" experience; both dynamic scenarios can be conceptualized as based on the individual's "internal group relations".

Although the outings intensified the patients' and nurses' experiences, making them visible, I think that in reality what they are doing is making manifest a vital aspect of psychotic experience that affects the patients and those around them constantly.

Notes

1. Outings are a complex work task. The nurses have diverse responsibilities as they need to:

» promote a particular model of patient care that involves taking the patients on the outings

» monitor at all times the patients' tendency to act out on the outings, while being mindful of the need to take care so as not to provoke the patients

» protect the patients from the consequences of their disturbing behaviour when they act out

» protect the patients from the disturbing impact that members of the public or other patients may have on them

» protect members of the public from the patients.

Considering all this, it seems very likely that, at some point, the nurses will feel they are failing, in some respect, the patients, the members of the public, or the task of implementing the outings.

2. In this example, social class and racial differences are particularly striking—other vignettes in the chapter present situations in the ethnically mixed and deprived inner-city areas where class and racial differences between patients and public were much less marked. The nurses' choice of Harrods is interesting. It was probably predictable that the differences between the patients and the members of the public would be more significant in this particular setting and therefore likely to provoke a reaction in all parties. However, it did not seem to me that the nurses were guided by a need to punish or attack their patients and themselves, or the members of the public, although such deeper motives cannot be ruled out. The ethos of the team was to help the patients to "go back" into society. The patients liked going to the shops, and although this outing proved to be one of those "difficult" situations, the nurses thought that the patients would enjoy and benefit from the visit to this famous and opulent store.

3. The nurse's concern that others would think she was abusive to the patient is one that is frequently voiced by nurses working with psychotic patients. I have observed in other staff teams that staff often expressed a worry that patients and their families, colleagues, and/or management would see them as being abusive to the patients (Novakovic, 2002). This tends to become a preoccupation when the nurses feel attacked and provoked by patients and when, in turn, they feel resentful towards the patients, particularly because of the disturbing feelings that they are made to experience, including the wish to retaliate. The nurses defend themselves against their vengeful feelings, persecutory guilt, and fear of being thought of as being harsh by appeasing and inviting patients to control them in a cruel way.

4. Some patients are peculiarly sensitive to being receptacles for what others have projected onto them—that is, they collude with these projections. Such patients lend themselves to this process; sometimes they seem to act out the (others') madness, and sometimes even to *act* it. In these situations, the public, family members, or even nursing staff can feel compelled to use and

abuse the patient as a projective depository for badness and madness. This has a broader reference, particularly to families where the more disturbed patient acts as a kind of container for all the madness in the family, but also in institutions where similar dynamics can pertain.

5. Although there are differences in the way Bion and Rosenfeld understand the role of introjection in psychotic states, they both describe complex dynamic relations suggesting processes that "go" in different directions. Bion (1957) notes that the expelled, projected fragments of the psychotic patient's personality can "enter into or engulf their objects" (p. 43). Rosenfeld proposes a similar dynamic in narcissistic object relations when he states that the object can be omnipotently incorporated and the self can omnipotently enter into the object. Bion refers to the "particle of ego" and Rosenfeld to "self":

» the particle of ego/self *enters* (Bion)/*omnipotently enters* (Rosenfeld) the object

» the particle of ego/self *engulfs* (Bion)/*omnipotently incorporates* (Rosenfeld) the object.

6. Klein (1952, 1958), in passing and quite tentatively, also seems to indicate that some processes or phantasies in infants might operate "simultaneously":

It is part of the complexity of early emotional life that a multitude of processes operate in swiftest alternation, or even, it seems, simultaneously (Klein, 1952, p. 66).

In the very young infant's mind the good breast and the bad devouring breast alternate very quickly, possibly are felt to exist simultaneously (Klein, 1958, p. 241).

7. Rosenfeld (1987b) found that "even in the very disturbed schizophrenic patient there are remnants of the sane personality with some capacity for normal thinking . . . [and it is] useful to consider that the schizophrenic personality is divided into many different parts relating to different objects and having diverse functions and meanings" (p. 221).

CHAPTER EIGHT

Psychotic processes in large groups

Caroline Garland

In this chapter, I give two examples of instances in the wider world in which the group-as-a-whole functioned in the grip of a psychotic process. In the first brief instance, in which little therapeutic work was possible, the events took place in a girls' secondary school. The second, which involved much of London in the immediate aftermath of 9/11, is an attempt to show something of the way in which a traumatized group can begin to gather itself up to think and act coherently once more. Both instances concern an attack upon an existing belief-system: one from within the same system, which was unsuccessful; and one from an alternative system, which was devastatingly effective in the shorter term.

The little girl who said she was a witch

During a training as a child psychologist many years ago, I was asked to see an 11-year-old at an inner-city comprehensive school. The school was a devout Church of England establishment for girls only. The pupils wore a sober uniform, at odds with the lively gear sported by many other comprehensive schools of the day. The school lived within the shadow of the large parish church to which it was attached, and there were frequent and intimate contacts between the two establishments: morning prayers, for example, were held within the church. Many of the staff were members of the Christian Union and attended meetings regularly.

The girl, from an immigrant group, was in the second term of her first year. She had not found it easy to make friends. The girl's divorced mother had been concerned to keep her daughter innocent of the facts of life, telling her only, when menstruation began (four months before I saw her), that from now onwards if she "went with men" she would fall pregnant. In the child's head was the usual mish-mash of playground lore, freshly awakened oedipal phantasy, and burning curiosity, but this was countered by a fierce internal prohibition against letting herself know that she was aware of any of it. Her mother had sent her to a school that strongly reinforced the values of the spiritual as opposed to the material, let alone carnal. This was a stance that required dedicated maintenance on the part of the staff in the face of the combined desires of several hundred adolescent schoolgirls.

Faced with clear and explicit instructions for denial of her sexuality both by Mother Church and by her parent, the child found a way to stand the whole situation on its head. She became a self-proclaimed witch. She turned the established tenets of the Church upside down and used them as her weapons. She became knowledgeable about all the ins-and-outs of sorcery and witch-craft and told her fascinated classmates that she had supernatural powers; that the Devil was her lover; that she had killed a child in her primary school through witchcraft; and that even now she was at work on the religious instruction teacher (an anxious and somewhat susceptible figure).

The girl became something of a *cause célèbre* in the school. Chil-dren drew ostentatiously away from her in the playground, and some of the parents forbade their children to talk to her. The child had transformed her helplessly friendless state into something active, managed by her. One might compare this with the *"Fort-da"* game described by Freud (1920g), in which the little boy converted the loss of his mother as she went about her busy life, something he could not prevent, into an active game in which he sent her away symbolically and then brought her back again, mastering through play the painful feelings her absence had provoked in him.

The situation in the school was less benign, and the referral was clearly of a very troubled child. The situation threatened to make matters still worse for her. The older girls began to claim that they were frightened to pass the room in which she worked. At the point at which I was brought into the story, some of the staff themselves had become caught up in her fantasy. "Of course I don't believe in witchcraft, but have you noticed her eyes? *They don't reflect the light!*", I was told in the staff room. Another teacher wanted her to meet someone "very, very holy" to help her understand the error of her ways.

It seemed that becoming a witch achieved neatly and forcefully the child's unconscious twin goals: that of defying the all-powerful mother (individual or institutional) and that of asserting her own sexuality. In *On the Nightmare*, Ernest Jones discusses the Devil as the personification of the child's conception of the malevolent aspects of the father (Jones, 1931). The central feature of the bond with the Devil is the sexual relationship from which the witch derives her magical powers. As Jones points out, the source of the whole idea is derived from unconscious incestuous longings.

It was unclear to what extent the child was caught up in this richly elaborated fantasy, which held the school in thrall for several weeks. The kind of help offered by me and my department was politely turned down—separately, both by the school and by the child's mother. I can therefore only touch on something of the processes at work.

This brave though intensely provocative attempt at opposition failed, as it was bound to do. There were several reasons for this, both personal and systemic. Speaking systemically, the child's failure to assert her needs and desires in contrast to those of the institution was because the base from which she launched her counter-offensive was the self-same base that supported the belief-system she was opposing. She was not saying, "I don't believe in your God." Instead, her position implied, "I too believe in God—*but I can destroy him.*" Thus the machinery of the Church itself (exorcism, prayer) was brought in to solve her problems. The possibility of help derived from an alternative belief-system (psychoanalytically orientated understanding, for example) was rejected by both parties. As Lyndal Roper points out, the belief in witches and the Devil's Kingdom in the European witch craze of the sixteenth and seventeenth centuries was shared both by the inquisitors and by many of their victims: "The confessions, far from having been extracted only under torture, were often made voluntarily and in elaborate detail" (quoted in Barkun, 1974).

An existing system of beliefs acts as a powerful screen against the detection of its own weaknesses or blind-spots. Those who would spot the flaws are often blinkered by their use of the basic premises of the belief-system they wish to examine. In a world that is coloured entirely blue, there is no possibility of knowing the nature of "blue".

London, post 9/11

This second, longer example concerns the kind of breakdown in thinking that inevitably follows a highly traumatic event. When an individual is traumatized by a sudden violent event, the impact on mental functioning is very marked. There is an immediate period of shock and denial—the event is too large and too horrible to be taken in all at once, and the mind protects itself by trying to shut down. When small children screw up their eyes looking at pictures of monsters they are doing exactly the same thing, titrating the dose. This shut-down alternates with periods when the event breaks through the mental barriers, and then there is an overwhelming sense of intrusion. In neither state of mind is conceptualization of the event, or thought about it, possible. At this time, the capacity (or what capacity there may have been) to trust in the goodness, safety, and predictability of the world and those that inhabit it is extremely limited. *Someone or something did this, or didn't stop it from happening.* There is an overwhelming sense of persecution and mistrust. The depressive position, in which thoughtfulness might be possible, is noticeable by its absence. Everyone is suspect. Fear and hatred, together with an impulse to *reverse the insult*, the trauma, can come to dominate functioning. The impulse is to adopt extreme positions— *tit for tat* on a global scale.

The longer-term effects are also marked. True thinking, the capacity to symbolize, does not work any more, at least in the area of the trauma. By thinking in this context, I mean the ability to represent events to oneself mentally in a way that enables them to be looked at without being plunged into feeling that they are happening all over again, which is what is known as a *flashback*. In a flashback, the ego is overwhelmed by what Bion (1962b) called beta-elements, the raw, unprocessed sensory elements of the trau-matic event—a sight, sounds, smells, emotions. With luck and time, this state of affairs settles down, and the traumatic event "shrinks" in terms of the amount of mental space it occupies. It can become a part of the individual's life, rather than being its central organizing feature.

The further problem is that this process is almost never completed. There remains an area in the mind—the "no-go" area occupied by memories of the trauma—in which true symbolization is never recovered. The breakdown between imagination and reality in this area is chronic. Those sensory stimuli, which might even include certain words themselves said out loud, do not any longer *stand for* the event in the past—they *are* the event in the present. They evoke the emotional and physiological responses suffered at the time of the trauma. At its least toxic, this shows itself in the way that the thoughtful observing aspect of the mind is overridden, and emergency action is taken, even if at the same time a small internal voice is saying, "That's fireworks, not gunfire", "That aeroplane is not aiming for this building". This is what Hanna Segal (1957) was the first to describe, calling it a *symbolic equation*. The gap between the symbol and what it represents is lost, and the symbol is taken for and acted on as if it were the thing itself. However, there is an even more problematical outcome.

To whatever extent there is an *inability to think about* a painful event, there is almost always a resort to an identification. Identifications following trauma come in two kinds: either they are made with the dead or damaged, perhaps in part so that one does not have to finally acknowledge the loss; or, more often, they are made with the agent or object felt to have caused the trauma. In both cases, identifications take the place of thinking. They are a way of solving the problems that thinking might make visible.

An identification with the traumatizing agent is driven by what feels like righteous revenge but can equally be thought of as something we might call a *projective imperative*. In a projective imperative, quite as important as notions of "justice" that fuel a belief in revenge as proper, there also looms the issue of the reversal of a narcissistic wound. The sufferer feels him/herself to be diminished and humiliated by his or her helplessness and suffering. To feel big and powerful once more, those awful feelings have to be shoved forcibly back at the agent of the traumatic event. Within a primitively functioning psychic economy (and that is what any of us can revert to in the early hours following a traumatic event), this need for reversal becomes formalized in the principle of talion law—an eye for an eye. If it is hard for *the individual* to distinguish between true injury, which needs to be addressed, and the narcissistic wound, which may have to be borne, it is even harder for *the group* to do so. A narcissistic injury to the group is compounded by its "group" nature and plays a large part in our unwillingness, which at times amounts to an inability, to be thoughtful about certain events—and to act (or not act) on the basis of that thoughtfulness.

The group

It is easy to be negative and rude about large groups. They have many weaknesses. When things go bad, they may go very much worse because they are happening to or within a group. Groups exert a powerful regressive pull against a hard-won depressive-position functioning in each individual. Each member can subsume his or her capacity for thought in the group's leaders, who may or may not be sane, or competent. Group members can become overwhelmed with the anxiety of *being excluded*, and, when *not being included* means the fear of being left to die, this can lead to crowd contagion or hysteria. The group behaves as if it were a single organism with a single notion in its head. In the United States, following the discovery that a rogue scientist had been hoarding a stolen batch of the anthrax bacillus, a mild localized version of this phenomenon was named *Cipromania*, after Ciprofloxacin, the antibiotic regarded as the only available antidote to anthrax. More dangerously, this kind of group hysteria can lead to mass slaughter. This was the situation depicted in Shakespeare's version of the murder of Julius Caesar, when the crowd becomes fired up by the thought of finding the evil ones, the conspirators, those responsible for Caesar's murder. This mob shows an active unwillingness to think. Rampaging through Rome, they latch on to an innocent citizen who has the same name as one of the conspirators.

> *Third citizen:*   Your name sir, truly.
> *Cinna:*   Truly, my name is Cinna.
> *First citizen:*   Tear him to pieces, he's a conspirator.
> *Cinna:*   I am Cinna the poet, I am Cinna the poet.
> *Fourth citizen:*   Tear him for his bad verses, tear him for his bad verses.
> *Cinna:*   I am not Cinna the conspirator.

Fourth citizen: It is no matter, his name's Cinna, pluck but
his name out of his heart and turn him going.
Third citizen: Tear him, tear him! Come, brands, ho! To Bru-
tus', to Cassius', burn all!

[Act III, Scene iii]

This is a group that has been whipped up by a powerful demagogue
to avenge Caesar's death, but they are also in the grip of terrible fear
and anxiety. If you stand out against the general mood, you yourself will be attacked and killed as another traitor. This is psychotic
behaviour on the part of the group because it assumes that to share
a name is to share a character and behaviour, in the same way that
a psychotic individual can believe he is Napoleon by naming himself Napoleon. In this case, "fight or flight", following Bion's theory
of the *basic assumptions* (Bion, 1961), is felt to be the only possible
course of action.

More modern examples are the genocides that follow the
demonization of one racial group by another, followed by wholesale slaughter. When a basic assumption has the group in its grip,
then the "work" function of the group is lost, and the ability of each
individual to think for him/herself gets subsumed into the generally psychotic group mentality. The group has lost its head. Caesar,
to go back to Shakespeare's example, was the man on whom the
masses were *dependent* (another of Bion's basic assumptions) and
into whom they had projected all their individual capacities for
thought, planning, and military and civic action. When that head
was severed, each individual within the group also lost at least
temporarily the ability to think for himself. At that point, mass
suicide becomes as plausible as mass murder. (One only has to
think of Jim Jones and the Kool-Aid self-massacre in Jonestown,
Guyana, in 1978.)

And yet, as individuals we are lost without the group. Groups
are a fact of life. If we are going to survive as individuals, we have
to learn to live within groups—those we are born into, those of
our own making, those we seek out, and those we find ourselves
stuck with. Even the hermit, as Bion pointed out, is defined as such
in relation to a group from which he excludes himself. This is a major
task for all human beings—to remain an individual, capable of
independent thought, and yet also a contributing part of the group.
Each will influence the behaviour of the other. Given that we are

stuck with groups, the task for each of us is to contribute to *main-taining the group in working order:* capable of task-directed thought and action. A group that is able to work at the task for which it came together without being dominated in its functioning by psychotic anxieties (Bion's three basic assumptions) can be a powerful force for change for the better. Contribution *to* the group and coopera-tion *within* the group will get the task done more effectively than individuals working on their own could manage.

The trauma

On 11 September 2001, the epicentre of the trauma was in New York, and New York became a traumatized city. This raises a crucial question. Given the damage to the capacity to think that follows a trauma, and given the severe compounding of that problem that fol-lows from the intrinsic nature of large groups, by what means can the group struggle to recapture its work function? And, above all, how can it do this in a thoughtful, non-paranoid, non-schizoid way, given the great regressive pull in that direction exerted by the nature of trauma, by the immense amounts of anxiety swilling around, and by the intrinsic nature of the group process itself?

In the material that follows, I hope to show some hints of the group's unconscious willingness to struggle to "put into thoughts" these same issues. This meant contemplating painful feelings of fear, humiliation, and defeat, rather than simply acting out by identifying with a hostile and perverse object in order to reverse the wound. This is the narcissistic aspect of the trauma, the aspect of it that aggravates nationalist fervour and cannot tolerate dissent or criticism of its leaders (Bennetts, 2001). In any large group, there will always be those who want to "kick ass", alongside stop-the-war movements and campaigns for nuclear disarmament, along-side those who don't know, who are still struggling with what to think or to do. That is the nature of groups within a democracy, which is itself a very particular way of group functioning. In this chapter, however, I hope to describe elements of the functioning of the group-as-a-whole which may be indicative of a capacity for something less split, less paranoid, and more hopeful. That is to say, a return to *working at the problems* the group faces, no longer entirely dominated by impulses to remain dependent, to engage in fight or flight, or to disappear into a pairing-up with some messianic and improbable solution. (An example of this last would be the slogan "All You Need Is Love".) I am saying that groups, too, are capable of achieving a depressive level of functioning. We do not have to function only as crowds, hordes, or mobs.

The "urban myth" and the "joke"

I suggest that what the newspapers call the *urban myth* (but which folklorists would call a legend) and *the joke* can both represent a part of the struggle of the large group *to regain the ability to think*. They are not simply to be ignored as the froth that accumulates at the top of the boiling national pot.

But before something can be thought about, the individual has to be able to *formulate* what has happened and then *represent* its nature to him/herself. If this is a difficult task for a traumatized individual, it is even more so for a group containing many disparate elements. Then there is the question of what the group feels about what has happened. And then—and at its best—there is an attempt to deal with what has happened and what might be felt about it through symbolic means rather than only through action. All this takes time.

One of the facts of the response to the 9/11 attack was that nothing precipitate took place during the immediate aftermath. For some days, whatever stayed the action, there was a delay that was crucial in allowing some opportunity for the large group to begin to process what had happened. In the case of New York, this was probably crucial in taking on board the scale of the grief and the mourning that was inevitable and necessary: that aspect of the event that represented the material wound, rather than its purely narcissistic aspects. These were losses of one's loved and valued *objects*, not just losses of *self*-image.

Clinical material

I have two pieces of clinical material in the form of "group" phenomena—that is, not attributable to a single individual. To that extent, they can be regarded as something akin to group day-dreaming, the fulfillment of a group wish. The first concerns the population of

London itself; the second concerns the United States, largely gleaned from the *New York Times* online and from Professor Alan Dundes, who was an invaluable source of information and comment.[1]

London

Ten days after the 11th, early on a Saturday morning, I had a telephone call from a young colleague who said, "Look, this might be nothing, but I've just had a conversation with my sister I want to pass on—just in case." A friend of her sister's had been in a London post office the day before where there was a man struggling to post a large parcel. He looked like a foreigner, and he seemed to be short of the right money. The sister's friend, behind him in the queue, gave him a hand, added the missing 30p, and thought no more of it until she left the post office, where she found the man waiting. He spoke to her in a heavily accented voice. "You have helped me. I will help you, but you must tell no one. *Do not go into Central London this weekend.*" She tried to question him, but he walked quickly away. She then went to the local police station and repeated this story. She was shown photographs of all the suspected terrorists in this country. "That's him", she said with confidence. "That's the one I saw."

Within a few days, several versions of the story were current (Leeds, Manchester, Bradford, "my friend's mother/sister/cousin", picked up the wallet he'd dropped/showed him the way, etc.) but all bearing a strong structural resemblance to each other:

> A woman helps a man. In exchange for her unsolicited and generous act he helps her in return, sparing her from his lethal power. He is identified by the authorities as being the real thing.

For some days, this story nagged at me. It had a familiar quality. Then I suddenly recognized it as—structurally at least—highly reminiscent of the story of Androcles and the Lion (Aesop again). Androcles, a runaway Roman slave, hides from the cruelties of his masters in a cave. A lion comes into the cave, and Androcles sees that he is limping because there is a large thorn in its paw. Although afraid, he extracts the thorn. Later when Androcles is recaptured and thrown to the wild beasts in the circus amphitheatre, the self-same lion recognizes him and licks and caresses him—and Androcles is set free.[2]

In its "terrorist" version, this story has a powerful appeal. The helpful woman has been included in the subset of those "in the know", where we all long to be (privy to the parental primal act), and now we, the latest recipients of the story, are there too. We are the privileged group. (The structural equivalence of women and slaves probably belongs in a paper of its own. . . .) The projective dart, the detail that ensures the story gets under the skin of someone already anxious, is the identification by the police of the man as a terrorist. However, I think the story says more than this. It indicates a belief that human beings are capable of acts of unsolicited kindness (which they are), and that kindness is repaid in kind. It says not all bad objects are all bad, and it therefore recognizes the possibility of *ambivalence*, as opposed to either idealization of the enemy's power or denigration of his way of life and capacity to destroy. Above all, it is a symbolization through words of a life-and-death situation, one that had half the world in its grip. Was the woman's action merely appeasement? I do not think so. It was important that her help was offered before she knew what he was. This is, I think, closer to the depressive state of mind than is a position characterized by "You're either with us or you're against us."

New York

I learned from Alan Dundes that there was a structurally related version of this story concurrently active in the United States. However there was an important difference between the two versions—namely, that the US version was sexualized. It involved penetration, which might say something about US preoccupations in general, but it might also reflect the way in which US boundaries and buildings were penetrated in a physical way by the assault whereas Britain's were not. This example comes straight off the Internet.

My friend's friend was dating a guy from Afghanistan until a month ago. She had a date with him around 9 September but was stood up. She was understandably upset and went to his home to find it completely emptied. On 10 September, she received a letter from her boyfriend explaining that he wishes he could tell her why he had left and he was sorry it had to be like that. The letter also BEGGED her not to get on any commercial airlines on 11 September and not to go to any shopping malls on Hallowe'en. As soon as everything happened on the 11th she called the FBI and has turned over the letter.

What are the significant differences, from an analytic point of view? It is already too late to avert the first catastrophe, but a second (Hallowe'en, six weeks later) can be avoided by being "in the know", let into the secrets of the bedroom. However, the favours (sexualized) she gave him have counted for very little: the woman has been betrayed. The sexual relationship indicates the degree to which the United States feels it is already "involved" in something that cannot be undone. Here I found Alan Dundes' essay *From Game to War* (Dundes, 1997) not just convincing but also unnervingly backed up by the freely circulating jokes and stories that gave expression to the unconscious meaning in the group mind of that terrible penetration. Dundes suggests that the unconscious phantasy behind male–male combat (whether in sport or in war) consists of penetration and sexual humiliation of the opponent, including castration.

From the point of view of making painful unconscious material available for thought, as all therapists working in war zones and refugee camps know, it may be easier to begin with drawings and pictures. The first drawings (by which I mean "made" pictures as opposed to photographs) were crude and not in the least funny, but in their raw way they were attempts at representing something that could not at that point quite be mustered as material for thought.

1. A mock-up photograph of a naked, submissive, and somewhat baffled Bush being buggered by a serenely smiling Bin Laden, also naked but for his turban. The caption says, "Make love not war".

2. Bin Laden in drag—that is, womanized. This *symbolizes* (i.e., does not enact) the reversal of the trauma, and the castration of Bin Laden via an identification with the aggressor.

3. Less confidently, Bin Laden with his turban off. The top of his head resembles a penis. This is a visual way of saying "dick-head", which acknowledges that he is male but is at the same time disparaging of that maleness. Again, this is a symbolic, rather than an actual, attack.

I take jokes in this particular unthinkable situation to have a particular function. They are not only thin disguises for fear and hostility (Freud, 1905c), in which the attempt is to belittle the enemy and make him look ridiculous—a figure of fun rather than a figure of fear. They also represent the very earliest stages in a struggle to establish an alternative point of view, one that is not simply part of a destructive coupling involving mutual hatred, mutual blame, and mutual attack. In this, they are related to achieving the position of observer, a third position (Britton, 1998), in which they are able to contemplate the terrible coupling depicted in the first dreadful images. Only in this position is thought-as-opposed-to-identification possible. It is perhaps relevant that at the same time some US commentators were beginning to be able to take a historical look at US behaviour from a third-world-eye point of view—to take a look at themselves as viewed by some others, and to think about it out loud, in spite of hatred of these activities in some quarters of the United States.

By early November, six to seven weeks after the assault, the jokes had become funny as opposed to merely macabre (see *The New Yorker* of 16 November 2001). By this time, they represented an oblique and ironic point of view on the United States's *own* responses to the events, as well as to the political realities. The emphasis on the sexual humiliation and castration of the enemy had faded, as some reduction in the sense of being helplessly buggered had receded. When the narcissistic damage can be tolerated, the real damage—the losses, and the pain of those losses—can be addressed.

Discussion

What is the function of these legends, these day-dreams, for the group as a whole? There is a small book in the Tavistock Library by Marie Bonaparte (1947) concerning the legends circulating in Europe during World War Two. One entire chapter is devoted to "The myth of the friendly enemy". The stories she collected are, in essence, exactly the same as the legends I have described. Bonaparte regards these group stories as containers for the group's enormous anxieties concerning the outcome of the war. Of this particular one she says, "the terror aroused in nations by the threat of enemy aggression gives rise to another mechanism, more primitive and even more simple, by which to control anxiety: the plain denial of the enemy's menace". This is clearly right. These stories describe a parallel version of reality, in which what Roger Money-Kyrle (1968) has called "the facts of life" can be ignored. The "fact of life" that is death— moreover, in this case, not *death one day from natural causes*, but *death now and at my hands*—is pushed to one side by the story that adds *"but not for me and my friends"*. However, this does not contradict my earlier suggestion concerning the group's wish to refind its ability to think about what has happened in a non-paranoid way.

In the "post-office" version described above, the capacity for mutual concern is located in both parties: help is repaid with help. (This is a considerable distance on from "The Corpse in the Car", a legend also collected by Bonaparte that expresses a simple wish for Hitler's death.)

Conclusions

In both instances I have given, the group found it hard to hold on to a sense of reality in the face of threats to its existence, whether spiritual (witchcraft) or bodily (the use of passenger planes as assault weapons). The fear of annihilation is the most fundamental of human fears. What gets called "crowd hysteria" is the process by which an emotion, perhaps particularly when one of fear, becomes self-feeding, growing exponentially in intensity as it spreads through the group. It is a massive and mutual resort to projective identification by a large body of people. There is, perhaps, an additional factor, that of "critical mass", which adds to the problem: when the group is too large for any one person to know all of the others by name, even by sight, the process can spread with the rapidity of an electric current.

This phenomenon would seem to be linked with Le Bon's (1895) original description of the crowd. Once in a crowd, individuals, he says, appear to behave in ways that bear no relation to their original temperaments, occupations, intelligences, or tastes. Behaviour becomes homogenized, tending to take on some features of a lowest common denominator. In the two instances discussed at the start in this chapter, fear lay at the heart of the crowd phenomena: fear of life (sex) and fear of death. It would seem as though the presence of too much of either life or death in phantasy can overwhelm individual judgement and discretion, at least in the short term. In the religious school, the fear of sex evoked both horror and fascination. In the staff mind, only someone "very, very holy" would do to free the child, and hence the school, from the grip of the Devil's over-heated claw. The precise size of the "crowd" was, perhaps, also a factor in this situation—of a size just large enough for a mass hysteria to get under way, and yet not large enough for dissenting opinions to exist and be voiced convincingly.

In the second instance, it was the fear of death that gripped the large group, evoking both sexualized and reparative phantasies. However, the "crowd" formed by the United States and Britain, and their combined media, is truly immense, composed of many very disparate elements. This was its strength, in the face of the trauma faced by the United States, allowing for a gradual resumption of its capacity to think. The crowd never became entirely homogenized.

In this situation, the significance of the mobile phone and the Internet cannot be underestimated. Their capacity to create a virtual "crowd", often with no perceptible leader, can become a power on the side of good, or a power on the side of bad. Already in several European countries, it is responsible for rapid mass gatherings, either to make hay, or to lay waste the hayfield. It played a significant and constructive role in coordinating the uprisings of the Arab Spring, and a very much less benign role in the 2011 riots in London. But it remains to be seen how these new kinds of virtually instantaneous groupings will evolve, in what ways they will be used, and what limits may have to be set on their powers.

Notes

1. I was helped and also entertained by e-correspondence with the late Alan Dundes, Professor of Folklore at the University of California, Berkeley. His vast and steadily accumulating library of folklore, urban myths, apocryphal stories, and jokes has provided me with crucial source material and many ideas (see especially Dundes, 1997).

2. "Androcles and the Lion" is, in fact, not a legend (Dundes, personal communication) but a standard folktale, an Aesopic Fable: Aarne-Thompson tale type 156, "Thorn Removed from Lion's Paw".

CHAPTER NINE

A community meeting
on an acute psychiatric ward:
observation and commentaries

In this chapter, we present an observation of a community meeting on an acute psychiatric ward; this is then followed by analyses from a number of different perspectives. The observation was conducted as part of a larger Observation Project (Novakovic, 2011), building on the work of Hinshelwood and Skogstad (2000a). The aim of the project was to gain, through a detailed study of the interactions between staff and patients, a deeper understanding of the complex issues faced by staff in this very disturbing setting.

We would particularly like to thank J.M. for providing the very detailed account. In the observation recorded here, we have not included the observer's experiences, such as his feelings and thoughts concerning his role as an observer, the participants, the meeting itself, or the wider organizational context. This is in order to present a more untainted, "unsaturated", account of the meeting so that the commentators could be as free as possible thinking about the interactions, themes, and dynamics in the group.

The chapter was inspired by a clinical commentary section in the *British Journal of Psychotherapy* (Blackwell, Bell, & Dartington, 1993), where transcripts were followed by analyses by a group analyst, a psychoanalyst, and an organizational consultant.

Ward observation

Upon entering the ward, I went to the nurses' office. The nurses were very busy with something and did not seem to notice my presence. After waiting for a short while, I said that I had come for the community meeting. One nurse then told me to go to the nearby large common room, where the community meeting group was about to start.

In the group room, five patients and one nurse were seated, in two circles. There was an inner circle composed of several chairs and one sofa, and an outer circle formed by several chairs scattered further away and one sofa near the wall of the room. After a short while, a second nurse entered and then a third nurse popped in just to ask for the TV to be switched off; she then went out, although she returned a little later. One patient said he did not want the TV to be switched off, and it remained switched on for a little while (I did not notice when it was switched off later on). One patient left the room, and then another patient also left and shouted very loudly just outside. One nurse then left, and the nurse remaining in the room at that time asked me if I wanted to introduce myself; I did so.

One of the patients agreed to write the minutes for this meeting, and a notebook was produced, but then he changed his mind and said that he did not want to do it any more. Another patient took on this task. Looking at the notebook, he said: "From last week there was nothing, we did not have a meeting." Patient A said, "What's the point of talking?" He went on to say that he really disliked the patients spitting on the floor—but none of the culprits who were dirtying things were in the room, so what was the point of saying anything.

Patient L, who was sitting in the outer circle, started laughing as he was reading the newspaper. Two nurses immediately reprimanded him, and he stopped laughing. Patient A said that he would be leaving the ward soon and he planned to do some voluntary work in a patient organization. He thought that patients were not really introduced properly to the ward activities and that patients needed to know where the general office was. Patient L started laughing again, and this time nobody paid attention to him. One of the nurses continued to gently prompt one of the other patients to speak, saying to him "Say something", but the patient remained silent.

One of the patients then said, "Oh I like the audiological department, music is played there, it's good to expose yourself to music." He then said that he would like to go swimming. The nurse said, "You can't go swimming here!" Someone said something about drowning in the swimming pool, and a few patients laughed. One patient said that this meeting should really be made compulsory, that everyone should attend.

By this time two more nurses had arrived. Patient A remarked that there were four nurses in the room and only three patients talking. He said that in this meeting there were more staff than patients. Another patient, B, came into the discussion saying, "Can we go anywhere, where can we go?" And again someone said something about swimming. A patient said, "The patients can drown, can't they?"

Patient A said, "You know what you can do if you're really bad, you can smash things." And he added with pleasure, "And I want to smash things!" Someone said that if you do that, you end up in P Ward (Psychiatric Intensive Care Unit). Someone else (I think it might have been a nurse) said that P Ward was a very difficult ward to be in. Another patient, Z, who had come into the room when the discussion about smashing things started, said "I want to go to P ward and I will smash my room." He loudly exclaimed, "I am bad." This did not produce any effect, and he said even more loudly "I want room service." A nurse said to him, "You are not in a hotel." Patient Z continued to say, "We should have breakfast every morning, in bed really, I really think we should do that."

Another patient joined in the discussion, saying to no one in particular, "Look, there are a lot of people around here who are out of order." Patient A said, "Yes! A lot of intimidating people around." I think Patient B said people actually come on to the ward and can't leave because they are on a section. Someone asked what a section was. Patient A explained that someone was sectioned when they did not want to be admitted on to the ward, and he then said that he had come voluntarily. He said that he was asked at the emergency reception if he would go into the hospital, and he said that he agreed because he knew that he was disturbed. Otherwise, if he had not wanted to go, he would have been sectioned. He said that at the time he thought that he was trying to kill the whole world. Then he laughed and said maybe it was the other way around and that he was trying to get the others to kill him.

Then another patient said that something of his had gone missing. He was asked what had gone missing, and he said that it was a mobile phone. The nurse said, "You really should not keep personal items of value unattended." Patient A said that another patient had lost two phones. Then he quickly lifted up his phone and said loudly and provocatively, "I nicked it off him!" There was an air of some surprise, mixed with excitement, but he then said that he was joking.

Patient B said that it was actually dangerous here. He asked: "What are these bars?" and somebody suggested they were for "health and safety". Then another patient said, "But the door has been locked!", and he went on to say that a few days ago there had been a real fire on the ward, and if there had been a big fire they would have all burnt down since the fire door was locked. The first patient said, "Look, how could you get out of this door?" He put his foot up, gave an imaginary kick with his leg in the direction of the door, and said, "Certainly I could not break that door." He said to the nurse "Don't tell me you can get out of it!" And the nurse said, "No, there is another fire exit." The patient contested this by saying, "No, there is a padlock on that other door, it is impossible to get out." The nurse seemed surprised about the padlock and said that they would have to see about that. There was a discussion about how they could actually all burn down and this needed to be looked into because the fire exits were locked.

Patient B said, "What about the grandeur?" Patient A explained something about a very good place where one could have a meal and can go anytime, something like a drop-in centre. He said that there was a day specially for women and there was a day for gay men, but three days per week one could drop in there. Patient Z asked, "Can you go if you are transsexual?", and everyone laughed.

Patient A said, "This is really a bad situation. Did you know that Trust X is going to take over our Trust?" One of the nurses asked how this related to this meeting.

Again the discussion returned to the issue of safety. Patient Z said "Look at that corner." We all looked and saw a damp and mouldy corner, from floor all the way to the ceiling. He asked the nurses mockingly how healthy was that mould and then jokingly said that it would certainly improve his bones and his breathing. They talked about the moss growing in different places like behind the sink and in the bathroom. One patient asked, "What about the cockroaches?" and the nurse said, "You know what, we have cockroaches because you eat in your rooms!" The patient asked the nurse if she ever had breakfast in bed. She replied, no she did not, and he said "No, you did!" She said, "No I didn't." The patient said, "You must have eaten in the bed at some point in your life, come on, admit it, don't say that you have never ever eaten in your bed." She replied, no, she has never eaten in her bed. Somebody then said that they even have rats.

Another patient said, "Oh here is Mother Teresa, but without sandals!" I presumed that this referred to Patient O, who was just walking into the room. Everyone then started talking at the same time; it was impossible to follow the discussion. The new patient, O, made a dramatic and loud statement: "Can a spark from my lighter blow up the whole hospital?"

There was a brief silence, no one responded to his question, and he slowly moved into the room to sit in the inner circle. He then said that he could not shower with hot water, he said it was impossible, it took only 15 seconds, and he has measured this, exactly 15 seconds before the hot water started. Somebody asked why he did not want the hot water and another patient asked him did he want a Jacuzzi. Unperturbed, Patient O said no. Patient O with deliberate slowness, and it seemed as if he was teasing, said, "Lord, I did not get the name of this gentleman, he is a good friend of mine." He then looked at all with some deliberation and said slowly but clearly and loudly that the only toilet that was clean was the one he used. Another patient said to Patient O, "That is not true, your room is the dirtiest one in the ward!". And suddenly all the patients and the nurses started telling Patient O that his room was dirty, and someone added that he was dirty, and his room was dirty. Patient O did not look affected by this criticism and nonchalantly said that, yes, it was so because somebody else lived in his room on the ward.

One nurse asked if anyone had any other contribution to make and, without waiting very long for responses, she announced that this was the end of the meeting.

Commentary I

David Kennard

My first reaction on reading this account was to identify with what I imagined was the experience of the observer, first on not being noticed when he went to the nurses' office, and then sitting in the room waiting for the meeting to start. It was the experience of being ignored, unrecognized, almost not existing. I was surprised at how these very disturbing ideas could be so easily aroused just by reading the opening lines of the account, which recalled some of my own experiences of ward meetings. It was a reminder of how powerful the effect can be simply of walking on to an acute psychiatric ward without a clearly defined role, of feeling excluded from the busy world of those with roles.

As the account went on, I found myself caught up in the interactions of the meeting, and my initial feelings subsided. I still experienced strong reactions, but now they were ones of interest, anxiety, irritation, or amusement at the unfolding drama of the meeting, until it came to its abrupt end. I share these initial reactions in the hope that they may be similar to some readers' reactions, and also because they may reflect some aspects of the experience of life on the ward.

The material we are presented with seems full of interpersonal and emotional meanings, which, like the patients themselves, are allowed to wander at will without attempts at understanding or interpretation, but within the boundaries set by the nursing staff. There are recurring themes. The most prominent is danger or risk of harm—from drowning, being killed, from fire, unhealthy damp, or explosions. There is a theme of escape from the ward—to go swimming, to go to the intensive care unit, to go anywhere. There is irritation with patients who are dirty or who don't come to the meeting. None of these meanings are explored with the patients.

The use made by the patients of the meeting appears to oscillate between attempts to set an agenda or raise matters of concern on the ward, such as the patients who make things dirty, how new patients might be better introduced to the ward, personal items going missing, alternating with dramatic, even melodramatic "show-stoppers", such as Patients A and Z claiming to want to smash things and later Patient O loudly asking if his lighter could blow up the hospital. The tone, at least until near the end of the meeting, remains largely good-natured, with elements of humour when the nurses are challenged over the padlocked fire exit or the mould in the corner of the room. The nursing staff maintain certain boundaries. They switch the television off, invite the observer to introduce himself, end the meeting, and comment on some realities of the environment—"you can't go swimming", "you are not in a hotel", "you really should not keep personal items of value unattended"—but otherwise allow the patients a free rein.

On the positive side, this is a lively meeting. Patient A takes the lead, several patients contribute, there is some interaction between patients, and a number of direct responses are made by the nurses to what is being said. I've certainly sat through less interesting or interactive meetings.

But there also appear to be missed opportunities. At the start, there are some attempts to get things off the ground—inviting a patient to take the minutes (the account implies this), reprimanding an individual who laughs at a newspaper he is reading, prompting one patient to speak. But following this there is little attempt by the nurses to support the healthy, socially aware capacities of the patients, by facilitating discussion, in the group, of issues of common concern. Neither is there any acknowledgement of the repeated expression of aggressive or fearful fantasies, at least to enquire what effect these have on the rest of the group. The staff do not interact with the patients. They restrict themselves to maintaining the boundaries of time and occasionally content. For example, staff question the relevance of the Trust takeover to the meeting, and they respond to requests or complaints in what comes across as quite an admonishing tone: "you are not in a hotel", "you really should not keep personal items of value unattended", "we have cockroaches because you eat in your rooms". Only on one occasion does a nurse engage at a more personal level in conversation with a patient, about whether or not the nurse has ever eaten in bed. And if the underlying, unasked question here is, "are the staff like the patients in any way?", the answer is a resounding "No".

An important question to ask is, was this meeting successful? The "success" of a meeting depends on its aims, which are not explained, but I shall take the liberty—and risk—of using my experience of mental health wards, therapeutic communities, and group analysis to speculate on what the aims of this meeting might be, and how far they were achieved.

At its lowest level, the aim of the meeting could be to provide a safe space for patients to meet together to "let off steam", which is a lot better than leaving them in isolation to wander or sit without stimulation or attention. In terms of ward-based group approaches, there is no particular conceptual underpinning, although its antecedents may include the therapeutic community approach (see below), Bion's attempts at conducting groups as described in *Experiences in Groups* (Bion, 1961), and Quaker meetings for worship. The patients are free and able to express their opinions, wishes, and fears to an audience of their peers and to get some recognition and response. Such an aim was successfully met.

Another "lower level" aim could be to "take the pulse" of the ward, so to speak—for the staff to check on the mental state of the patients and on issues or tensions that might need watching and managing by the staff in the day ahead. This aim contributes to better ward management and so, indirectly, to benefit for the patients.

A more ambitious aim, using the *therapeutic community approach* (Clark, 1965; Kennard, 1998), is to engage patients in the day-to-day running of the ward. The potential benefits of the therapeutic community have been well summarized by Haigh (1999): to provide a sense of belonging, to provide emotional containment and safety, to foster open communication within and between the staff and patients, to learn from involvement in the day-to-day problems of living together, and empowerment through shared decision-making. Arguably the meeting meets the first two of these aims, the third to a limited extent (limited by the absence of some patients and the non-communication of the nurses), but not the last two aims. There is no attempt to foster discussion between the patients on the problems of shared living or to engage the patients in thinking about how things might be improved on the ward. The references at the start of the meeting to minutes being taken and read out, to the absence of those individuals whose dirty habits need talking about, and to the need for a better introduction for new patients to ward activities, all suggest that there is some initial expectation of patient involvement in decision-making, but on this occasion, at least, none of the staff take this up and the expectation lapses.

From a *group analytic perspective*, the aim might be to help the group to develop more free-flowing communication, overcoming the isolation of individuals, and to "translate" the grandiose or fearful fantasies into a common meaning that can be shared and talked about. One of Foulkes's best known descriptions of this process is quoted by Pines (1983), referring to both neurotic and psychotic disturbances: "The language of the symptom, although already a form of communication, is autistic. It mumbles to itself hoping to be overheard; its equivalent meaning conveyed in words is social" (pp. 276–277). In the meeting, the various fantasies about drowning, smashing things, being burnt, or affected by the damp could be translated into a common language as expressing a need to feel safe. This is a basic concern of any group, especially in its early stages, and the turnover of a ward-based group is such that it is likely to return frequently to these early stages in the life of a group. (Stock, 1962, has given a classic account of the different concerns that members have about potential harm in the early stages of a group.)

It is unrealistic to expect ward staff to use a group analytic approach unless they have had relevant training. However, the use of a community meeting as part of a therapeutic community approach is more likely to be within the competencies of the nursing staff. Elements of a therapeutic community approach in the meeting are visible: the attempted involvement of patients in taking and reading minutes, the invitation to the visitor to introduce himself, the wish by some patients to discuss the problems caused by those who dirty the ward, even the perfunctory request at the end for any other contributions. But beyond this, the nurses opt for a largely passive role, apart from offering occasional reality checks and admonishments. The patients do perhaps have the experience of a safe container in which to play out their fantasies and frustrations. But they do not have the experience of re-connecting with others through communication about shared concerns, which is potentially available in a ward-based community meeting.

Commentary II

Julian Lousada

The poverty of relationships

The "observation" presents a vivid description of a community meeting in which the patients demonstrate their disturbance and frustration. For the most part it is only their voices that we hear. So, from the outset, I found myself wondering what was understood by the term "community", and whether the patients or staff belonged to it in any meaningful sense. The theme of anonymity and the poverty of relatedness pervades the account from the very outset. For example, I was struck by the generic reference to "nurse", as if the nurses could not in any way be differentiated, by gender, age, or ethnicity or indeed by name. The ward manager's absence from the community meeting seemed to express something powerful about the utility of this meeting in the manager's mind. What is revealed systemically is a repeated failure of connections or communications, and an absence of relatedness between those involved.

From the outset, both the task and the activity are sabotaged. The two circles made for a confusing "setting", perhaps indicating an inner and outer state of mind or an atmosphere in which there was no expectation that the nurses and the patients might find a way of connecting such that a community could be experienced. Certainly the boundary and container of time was damaged by the nurses' inconsistent arrival; three were present and then, as the meeting began, two left. The coming and going of both nurses and patients has a restless pacing quality, as if checks are being made on whether or not the community has formed only to discover it hasn't, but nevertheless the meeting continues, with the nurses enquiring about the minutes from the previous meeting when no decisions or comments had been made.

The meaninglessness of the notebook for the minutes is raised by Patient A, who asks "what's the point?" given the absentees. Patient L is then reprimanded for his laughter and subsequently ignored. When two further nurses arrive, now outnumbering the patients, another patient suggests that attendance should be compulsory, a comment clearly directed towards the staff "community" members. It is as if the patients are more in tune than the nurses, not only with the lack of containment, but also and critically with the absence of a belief in a task that involves all in the community.

The community meeting seems like a rudderless ship battered by disturbance and lacking any capacity to navigate towards a place of purpose and safety. The atmosphere becomes progressively more disturbed, and the patients reflect this by discussing the wish to smash things and the desire for containment on P (the locked) Ward. The need for and the absence of authority, a captain, as it were, seems to be implicitly and repeatedly referred to.

There is some evidence that the patients are "engaged" but in the context of inattentive parental objects, who are too anxious to be able to detoxify their own and the patients' disturbing thoughts. The meeting produces more, rather than less, rigidity of role. The patients are trapped in free-floating association and disturbance, while the nurses are trapped in a concrete state of mind where symbolization is not available for thinking.

In the psychiatric ward in question, I am left curious about the experience of the nurses who are running the community meeting. What are we to make of their late arrival? their coming and going? the absence of the manager? the gap between their contribution to the content of the meeting and that of the patients? In short, what can we speculate about their emotional experience and, as such, their relatedness to both the community group and the wider organization?

From the limited material we have, I would suggest that there is a sense not just of individual disconnectedness, but of two groups each of which is unable to use the other to establish a fuller picture. Both groups seem to be trapped in a place where the "other" is unable or, indeed, unwilling to "venture out" for fear of entrapment or contagion. This, then, is a situation in which neither group can conceive of the possibility that the experience of the other might illuminate their own, and, indeed, without such access to the other's experience no transformative experience is possible. At the simplest level, group activity depends on individuals bringing themselves to a collective task. The community meeting is, one supposes, intended to make connections between the experience of staff and patients which in turn depends on the presence of individuals engaged in an activity *together* for the purpose of learning from the outset. This requirement is not met, and so the "idea" that underpins the community meeting is not discovered.

David Armstrong (2005) refers to a situation of

> "organizations locking themselves in" in those circumstances where they are unable to entertain a new idea: whether it (*the idea*) comes from outside or inside or through the pores of sensitivity to the presence of the not-known. But we can easily lose sight of the fact that any new idea requires a host through which it is disseminated, but is also made available throughout the community. . . . Ideas are precious; they do not necessarily emerge fully formed or in a way that is fully understood. [p. 26]

I think that what is "locked in" is the ward's "requirement" to have a community meeting without the understanding that the meeting needs individuals in their roles to be present and to be curious about each other.

The absence of task and the continuation of method

What emerges is a loss of "task", but nonetheless a continued commitment to "method", without an agreement about what the community meeting is meant to achieve. The commitment to "method" without a sense of purpose is not simply a managerial failure; it is also a bewildering and alienating experience for those who are expected to work within the "method". In these circumstances there can be no way of deciding how to work together or, indeed, of determining what has gone on and its quality, or lack of it, or knowing what has been achieved. The organizational mind is seriously weakened by the absence of the reality provided by the task or purpose.

The evacuation of purpose from the method is endemic in the system. Activities become bureaucratized—that is to say, they become part of a routine that has no aim. The nurses in the meeting are present but without any sense of purpose. What has seemingly been lost is the idea of what a connection between staff and staff, patients and patients, and patients and staff actually entails. Being physically present without a corresponding psychological presence is not enough. The unconscious working assumption seems to be that these patients are so disturbed that to engage with them is to run an unacceptable risk. There is no exploration of whether this assumption is right or whether just possibly the disturbance in the meeting is a product of the experience of being present within it.

Many writers have drawn attention to the vulnerability of teams and organizations to acting-in with the disturbance of the patients or the activity they are required to undertake. Most famously and certainly most influentially, Isabel Menzies Lyth (1960b) developed the concept of "social defences" as a way of explaining the organized but often unconscious ways in which those providing welfare services erect defensive manoeuvres to protect themselves from their unacceptable feelings associated with their role and task. As Paul Hoggett (2010) writes:

> These defences are both adaptive, enabling workers to cope, and, usually, simultaneously dysfunctional. They can be defences against seeing and facing suffering, feeling the suffering or thinking about it. [p. 203]

In the context of an acute psychiatric ward like the one we are discussing, it is hardly surprising that well-intentioned staff erect social defences. The role of nurse is a complex one, not least because it is imbued with the maternal functions of physical and emotional care combined with a requirement for compliance with the doctor's authority. The role does not come "ready-made"—it requires considerable capacity for thought and judgement. Such a capacity can be undermined by the organizational dynamics and by the nature of the patients being treated. The more disturbed the patient, the more the capacity to think is put under strain:

> Patient L started laughing again, and this time nobody paid attention to him. A nurse continued to gently prompt one of the other patients to speak, saying to him "Say something", but the patient remained silent.

The point is not that there is a correct interpretation of the communication of the above material; rather, that a therapeutic benefit is derived from the clinician's attempt to give it meaning. It is this "attempt" that would be noticed and responded to. This is not an easy process; it requires knowledge of the psychotic state of mind, but also some knowledge of how to use oneself, and an expectation of support. In discussing a similar group of staff, Hinshelwood comments:

> Hence staff working with such disturbed people need some understanding of communication processes which are not abstract or symbolic. Staff need to explore the "Language of Action"(Hinshelwood, 1987). Relationships that occur in "activities" are likely to be more significant in care institutions that look after people with severe mental disturbance. [Hinshelwood, Pedriali, & Brunner, 2010, p. 27]

All activity requires roles to achieve its purpose. When roles become invisible or undifferentiated, development in object-relating becomes increasingly difficult. It is through the exploration of the boundary of the role and the discovery of the skills associated with it that colleagues discover what they individually bring to the role, how to work together, and what they require to sustain the quality of their work. This reflective activity is an essential *part* of the work in order to protect the task and the organization from the distressing projections they are subjected to.

Implicitly in this account, there is an *idea or method* called "community meeting"; however, for some reason it does not appear as an idea whose history is known and cherished, and this inhibits the ability to transform it into a valued and purposeful activity that can be explored, understood, or worked on. In effect, it has no "contemporary" meaning. The organizational context, the primary task of the ward, and indeed the task of the community meeting are strangely absent, as if they are so obvious that they do not need to be commented upon and, as such, would add nothing of value to an understanding of the task and the observation. In this way, we see how the nurses' actions mirror those of the patients, who also have thoughts that they wish to act on but cannot find meaning for (swimming, making the meeting compulsory, and smashing things up).

How does the nurses' behaviour reflect the task they have in their minds, and how does the "way" in which they worked help us understand something of what is happening? Vega Roberts (1994) writes:

. . . it can be helpful to ask what are we behaving *as if* we were here to do? Identifying this "as-if" task can provide clues about the underlying anxieties, defences and conflicts which have given rise to the dysfunctional task definition and associated dysfunctional boundaries. [p. 38]

There is little doubt that the patients in the community meeting are very disturbed and that their contact with reality is at best tenuous. The nurses' anxiety is understandable, as is the need, as they see it, to hold on to reality as far as possible. I imagine that the purpose of a community meeting is to do what can be done to put into words the relatedness between what is said and what might be the more hidden—that is to say, the unconscious communication relating to the patients' experience *as community members*. However, to engage in this communication it is necessary for the nurses themselves to accept that they also have an experience *as community members*; this is the site of potential connection, but it requires the nurses to use themselves, and it is here that the risk to their own state of mind feels most acute.

The casualty in this ward is twofold. First, curiosity and the capacity to have experiences that can be made sense of are lacking. Second, there is no belief in the possibilities of connections between people such that engagement within and across the boundary or role could be explored systemically and therapeutically, which would enable a community meeting to take place for the benefit of all concerned. This is a suffering system for all concerned.

Commentary III

Mary Morgan

This observation of a community meeting in a psychiatric hospital might not immediately present us with material about couple relating—there is only one brief interchange between a patient and a nurse that might constitute a couple interaction. However, I think it is possible to take this interchange and also the general exchange between the staff and patients on the ward as examples of couple interaction. In particular, these illustrations show us some of the psychotic elements that occur in poorly functioning relationships.

Before describing these processes, I will put this in the context of the idea of creative couple relating (Morgan, 2005), in which a genuine and creative intercourse takes place. The capacity for "creative couple relating" comes about as part of psychic development and contributes to a belief that by allowing different thoughts and feelings to come together in one's mind, something new and potentially creative can develop out of them. As well as being an internal capacity, relationships with external others are affected. The different, or sometimes opposing, perspective of the other is not felt to obliterate one's own view but can be taken in to one's psyche and allowed to reside there and mate with one's own thought. In this way, the individual's own psychic development can be enhanced through engaging with another person. There develops a state of mind in which two minds can come together and create a third, a new thought. When this state of mind is possible, there is a genuine curiosity about the other and what is in his or her mind, and how what is in the other's mind may not only be valuable in itself but may transform something in one's own mind.

A capacity for creative couple relating comes and goes; it is not a fixed state that can be maintained at all times. But I do think that once it has been discovered, it resides somewhere in the psyche as a state of mind that can be evoked. This observation helpfully illustrates the kinds of states of mind in which this is not possible.

The interaction between the nurse and the patient about cockroaches is a good example of non-creative relating. The patient who talks about cockroaches picks up something about dirt that permeates the observation; the patients spitting on the floor, fears about health and safety, damp and mould. A patient asks, "What about the cockroaches?" The nurse responds as if attacked and then accuses the patient: "We have cockroaches because you eat in your rooms." What follows is accusation responded to by accusation about who has (ever) had breakfast in bed. Something, represented by the cockroaches, has disturbed both patient and nurse, and there is an attempt by each to forcibly project this disturbance into the other: "you are the one who eats in bed and brings the cockroaches". This kind of exchange is typical of a couple who each feel the other is trying to drive them mad. One partner feels disturbed and frightened by something inside them, "a dirty cockroach". In the absence of the capacity to think about this or feel there is another who could help them think about it, the only possibility is to try to rid the psyche of what feels unbearable by forcibly projecting it into the other. When the partner is used in this way, as a kind of psychic dumping ground, the relationship is sacrificed. Using the other in this way restores a sense of psychic equilibrium, the disturbing thought or feeling having been evacuated into the other. The problem (or, one might say, advantage) of projecting disturbing psychic content into one's partner is that it does not go far away, and there is then a constant need to keep it located in the other. Working with couples, one see this vividly as each partner tries to keep the other's projections out while at the same time trying to force his or her own projections in.

Some couples, perhaps like the nurse and patient in this example, are caught up in this kind of gunfire of mutual projection. One can see how this starts to escalate as the patient tries to force the projection by telling the nurse that she's the same as him, and the nurse tries to reproject this unwelcome thought or feeling by saying no, she is different, claiming that she has never eaten in her bed. There is an absence of any kind of container, either internally or in the relationship. In this situation, there is a tendency to get rid of what feels emotionally unmanageable, project it into the other, and try to keep it there. The proximity of the partner who carries unwanted projections, while often experienced in the couple relationship as

tormenting and persecuting, may also protect against fragmentation, the relationship functioning as a kind of asylum.

Relationships, especially intimate relationships or those in
intensive work situations, are a fertile arena for projection. The
object or group with whom one is in a relationship, often coloured
and intensified by transference, is projected into because of its proximity and because boundaries are more permeable. Many couples
come for help in a state of mind in which they feel unable to think
about their own and their partner's unmanageable feelings and
what is happening between them. They feel overwhelmed by their
own emotions, and in this state of mind it is easy to see the other
as responsible for disturbing them in this way. In this observation,
both nurse and patient try to lodge the "dirty feeling" in the other.

This can occur in couples when there is anxiety that neither
can process, either separately or together. One couple was worried
because the nursery had reported to them concerns about their
youngest son. They were told that he could not cooperate in play,
was being aggressive, and was snatching toys away from other
children and spoiling their things. Quite typically, for this couple,
the concern was not brought up directly. Instead, they started to
attack each other in the session. The husband complained that his
wife was too preoccupied with her job and didn't look after things
at home—he said she was untidy and disorganized and he couldn't
stand it. He had tried to help her be more organized, but it was
hopeless. The wife was furious about the accusation and said that
she was tidy and that he had no idea about what it was like managing her job and looking after the children—things got messy, but
she tidied up eventually. The problem was that he was so obses-
sive in his tidying up that she often could not find things, and this
drove her mad. She wondered if he was throwing her things away.
He responded that he was not throwing them away, he was putting them away, and if she was more organized she would know
where they were. He then gave the therapist several examples of
how chaotic his wife was and how other people had commented on
it. The wife said this was a lie and that he was mad—she actually
thought he had a disorder of some kind, and she was trying to get
him to see his GP. As with nurse and patient in the ward example,
the other is the bad/mad/dirty one, not the self. The therapist had
heard similar arguments before, but she noted that on this occasion
their familiar argument about the state of the house had reached
new heights. She interpreted the couple's anxiety that they felt in

a mess that neither felt able to deal with, and that they each felt the other was to blame for it. She wondered what the mess was. After several more accusations between them, in which each now began to feel humiliated and despairing, the therapist suggested that there was something quite unbearable they were struggling with and wondered what had happened in the week. The couple eventually began to talk about the report from the nursery, and the therapist tried to help them think about their son and to stay with their difficult feelings about what was going on rather than start again the process of evacuating them into the other.

The second example of couple relating in the community meeting which I wish to consider is found in the general dynamic between nurses and patients where there is no curiosity and no belief in the possibility of a creative intercourse. There are many examples of this. One patient talks about liking the audiological department and says that he would like to go swimming. A nurse responds "you can't go swimming here". Another patient says "I want to smash things" and another patient responds "if you do that, you end up in P Ward". A patient says "I want room service" and a nurse says "you are not in a hotel". A patient talks about something of his that went missing, and a nurse responds "you really should not keep personal items of value unattended", and so on. There seems to be a complete lack of curiosity about what anyone is saying, why they are saying it, and what it might mean. There also seems to be enormous anxiety about opening anything up, and one must ask why. The presence of the observer is not commented on either, even though one imagines this might stimulate some fantasies. There are couples just like this who come together not to engage with the otherness of the other, but to establish and construct a relationship to defend against anxiety.

For example, the female partner in a couple was trying to talk to her male partner about money and the fact that she earned quite a lot more than him. He responded with a rational plan for how they could deal with this and both feel OK: they would buy a house together with her money, they would jointly decorate it and make a home; she would of course own it, but it would feel like theirs. As they talked and became quite excited about this plan, it became clear that they could not touch on how difficult this situation was for them both, how emasculated he felt, and how disappointed she felt and all the resonances this had with earlier events in their lives. As they continued talking, the excitement about this plan faded and the atmosphere changed to something flat. The therapist sensed that there was immense anxiety just beneath the surface and wondered whether the couple would be able to bear getting in touch with this or whether they would try to construct another defensive strategy for keeping painful feelings at bay.

The community meeting observation shows, in extremis, the flat uncreative quality of such relating. One is left feeling nothing much has come out of the meeting and nothing ever will, and that that is what everyone expects. As with the couple, if there was anyone present to wonder about this, that person would feel there is something extremely defensive taking place.

The observation and these brief vignettes of couples highlight the fact that relating to another is not always in the service of wanting to get to know the other, be known by the other, or share an experience. Sometimes relationships are used as a way of getting rid of unbearable thoughts or experiences that are too difficult to know about or to stay within oneself. Equally, a lot of support both internally and externally is required for the recipient of these evacuated contents when working in an environment in which disturbing projections are rife. Otherwise, the relationships degenerate into systems of rapid projections and reprojections, or defensive structures are set up so that the projection cannot penetrate, and curiosity about the other is absent. Couple therapists see both kinds of relationships, the former in presentations where the partners try to drive each other mad and the latter in those where the relationship has become flat and uncreative.

Commentary IV

Wilhelm Skogstad

This ward observation is both interesting and disturbing. The reader is given the raw observation material of a moment in the life of a psychiatric ward, with acutely psychotic patients and their ward staff. One hears nothing of the observer's emotional response or of the wider context, and one has no way of gaining answers to the questions one would like to ask. It is a disconcerting glimpse into a world of madness.

What are we to make of this? The kind of institutional observations Hinshelwood and I proposed (Hinshelwood & Skogstad, 2000a) would take place over a considerable period of time. In trying to make sense of an institution, such as a psychiatric ward, one would take account of the particularities of negotiating entry into the organization, of what is directly observable in the sessions, the observer's emotional responses to the observation, as well as the processing of all of these together in a seminar, with the minds of others as sounding boards. Even with such wider material, any hypotheses coming out of the process would need to be treated as tentative. They might be confirmed or disconfirmed by further observations, but they would never have the same validity as in psychoanalysis, where the patient's responses to interpretations provide important and often illuminating additional material. With one observation alone, as in this case, and no chance to check things out further, one is limited to speculative thoughts and might easily be drawn to false conclusions.

Even with this caveat, one gets the sense of entering a world of madness. This is very different from the "world of bodies" I encountered when I observed a medical ward (Skogstad, 2000). There, the task of dealing with bodies and physical illness seemed to create a way of relating to people in a concrete, bodily manner,

167

as if they were not people suffering with anxieties and pain, and the anxieties about illness and death seemed to lead to a defensive culture of manic excitement. Here, on a psychiatric ward, dealing with people's madness creates quite different anxieties, and the culture and atmosphere appear quite different, closer to that observed in previous observations of psychiatric institutions (Chiesa, 2000; Donati, 2000; Rees, 2000). One of the hypotheses from those observations was that there was an unconscious assumption in staff that any lively interaction could lead to the outbreak of madness and therefore had to be curtailed (Hinshelwood & Skogstad, 2000c).

The observer enters the ward to attend a community meeting. He is not noticed, and when he eventually draws attention to himself, saying he has come for the community meeting, he is directed to the common room. I had the sense (which may be wrong) that staff did not know this observer and that it may have even been his first visit to the ward, and so it is remarkable that no question is asked. This gives an impression of a lack of boundaries as well as a lack of ordinary human relatedness and curiosity. Is this what awaits a patient entering the ward? Are they just expected to fit in, no questions asked? In fact, one patient, who is about to be discharged, refers to entering the ward. It seems to have been a disorientating experience, with the patient not even knowing where the general office was—that is, where he would find the nurses.

One would expect a community meeting to have clear boundaries in terms of space, time, and membership. In this case, the space is clear: it is the ward's common room. Yet otherwise there seems to be a troubling confusion: one nurse pops in and out, another leaves, some are late, patients wander in and out, and it seems unclear who is expected to attend the meeting; a patient says it should be made compulsory. The TV is left on for some time, and it is unclear who has the authority to say that it should be switched off. Are staff afraid of asserting their authority and establishing clearer boundaries? Does this confusion serve a defensive purpose?

The ward, this involuntary or only half-voluntary temporary "home" for patients, seems to be represented in their minds in different ways. Some express fantasies of the ward as a bountiful breast, a place with "room service", "breakfast every morning in bed", and a swimming pool. On the other hand, it is felt to be a disgusting place, with cockroaches, rats, and people spitting on the floor. Some express terrifying persecutory anxieties about the ward as a place where they are locked in by bars and padlocks, where they might all burn down or drown. Patients communicate violent impulses towards this place, the wish to "smash things" or to "blow up the whole hospital", and their sense that containment for such impulses cannot be offered here, only somewhere else, "in P Ward".

In this way, the patients express vivid psychotic fantasies, which are partly based on severe splitting, and the accompanying perse-cutory anxieties. Yet the nurses respond in a highly restricted way, always emphasizing a limited, almost banal kind of reality: "You are not in a hotel", "you can't go swimming here", "we have cock-roaches because you eat in your rooms", or "P Ward was a very difficult ward to be in".

Similarly, when an anxiety about the place being taken over by a powerful organization, Trust X, is expressed, it is, more or less, dismissed as not relating to the meeting.

The impression I gained from this observation is that, in this setting, there is no real space for the patients' mad (or even not-so-mad) fantasies, impulses, and anxieties, that staff are unable to understand and contain them. The nurses seem desperate and helpless in their attempts to bring the patients down to the level of a superficial physical reality. In this way, it becomes a mad world in itself, a world of concrete objects with no meaning. In this "mad world of reality", even the real dangers get ignored, like when the fire exit is locked or when the risk of another NHS Trust taking over is treated as irrelevant.

This state of affairs is, I think, a reflection of the terrifying anxi-ety that the patients' madness, their psychotic world, engenders in staff. They might feel the need to defend themselves against the contagion of madness. The lack of human relatedness and the lack of boundaries I noticed at the beginning may now be better understandable. If close human interaction can bring one disturb-ingly in touch with madness, it may feel better to stay at a distance; if establishing authority and boundaries might stir up violence and madness, it may feel safer to shy away from them.

Community meetings on such wards may have been established because of an idea that bringing people together in an ordinary and democratic way is helpful—a friendly, humane face of psychiatry. And yet, as we can see, getting close to psychotic people stirs up deep anxieties, which staff would need training and support to understand and contain. Yet in this setting, they seem left with their own anxieties, and as a result, rather than being helpful, the meeting turns into a defensive procedure, geared more to helping staff manage than to helping patients deal with their anxieties.

It is encouraging, though, that the project that produced this interesting and rich observation also led to the recommendation that staff need training and ongoing support.

CHAPTER TEN

Asylum and society

Elizabeth Bott Spillius

Since first publishing the paper on which this chapter is based (Bott, 1976),[1] 1 have changed my view of what its central theme should be. The original research was a study of a typical large British mental hospital carried out somewhat intermittently between 1957 and 1972. Originally the paper had two main themes: the persistence of chronic hospitalization and the presence of endemic conflicts in the hospital. I devoted a great deal of discussion to the first theme because it was assumed in the 1960s that the number of long-stay "chronic" patients was rapidly declining. The big old hospitals in the country were to be closed down and replaced by psychiatric wards in general hospitals for short-stay "acute" patients. The remaining chronically psychotic patients would be housed in a reduced number of the old country hospitals or, better, in some sort of facility provided by local government authorities. "Community care" was a fashionable idea, though little real effort was made either by the National Health Service or by local government authorities to make concrete plans for it.

By the time of writing this chapter, 2011, it has become clear that long-stay patients, including young long-stay patients, are still accumulating and that providing treatment and care for them is a continuing social problem. Interest in mental health circles no longer focuses on whether services for the chronically mentally ill will be needed but on what form these services should take, specifically on whether and how chronically ill patients can be cared for in the community, near their homes (Clifford, 1988; Griffiths, 1988; Wing & Furlong, 1986).

In this version of my original paper, I focus, as before, on the hospital as I knew it in the 1960s and 1970s, and I continue to describe its practices in the present tense, even though the hospital I studied, like many other large mental hospitals, no longer exists. I suspect, however, that the care of mentally ill patients at the present time may still involve some of the difficulties and contradictions that were present fifty years ago. I found, for example, that there was usually a basic conflict between the patient and his or her close relatives, and that this conflict had an effect on the organization of the hospital. The staff at the hospital, however, did not usually see the link between the conflicts between patients and their relatives and the conflicts in the hospital. In spite of the two types of conflict, familial and institutional, the hospital I studied had an excellent reputation and was generally considered to be run in a benign and thoughtful way. Even today, when "old-timers" happen to encounter each other, their discussions of the hospital usually express a mutual feeling that something valuable was lost when the hospital was finally officially closed in 1998.

The hospital as I first encountered it

By British standards the hospital was large, its mean annual size between 1905 and 1972 having been 1,840 patients. It was situated in beautifully kept grounds in the countryside close to a village, which the hospital dominated, and near an industrial town where many of its patients worked, though neither the village nor the town belonged to the hospital's catchment area, which was some 20 miles away in north London. The hospital was divided into two main buildings, one containing 24 long-stay wards for patients of all ages, including admission wards for patients over 65 years of age, and a second building consisting of 8 short- and medium-stay active treatment wards for patients under 65 years of age. There were 18 medical staff, of whom 4 were consultants; 1 of the 4 consultants was also the Medical Superintendent. There were 4 other relatively senior doctors and 10 junior staff members in various stages of training. There was a high turnover among the nurses, particularly among unqualified nurses. There was a handful of psychologists and social workers and 20–30 occupational and industrial therapists. My initial study was based on interviews, group discussions, and observations of the wards of Dr Dennis Scott, one of the 4 consultants.

Over the course of the study, I examined the various new methods of physical and social treatment that were being adopted in the 1950s and 1960s and related them to trends of change in the admission and discharge rates of patients. The lack of fit that soon became apparent led me to conclude that I had been paying too much attention to what was going on inside the hospital and too little to the hospital's connections with its environment. Despite the usual assumption in psychiatric circles at the time that long-stay patients were no longer being cared for in sizable numbers, I found that among people under 65 there was only a slight trend of decline in the rate of chronic hospitalization between 1934 and the late 1960s. This indicates a comparatively stable aspect of the relationship between the hospital and its environment, a relationship that had not been much affected by changes in psychiatric fashion, the redefinition of madness as illness, or such environmental changes as alterations in family and network structure. It may indicate an unchanging core of mental illness, but it is more likely that chronic hospitalization is not a reliable indicator of such illness, but a result of the pattern of relationships between the patient, his or her significant others, and the hospital. Whether a patient eventually ended up inside or outside the hospital appeared to depend on which offered a more viable social place.

The admission process

At the time of my study it had become customary to speak of the use society made of mental hospitals and the function such hospitals performed for society. Admission was the crucial transaction in which the nature of this usage became manifest. I did not study admission directly. My discussion was therefore based on the work of others, particularly that of Dennis Scott and his colleagues (Scott, 1973, 1974; Scott & Ashworth, 1965, 1967, 1969; Scott, Ashworth, & Casson, 1970; Scott, Casson, & Ashworth, 1967). All his published papers deal with the process of admission and the part it plays in the relation between the patient and his or her significant others. I have also been much influenced by Erving Goffman's (1969) paper "The Insanity of Place", which describes with painful acuteness the destruction of one's sense of self by the madness in another about whom one cares. His paper is unique in describing the process before hospitalization—a corrective to retrospective accounts from inside hospitals, but a corrective also to facile assertions that the typical situation is one in which an innocent deviant is victimized by persecutory relatives and an over-conventional society.

The behaviour called mental illness is a form of social deviance. Like other forms of deviance—genius, crime, rebellion—it arouses strong reactions, usually negative, because implicitly it attacks the norms people live by. It differs from other forms of deviance in that it is not supposed to be the patient's fault. In this respect attitudes towards mental and physical illness are similar, for in neither is the patient blamed or held responsible for their state. But in physical illness the disability is restricted to the body, whereas mental illness affects the person's sense of self. Furthermore, as Goffman so poignantly describes in the paper mentioned above, the person behaves in a way that attacks the sense of self of the people close to him. As well as feeling guilt and a terrible sense of failure, relatives begin to feel that something absolutely crucial in themselves is being attacked. This is why the relatives of the psychotically disturbed person can become wildly distressed, sometimes over things that seem trivial to an outsider. The interactional framework that has defined the relative's sense of self is being destroyed. Scott puts it in slightly different language: "Physical illness is a role but mental illness is an identity." One *has* a physical illness; one *is* a mental illness. And between the person who will become a patient and the relatives there is what he calls "identity warfare"—a battle for psychic survival (Scott, 1974).

Usually it is a relative who makes the first crucial decision in which the patient's behaviour is defined as "ill". Distressing though this is, it takes some of the pain out of patients' behaviour, for it makes it unintended; he (or she) does not mean it; he is not responsible for himself. However, it also annihilates a person's identity as a responsible adult, and, for the relatives, it is fraught with often unacknowledged anxiety and fear of revenge. The fault is defined as residing in the illness, not in the person. What used to be a relationship is dismembered into illness in the patient and health in the relative. The patient may obligingly and even cunningly contribute to this process.

At the time of my study of the hospital, calling madness "mental illness" was a comparatively recent phenomenon. It was part of a humane attempt to take away its stigma and accord it the same dignity and respectability as physical illness. This redefinition assumes that the illness is a concrete disease inside an individual that is—or will one day be—treatable and curable in the same way as many physical illnesses are. Sociologists and many psychiatrists have criticized this definition of madness as a concrete disease entity inside the individual (Cooper, 1967; Goffman, 1961 [and especially 1969]; Laing & Esterson, 1964; Scott, 1973, 1974; Scott & Ashworth, 1969 [and Scott's various papers, especially Scott, Casson, & Ashworth, 1967]; Szasz, 1961). Their criticism is based on the fact that behaviour that is labelled mentally ill is crucially involved in and defined by interaction with other people. On the matter of causes as distinct from effects of the disturbed behaviour, the various authors disagree. Both Laing and Cooper regard mental illness as a form of social deviance created by families and society. My view (which is also Scott's and Goffman's) is that, whatever the cause, the view that madness is only deviance from conventional norms fails to appreciate the destruction the mad person—or, more accurately, the mad part of the person—wreaks not only on conventional society but on *any* form of society. The view that the patient is an innocent victim ignores the extent to which he or she controls and manipulates both associates and self to destroy the basis of thinking and gratification for both.

When relatives seek hospital admission for their potential patient, they are not merely seeking relief from an excruciatingly painful conflict. They are rarely satisfied if a doctor promises to admit the patient because the behaviour in question is intolerable. Typically, relatives want a clear statement that the patient is *ill* and that this is why the patient is being admitted. Only then can they feel at least partially absolved of responsibility. If need be, they can tell the patient (and themselves) that they did not want to get rid of the patient; it was the doctor's decision; it was "because of the illness". They can assure themselves that the madness is in the patient, not in themselves, for relatives are tacitly pronounced "well" by the same act that pronounces the patient to be "ill". Henceforth, responsibility for the care, control, and treatment of the patient is placed squarely on the shoulders of the doctor and the hospital for as long as the patient remains in hospital. It has become a medical not an interpersonal problem.

While relatives say and usually also feel that they want help for their patient, they act as if the help has to take the form of removal, control, and care. They will accept treatment easily only if it does not threaten their own status as "sane" and if it avoids making explicit the hatred of and dependence on the patient that the relatives have secured the admission to get relief from.

Having an illness absolves patients from responsibility and entitles them to care. But the stigma is enormous, and admission to the hospital, especially for the first time, is a catastrophe. It irrevocably alters the person's sense of self—a fact of which people who work constantly in mental hospitals tend to become almost unaware. Accepting the labelling of oneself as ill—or even as a person with difficulties or disturbance—is usually impossible. Patients are unwilling to say how the hospital might help or that they need help in any case, or even why and how they have come to be in the hospital. But usually they do not try to leave the hospital; thus, they act as if they find it a relief to be away from their relatives: they use the hospital as a refuge but cannot say so.

In spite of its degradation, the status of mental patient gives a person considerable power. Every act, however mad, that challenges the former *status quo* in one's relation with relatives still lacerates their sense of identity, even once the patient is in the hospital. The patient can continue to use supposed mindlessness to attack not only relatives' sanity but also his or her own. And every self-damaging act hurts the relatives yet again. The patient has certain advantages in the identity warfare. A growing body of work in the United States in the 1960s established that mental patients, including chronic patients, are able to modify their behaviour to secure the ends they desire (Braginsky, Grosse, & Ring, 1966; Fontana, Klein, Lewis, & Levine, 1968; Ludwig & Farrelly, 1966; Towbin, 1966). Patients who want to stay in the hospital know how to behave as if they were more ill, and patients who want to leave know how to behave so as to seem less ill.

In his relations with nursing and medical staff, the patient has a similar advantage. One of the important elements of what Talcott Parsons (1951) has described as the "sick role" is that patients, though not held responsible for being ill, *are* held responsible for cooperating with the doctors who are trying to help them get better. In the case of patients in mental hospitals, these two expectations lead to a built-in contradiction: the patient is expected to cooperate with doctors and nurses but cannot be expected to cooperate, since the ill state involves his whole identity. He (or she) is assumed not to have enough mind to cooperate with. Erikson (1957) makes the same point in a slightly different form. Certain patients make the fullest use of the opportunities for evasion and confusion that these contradictory expectations allow.

To the ordinary citizen, the redefinition of madness as mental illness has not had much effect. Anything that involves destruction of predictable behaviour and capacity to think is not regarded as similar to physical illness. Studies of public attitudes to mental illness show that people in general, like the patients' relatives, are reluctant to label people as mentally ill and will tolerate behaviour deviations as "eccentricities" for some considerable time; but once the label of "mental illness" has been assigned, the impulse to reject the person so labelled becomes intense (Sarbin & Mancuso, 1970). The term mental illness has thus suffered the fate of most euphemisms: it has come to mean the same thing as the term "madness" it was intended to replace. Stigma still attaches to mental illness and to the hospitals and people that deal with it. Public attitudes towards mental hospitals fluctuate between a wish not to know they exist and sudden concern over the welfare of their inmates, with occasional bouts of fear that dangerous madmen are being irresponsibly released into the community.

The admission process is crucial to the definition of the hospital setting. Before a patient can be put into the hospital, someone—usually a relative with the support of a general practitioner or social worker—has to get a hospital doctor to agree to the admission. What general practitioners and hospital doctors are asked to do is give the sanction of expert medical opinion to a lay decision that the patient's relatives have already made. By agreeing to admission, they confirm the relatives' view that the patient is incapable of accepting responsibility for his or her behaviour and that the hospital doctor and staff should accept responsibility for care and control. Furthermore, the admitting doctor tacitly confirms the relatives' belief and hope that the trouble is a medical matter, that it consists of a concrete disease entity inside the patient as an individual. An admitting doctor also undertakes, tacitly or explicitly, to provide treatment and to try to cure the patient. For the doctor and the hospital, all these aspects combine to form a fateful decision, which inevitably leads to conflict within the hospital, a conflict that is often as unacknowledged as the conflict between relatives and patient or the conflict within the patient's own self.

The process of admission would be more straightforward if the relatives could make it clear to the patient that it was they themselves who wanted the patient sent to the hospital because they found the patient's behaviour temporarily impossible, perhaps also with acknowledgement that the patient also found the situation intolerable. But such direct acknowledgement of conflict and hatred contravenes the implicit rules of social interaction, as well as being especially intolerable to people who are frightened of madness in themselves and each other. If a doctor refuses to grant admission except on the basis of such acknowledgement of need for mutual respite, the relatives are likely to feel very persecuted, especially if there is no other hospital to which they can send their patient.

There is, thus, a dishonest element in the work expected of doctors and mental hospitals, though hospitals and their doctors usually comply without protest, even without realizing the contradiction implicit in what they are expected to do, which is to treat the patient's illness in order to help the patient but also to control the patient on behalf of the people with whom the patient has an untenable relationship.

There is a consistent thread of feeling running through all the social and personal attitudes towards mental illness, mental patients, and mental hospitals. All concerned act as if they agreed, without having to reflect on it, that madness cannot be contained and accommodated as part of ordinary personal and social life. It is beyond the pale. If it is kept inside, it will destroy—destroy the individual, the family, the fabric of society. It must at all costs be separated off and sent somewhere else, and the main task of the mental hospital is to be that "somewhere else".

On discord between patients and relatives and its expression in the hospital

Although neither Scott nor I made a systematic comparison according to psychiatric criteria of the severity of symptoms among hospital-centred and community-centred patients, it was clear from ordinary clinical practice, both inside the hospital and in outpatient clinics, that some patients who got stuck in the hospital were not especially severely disturbed, whereas some of those who went home to their families were too incapacitated to work or to lead independent lives. It is difficult to know how prevalent such disability is, since ordinary clinical practice does not provide accurate information about what happens to patients once they go home (cf. Brown, Bone, Dalinson, & Wing, 1966). I believe that whether patients end up inside or outside the hospital does not depend primarily on the severity of the psychiatric disorder, but on the type and severity of discordance between patient and relatives, and thus on whether home or hospital offers the patient a more viable social place.

Organically oriented psychiatrists consider that chronic hospitalization occurs because the disease process involved in madness incapacitates patients and prevents them from occupying their social places outside hospital. In the 1950s and 1960s, the popular psychiatric view was that mental hospitals "institutionalized" patients and thus incapacitated them for life outside hospital. Scott's work, and to some extent that of Goffman, Szasz, Laing, and others, suggests that the crucial factor in chronic hospitalization is the nature of the relationship between the patient and the society in which he or she lives, especially his or her relationship with relatives. If the patient and relatives are in a severely discordant but mutually dependent relationship, the patient is likely to end up permanently in the hospital. For the patient, the hospital is an asylum; for the relatives, it acts as a place that contains and controls the madness and its destruction of their own sense of their identity as sane. In cases in which a patient is socially isolated, particularly if the relatives die or withdraw themselves from contact, the patient may use the hospital as a substitute for a world in which he or she feels unable to make a place. In brief, chronic hospitalization occurs when a hospital place is accessible and appears to the patient to offer a more viable social place than could be found outside.

It seems extremely unlikely that society or its health services can eliminate either the mad aspects of familial relationships or madness in individuals. But finding the best place to contain and care for madness poses considerable problems.

Control, care, and treatment

My thesis is that the admission process, combined with the way the hospital is connected to its environment, leads to the development inside the hospital of conflicts ultimately deriving from the basic conflict between madness and sanity, between the patient and his relatives, and, putting it in more generalized terms, between patient and society. When my study began, there was no open controversy or awareness of conflict over this issue, only an occasional voicing of an ill-defined feeling that something confusing was going on that made staff, especially doctors, uneasy and dissatisfied without knowing why. "This is a marvellous place to work because of the permissive atmosphere, but there is something odd about it. I don't know how to describe it", said a young doctor who had recently come from a much more authoritarian hospital. "The hospital is like schizophrenia itself," said another, "split up in bits, projections all over the place, parts not communicating with other parts. Things are always getting lost in this place—people, ideas, decisions. There is an overpowering sense of inertia." Or another, in 1961: "Do you want a chunk of my private paranoia? Trying to change anything here is like falling into an animal trap. Once you get outside your own ward, everything is chaos. Each misunderstanding is understandable, but there are just too many. It couldn't be chance. But I stay here, don't I?" More recent studies indicate that these feelings of discomfort, even demoralization, have not altered much in the past thirty years (Donati, 2000; Hinshelwood, 1979, 1986).

With hindsight, I think that what was making these doctors uncomfortable was an unarticulated sense that something the hospital was doing was not straightforward. There is a sort of dishonesty in (albeit unknowingly) allowing the hospital to be used to treat and house individuals who are acting as the receptacles of the madness that their relatives cannot bear to face as part of their family or as part of themselves. Malaise was aggravated by certain organizational features peculiar to this research hospital, but I believe that the basic dilemma was built into the organization of all mental hospitals that used the traditional definitions of why and how patients are admitted, because these definitions land the hospital in a situation of trying to help an individual on behalf of a society that does not recognize its wish to get rid of its mad individuals as well as to help them.

In the formal medical–nursing model, the functions of control, care, and treatment are supposed to act simultaneously in the interests of patient and society. Yet it is usually thought that control and care operate in the interests of society and that only treatment operates in the interests of the patient. It is, however, widely recognized that patients, relatives, and staff sometimes regard treatment as punishment meted out by the hospital on behalf of society—hardly surprising in view of the ferocity of the early physical treatments—whereas custodial care is sometimes regarded as a refuge from society. Furthermore, many doctors have come to regard ward regimes and nursing care as a major component of treatment—the only treatment in some programmes.

The *control* component of hospital activities consists of a set of regulations and restrictions originally designed to prevent patients from escaping or hurting themselves or causing offence to others. The regulations and rules are usually thought to be carried out for the benefit of society rather than to help the patient, except in the sense that preventing suicide can be considered helpful to the patient.

The general public has different views of the need for control from the views of people who are closely acquainted with mental patients in mental hospitals. The cultural stereotype is still that mental patients are dangerous and would all try to escape if they were not locked up, whereas for patients, relatives, and hospital staff it is inertia rather than violence that is the typical problem. The difficult issue was to get patients to leave the hospital, not to keep them in.

Doctors carry overall responsibility for the control function, but it is the nursing staff who immediately exercise it and, unless the doctor is particularly active in defining the way he or she wants the nursing staff to exercise control, they regard themselves as being responsible for the control function to the senior nursing staff and the medical superintendent; ultimately, though more tacitly, they regard themselves as responsible to the external society.

Standards of control used to be much more stringent than they were even in 1957, when my study began. Preventing suicides and escapes was no longer a major preoccupation of the nursing staff, and standards of cleanliness and order were less exacting than they had been during the 1930s. But even at that time, nursing staff regarded themselves as—and felt they were regarded by others as—responsible for maintaining something close to the usual standards of control, care, and cleanliness. Sometimes nurses made the social basis of their anxiety about patients' freedom very clear, as when a former nursing officer complained that the medical staff were allowing certain wards to run riot with permissiveness. He was worried that it would end with the nursing staff in court if there was a suicide. Another nurse complained about not having a proper programme for the care of patients, saying he knew it was designed to make the patients take responsibility for themselves but thought it damaging to the ward nursing staff to see the ward and the patients get into a filthy, disorderly state. Again, adherence to the control function showed itself in the content of the rumours that usually circulated when a ward was starting a new programme. The typical content of such rumours was that patients were being allowed to indulge themselves sexually or to be violent—the two instinctual urges that it is traditionally the task of society to keep under control.

Although hospital doctors are ultimately responsible for the control function, most of them do not like it. Many try to avoid it because they feel it interferes with treatment. But in the hospital situation, control and authority were always a crucial part of the treatment setting: it is a doctor who decides whether a patient can come into the hospital; a doctor who decides—or is at least in charge of the team who decide—on a patient's general ward programme, work regime, and treatment; it was a doctor who used to determine a patient's "privileges" and "passes"; and it is a doctor, or a team headed by a doctor, who usually decides when a patient leaves the hospital. In law, in the eyes of the general public, in the opinion of relatives and of patients, the doctor is the ultimate authority and holds this authority on behalf of society. Control is an integral part of the job.

If a hospital doctor denies this social and administrative authority or avoids its implications, he or she is sure to run into trouble. Some doctors at the research hospital tried to get their nursing staff not only to exercise the control function, but also to take responsibility for it in the eyes of the patients, so that the doctor could be devoted entirely to psychotherapy; this procedure led to conflict between nurses and doctors. In some hospitals, the responsibility for the control function may be assigned to administrative doctors and the treatment function to clinical doctors, which leads to conflicts between the two groups, as at Chestnut Lodge (Stanton & Schwartz, 1954). In group or community therapy, a doctor may allow the group to exercise control, which leads to experiments by patients to discover what sort of violence they need to perpetrate in order to force doctors to show their hand (Rapoport & Rapoport, 1957; Rapoport, Rapoport, & Rosow, 1960). A doctor may collude with patients in idealizing the therapeutic endeavour of his or her own unit while locating the control function in the parent hospital or the parent society (Cooper, 1967). Doctors may differ in how they express their responsibility for the control function, but they cannot get rid of it.

The hospital provides *care* as well as control—shelter, food, work, recreation, a social round of sorts—the framework of a life that would normally be provided by patients themselves or by their relatives and society. It is the nursing staff who provide the care, though other staff and patients may help. Everyone agrees that care is provided in the interests of the patients, though opinions differ sharply on what their interests are. Although nursing staff are expected to provide the care in the interests of the patient, their frequent contact with relatives reminds them that it is the relatives and society to whom they are responsible for providing the care. If the desires of patients and their relatives differ, the nursing staff are caught in the middle. There is likely to be competitiveness between relatives and nurses because the nurses carry out functions that relatives would be executing if the patient were at home. Relatives often feel guilty about not looking after their patient, though without admitting it to themselves; hence they sometimes accuse the nursing staff of the neglect and other faults in providing care of which they themselves feel guilty. Sometimes, of course, nurses *are* neglectful.

To chronic patients, the hospital becomes home. They resist being banished from it. This is the "institutionalization" so much criticized in the 1950s. In the research hospital, many nursing staff on chronic wards thought it would be cruel to send patients outside. They felt that the young doctors who were trying to clear out the chronic wards were trying to enhance their own reputations and save the Health Service money rather than helping the patients. The young doctors thought the nursing staff were trying to hold on to their ward workers. Most relatives wanted their chronic patients to stay in the hospital; a few were willing to try having them at home; some had lost contact. Patients wanted things to stay as they were, but with the provision of more recreational facilities. One patient who had lived in the hospital for many years caused much amusement by saying, "There are so many changes and upsets here now that I might as well go home."

Treatment is usually thought of as the special province of the doctor, though nurses, psychologists, social workers, occupational therapists, and industrial therapists may help. In theory, treatment is supposed to benefit the patient, relatives, and society. Often it pleases none. It depends on the situation and the type of treatment. No conflict arises if the doctor sticks to forms of physical treatment and ward management that require only a minimum of cooperation from patients and relatives, though even in the case of the gentlest physical treatment patients may avoid treatment by not taking it, as in the case of medication.

If the rift between patient and relatives is not deep, a traditional programme of admission-ward activities combined with drugs will usually repair the damaged relationship sufficiently for the patient to return home. Even before the use of physical treatments, "cures" were frequently achieved merely by the refuge and cooling off provided by the process of admission. "Patients come in raving", said an admission ward doctor in 1958, "and then get better, I really don't know why. I feel that all I'm doing is superintending a process of spontaneous remission. Anyway, I haven't time to do anything else."

When the relationship between patient and relatives is untenable, the doctor is caught in conflicts of loyalty to the patient and to society, and treatment in hospital becomes virtually impossible. "We know you have your methods" is a not uncommon remark by a relative, meaning that he thinks the doctor ought to use treatment to punish the patient and make him conform. It is not surprising that patients do not want such treatment, or that many sociologists, adopting the patient's point of view, hold that doctors delude patients into thinking they are ill instead of only socially nonconforming. If, on the other hand, a doctor provides a form of treatment that the patient accepts but the relatives do not, the relatives may attack the doctor and appeal to a higher authority to try to obstruct the process. If the relative and the patient have a deeply untenable relationship, then a doctor who uses a form of treatment that requires the cooperation of both patient and relative will be opposed by both. Whatever their differences with each other, neither relatives nor patient want to face the painful issues they are trying to use hospitalization to avoid. One might think it reasonable that such relatives and patients should agree to lead separate and independent lives, but this, too, is often unthinkable to them, for their mutual dependence is as intense as their unacknowledged hatred. Thus, in cases of acute discordance between patient and relatives, no method of treatment that ignores the discordance can have much effect; however, treatments that take the discordance into account are likely to arouse strong resistance, certainly from relatives, and usually from patients as well.

Life on the "chronic" wards

The Chronic Hospital was the most peaceful part of the system, despite the many changes introduced into it during the period of my study. It was located mainly in a very large old building containing 24 wards of long-stay geriatric patients, including their admission wards. This building also contained the offices of the medical superintendent and all the other senior staff except the other three consultants. It was ten minutes' walk to the Admissions Hospital, but socially and emotionally the Chronic Hospital was in another world: peaceful, orderly, and dominated by the ethos of the nursing staff.

The medical superintendent and an experienced senior hospital medical officer were in charge of the geriatric wards for women. The doctors on the other wards in the Chronic Hospital were mainly junior, temporary, and inexperienced in psychiatry, though each ward doctor was responsible to one of the three consultants. But the sisters (those female nurses in charge of female wards) and charge nurses (those male nurses in charge of male wards) thought of the junior doctors mainly as general practitioners who were dealing with their patients' physical ailments. The nursing staff looked to the senior nursing staff as the people to whom they were responsible. In this respect the socio-medical organization of the Chronic Hospital was similar to the organization of the whole hospital during the custodial period, when the nursing staff managed the wards under the leadership of the senior nursing staff and the medical superintendent, with the doctors acting as visitors to individual patients but taking no part in ward management.

Only the doctors—especially the young ward doctors, and occasionally a social worker—felt vexed by the inertia of the chronic wards; they thought relatives and patients were virtually malinger-ing and that many patients should have been having a go at life outside. Nurses did not like being accused of institutionalizing patients, but the young doctors soon left to do their stint in the admission wards. In spite of the general atmosphere of changeless-ness and tranquillity, many changes were adopted on the chronic wards in the 1950s and 1960s: nearly all ward doors were unlocked; patients were accordingly regrouped; patients were given indi-vidualized clothing; tranquilizers were introduced; more recreation was provided; and an extensive programme of occupational and industrial therapy was developed. New programmes were read-ily absorbed into the even tenor of chronic-ward life. The new activities made life more pleasant, but they did not lead to a vastly increased number of discharges of chronic patients.

Over the years, the chronic part of a mental hospital develops a chronic culture—a set of customary methods of living with mad-ness and disablement. Compared to the mental hospitals in the United States described in the sociological literature, the chronic culture of the hospital I studied was kindly and humane, though slow-moving and sometimes tranquil to the point of unreality.

Nurses usually adhere to the cultural definitions of madness as something to be shunned, and, even though they know that many of their patients do not typically behave in a mad way, the fact that patients have been medically defined as ill means that it is legiti-mate to regard all of them as mad. Since nurses cannot get away from the madness physically, they get away from it emotionally: they develop some form of relationship that locates madness in the patient and sanity in themselves, with a barrier to prevent contami-nation (see also Hinshelwood, 1986). This arrangement allows the nurses to stay in the situation without feeling that their minds are being damaged. It justifies the use of control by the nurses, entitles patients to care and refuge, and is a virtual guarantee that they will continue to be thought ill and will therefore not be sent outside.

The basic method by which nursing staff stay physically in contact with patients while leaving emotionally consists of some form of routinization—a concentration on activities rather than on the people who do them (cf. Cohler & Shapiro, 1964; Coser, 1963; Donati, 2000; Hinshelwood, 1979, 1986; Moss & Hunter, 1963; Tudor Will, 1952, 1957). All these authors discuss in various ways the anxieties and defences involved in nursing psychotic and/or chronically ill patients.

The simple realities of life on an understaffed large chronic ward provide ample opportunity for concentration on routine, which is simultaneously used to avoid contact with patients and to get the work done. One of the characteristic expressions of concentration on routine was the attitude towards talking to patients. If there were two nurses on a shift, they talked to each other, not to the patients. Several students who worked temporarily on chronic wards reported that if they talked with patients too much, the sister or the nurse would say, "You're supposed to talk to me!" Talking to patients is considered dangerous because it threatens to puncture the barrier that keeps sanity and madness in their proper places.

There were two main forms of routinization, one involving an *authoritarian regime* based on strict rules, the other based on *a form of unconscious collusion* between patient and nurse.

The *authoritarian regime* was most common on male wards—especially on wards where the patients were young or middle aged. On such wards, there was an undercurrent of tension and fear. The atmosphere was often military, sometimes quite explicitly so; frequently the charge nurses had been in the army. The role of army sergeant was one of the few acceptable models for a male charge nurse, one that countered the public stereotype of nursing as a female occupation. Many of the male nurses I talked to were very contemptuous of what they called the "Florence Nightingale" approach of the female nurses and made it clear that themselves had more realistic as well as more conservative attitudes towards the whole situation of mental hospitals and patients.

The other form of routinization, the *collusive* type, was more common on female wards. It involved a curiously peaceful but unreal atmosphere in which the nurses were thoughtful, even tender to patients, and patients seemed passive and dependent on the nurses, especially the sister. When she passed by, their faces lit up; when she was not there, they lapsed into apathetic withdrawal. It seemed probable that this sort of relationship was based on unconscious collusion between patient and nurse, which can be described as reciprocal projective identification (for a discussion of projective identification, see Spillius & O'Shaughnessy, 2011). The nurse acted as if she were the psychological recipient of the patient's capacity to think, whereas the patient acted as though she were the recipient of the nurse's *unwanted* feelings. In this way, madness was safely lodged in the patient; the fear of the patient contaminating the nurse with it was reduced by the sense that the patient was helpless and dependent because the nurse had absorbed all the available willpower and capacity to think.

Many sisters and a few charge nurses expressed considerable emotional satisfaction from having this sort of relationship with patients, though they were not aware of their use of projective identification or of the collusive element in their adaptation. The closest anyone came to expressing it directly occurred in the case of a sister who said she liked looking after psychotic patients because they were helpless and needed care, and that many of her personal problems had disappeared or become less troublesome since she had taken up psychiatric nursing. Sometimes patients pointed out a sister's or nurse's use of projection. One such patient on a disturbed ward had a fit of temper and broke a lot of dishes. The assistant matron looked at her angrily and said, "*Now* look what you've done!" to which the patient replied, "That's not my bad temper. That's sister's bad temper, and I'm letting it out for her." The junior staff and several patients exploded with laughter, because everyone knew that that particular sister had trouble controlling her temper.

The chronic wards I observed gave an impression of being bare of an indigenous patient culture and informal social structure, a state of affairs that Sommer and Osmond (1962) aptly describe as the "schizophrenic no-society", though one might equally well describe it as the "chronic ward no-society". There appeared to be none of the inventiveness and zest that one finds among normal people, even in prisons and other conditions of deprivation. Shared perceptions and shared interpretations of them, which form the basis for the growth of culture and social structure, did not appear to be present in their usual forms. Insofar as a patient culture operated, it seemed to be mediated through the staff. In terms of my hypothesis, this occurred because patients, through the process of projective identification, lodged much of their capacity to think in the staff.

In Britain, there are sometimes reports of individual instances of cruelty to patients. It seems inevitable that the structure of the nursing situation should lead to occasional outbursts of violence from both nurses and patients. In the authoritarian form of routinization, violence is always just below the surface. In the collusive form, the helplessness of certain patients is likely to stir such feelings of guilt in the nurse that she or he may lash out in rage at the offensively submissive object. Sometimes patients, safe in their cloak of illness, may provoke the staff, knowing that staff are not supposed to retaliate and may be punished for it.

It is my view that the problems of living with madness and disability will arise in any form of socio-medical organization—in hostels, in foster families, perhaps in group homes. But defining personal disablement as a medical problem has a debilitating effect, which could perhaps be mitigated in a different form of organization.

The Admissions Hospital:
conflict, defence, and painful change

The task of the Admissions Hospital was to treat patients and send them home if possible. It contained four wards for women and four for men, in each case consisting of a psychotic admission ward, a neurotic admission ward, and two medium-stay wards. Patients who became long-stay were eventually sent to the chronic wards.

The three consultants (excluding the medical superintendent) spent most of their time in the Admissions Hospital, though each was also responsible for a number of chronic wards. Each consultant led a *"firm"* (team) of four or five doctors who were in immediate charge of the wards. Compared to the Chronic Hospital, the Admissions Hospital was lavishly staffed with nurses, psychologists, social workers, and occupational therapists, as well as doctors.

In the socio-medical organization of the Admissions Hospital, the consultant was the leader of his team of doctors, and there were frequent meetings both of this group and of a larger set of staff, including nurses, occupational therapists, psychologists, and social workers, depending on the plans of the particular therapeutic programme. The ward doctor and/or consultant was the leader of the ward, and the sister or charge nurse was immediately responsible to the doctor rather than—or as well as—to the senior nursing staff. It was universally agreed in the Admissions Hospital that a major aspect of any treatment programme was the way the ward was run—its organization as a group, its activities, its rules, its personal relationships. In some programmes, it was the *only* form of treatment. The doctor was no longer only a visitor of patients as individuals; he defined his job as manager of a group enterprise the purpose of which was therapeutic. Thus by the late 1950s it was clear that a major change had already taken place in the definition of treatment as a social enterprise and in the role-relationship of doctor and nurse.

Because of the doctors' interventions in ward management, the executive management function of the most senior nursing staff on treatment wards had declined, and their job, so far as the Admissions Hospital was concerned, came to consist of staffing the wards with nurses, whom they also recruited and trained. The senior nursing staff thus provided a central service for the several medical teams or the hospital. They played no executive role in forming the therapeutic policies of the various medical teams, and conflict therefore easily arose. The medical teams were likely to think that the nurses essential to their therapeutic policies were being arbitrarily shifted about in order to obstruct the therapeutic goals of the doctor's team. The senior nursing staff tended to think that the consultants were wilfully ignorant of the demands of the other teams, of nurse training, of the nursing profession, and of the standards and expectations of external bodies. To "improve communication" in matters of this sort involved everyone in endless meetings. Because they wanted to get on with their clinical work, the consultants were content to let the medical superintendent "bring the matron round".

Several new methods of physical and social treatment were adopted during the period of my study. All these innovations aroused considerable enthusiasm, but none was spectacularly successful in the research hospital or elsewhere—nothing comparable, say, to streptomycin as a cure for tuberculosis. Drugs and other physical treatments relieved symptoms. Psychotherapy was not practicable or effective in a mental hospital setting because it conflicted acutely with the control function and in any case could not be used on a wide scale. Industrial therapy, at least at the research hospital, improved the quality of life of both patients and staff but did not increase the outflow of chronic patients. Ward community therapy aroused immense enthusiasm for a time, but the results were not of such obvious efficacy as to be adopted by the unconverted; such ward programmes were extremely arduous for the staff without giving any clear evidence that the effort inside the hospital had improved patients' ability to cope with life outside.

My impression was that several customary features of hospital practice were acting not only as methods of getting the work done, but also as defences against the anxieties inherent in the mental hospital situation—especially anxieties concerning the use made of the hospital by society and anxiety that existing treatments were not as successful as people wanted them to be (see Jaques, 1953; Menzies Lyth, 1960a).

At various times it seemed that there was, throughout the hospital, a defence of "not knowing"—a disinclination to find things out, especially anything that might threaten the prevailing *modus vivendi*. No systematic attempt was being made, for example, to evaluate various treatment methods. The nature of therapeutic work with patients is such that meaningful measures of effectiveness are exceedingly difficult to devise. In the research hospital, it was striking that even simple crucial facts were not known. Records, for example, were kept in such a way that no one knew how many patients were becoming long-stay or whether the various therapeutic programmes were having an effect on chronic hospitalization. Until my investigation, no one knew that the first-admission rate had stopped increasing in 1955, before the introduction of tranquilizers and the more radical forms of social therapy. It was difficult to get figures on the hospital population according to age and length of stay, in spite of the fullest cooperation from all the staff concerned.

Because society's expectations of mental hospitals are equivocal, and because indications of the success or failure of treatments are so difficult to evaluate, treatments and methods of care may be adopted or abandoned for reasons that have little to do with their stated aims: because they fit in with the doctors' value system or wish to cure; because they offer hope in the face of uncertainty; or because they give some protection against a half-felt sense by doctors that their skills are being misused. Psychiatrists and mental hospitals are therefore notoriously susceptible to ideological controversy and to bouts of optimism and despair.

Idealization and denigration appeared to be commonly used defences. When a particular ward started a new therapeutic programme, the ward staff usually became utterly dedicated to the new venture, which became almost sacrosanct: their hostility and uncertainty were projected onto outsiders in other wards, whose staff were felt to be hostile and interfering—which indeed they sometimes were. Envy of inventiveness and jealousy of the special attention paid to other parts of the hospital are endemic in the hospital situation. Finding an external enemy appears to be a very common development in almost all types of therapeutic innovation; if it is not the parent hospital who is wrong, it is the parent society, or people who adhere to other points of view.

It seems likely that seemingly inefficient arrangements may be retained precisely because they make communication difficult, for peaceful coexistence in an institution is often preferred to confrontation. Indeed, when confrontation and change did come, they were thoroughly unpleasant. Although several of the hospital's experiments in social therapy had established new links with the community, it was not until Scott and other senior doctors pressed on to a more radical redefinition of the unit of treatment as the patient in his environment that change inside the hospital became extensive, leading to regionalization and the breakdown of the amicable *modus vivendi*. Regionalization was a painful process, with sharp differences of view on what the relationship of the hospital to society was and should be, and with acute conflict over the extent to which the regionalized units should be administratively autonomous.

So long as people in the external society have feelings of horror and dread of madness, mental hospitals will be pressed into accommodating madness in a way that will relieve society of responsibility and allow its members to regard themselves as sane. If, like the research hospital at the beginning of my study, a psychiatric institution accepts patients for treatment as individuals on medical grounds and also provides a home for those who fail to improve, it will have divided loyalties to the patient and to society, and the stage will be set for a debilitating form of conflict inside the institution. If a hospital provides medical treatment for patients as individuals but refuses to provide long-term care, it is likely that many patients will drift from one hospital to another in search of a resting place. This appears to be occurring in the case of the psychiatric clinics in general hospitals, though I have not made a close study of this process. If the institution refuses to allow its treatment facilities to be used to treat patients as isolated individuals, there will be protests from relatives and the other social bodies to whom they complain. Finally, if an institution frankly accepts its task as providing a home for social rejects, it will be stigmatized as a hopeless chronic institution inappropriate for medical service, however much the social refuge may be needed by certain patients and by society.

None of these institutional forms is entirely desirable from anyone's point of view. All involve either constant conflict or shutting one's eyes to what one does not want to see. Perhaps a first step in planning might be to accept madness and the dread of it as social and personal facts. Then one would at least be in a better position to work at devising institutional forms that would make madness, in both patient and society, bearable rather than curable or beyond understanding.

Concluding remarks

Like most of the large mental hospitals, the research hospital gradually declined; it was officially closed in 1998, to be replaced by smaller and more temporary units in general hospitals closer to where patients lived and by hostels for chronic patients. Other changes have apparently followed. I have not studied the effects of this process of transformation, so I am not in a position to compare the new with the older method of handling the difficult conflicts involved in the care and treatment of psychotic patients and their families. But I would expect that the difficulties experienced by patients, relatives, and their various medical helpers in accepting the realities of conflict will have continued to play an important role in the provision of treatment and care.

Note

An earlier version of this chapter, called "Hospital and Society", was published in the *British Journal of Medical Psychology* in 1976. The present chapter is a shorter version of a chapter, "Asylum and Society", published in *The Social Engagement of Social Science, Vol. 1: The Socio-Psychological Perspective*, ed. Eric Trist & Hugh Murray (Philadelphia, PA: University of Pennsylvania Press, 1990), pp. 586–612. [Note: I did not call myself "Spillius" until after 1976.]

CHAPTER ELEVEN

Schizophrenia, meaninglessness, and professional stress

R. D. Hinshelwood

Professional men, they have no cares
Whatever happens, they get theirs.

Ogden Nash

The central contention of this chapter is that, in fact, professionals do care, in contrast to Ogden Nash's popular conception. However, caring for psychotic persons is problematic. It takes its toll on both families and professional carers, and the retention problem among psychiatrists and psychiatric nurses suggests that insufficient attention is paid to the low job satisfaction in our work. Demotivation and demoralization seem to be endemic.

I want to examine more precisely the nature of this stress and its consequences for the individual carers. In addition, given that stress is the business of mental health organizations, we can examine which features of the services themselves, although arising from the collective ways individuals try to cope with stress, obstruct the organization in its work.

Joe Berke, co-founder of the Arbours Association, once quipped that "Schizophrenia is an expertise in producing disquiet in others" (Berke, 1979, p. 33). Berke was well aware of the stress of his therapists and carers and of what they had to withstand. There is a specific kind of stress in confronting psychosis which, not surprisingly, has deleterious effects on the individuals involved, on their job satisfaction, and on the organization as a whole. Freud noted the difficult feelings these patients evoke:

> I did not like those patients. . . . They make me angry and I find myself irritated to experience them so distant from myself and from all that is human. This is an astonishing intolerance which brands me a poor psychiatrist. [Freud, 1928,[1] quoted in Dupont, 1988, p. 251]

On the one hand, Freud regarded the schizophrenic patient as outside ordinary human experience, while on the other hand he conveyed his own unease, recognizing that this is an inappropriate stance for a psychiatrist.

However, it is not only professional carers who are disquieted, though they may be more articulate about it. When Samuel Beckett went to the Tavistock Clinic in 1934 for psychotherapy with the novice therapist Wilfred Bion (see Anzieu, 1989), he took an interest in mental illness and visited the Bethlem hospital. His verdict about a schizophrenic patient he encountered was:

> [The patient] was like a hunk of meat. There was no-one there. He was absent. [Samuel Beckett 1935, quoted in Knowlson, 1996, p. 209]

There is something both recognizable and shocking about this reaction, the disconcerting and distressing sense of not knowing how to relate at all.

Freud thought that psychotic patients could not make relationships with others (Freud, 1916–17).[2] And as these quotes attest, a "non-relation" is, paradoxically, a powerful experience. Schizophrenic patients do make an impact, and often those who meet them pull away from personal contact. This is true of friends and of the families who may express this through their need to have their relative removed to a psychiatric service. The professional role requires impartiality, which is inevitably at odds with the powerful feelings of bewilderment, uncertainty, and defeat that are typically evoked.

It is not only friends, relatives, and staff who reduce the patient to a non-personal status, for the patient himself is invested in his own self-"objectification"—in effect, a depersonalization of himself. Thus, there is a collusion between the patient and those who care for the patient that demolishes his existence as a human being (Hinshelwood, 1999).

Objectification

Psychiatric personnel inevitably find it easier to maintain a neutral scientific attitude towards their patients, a professional stance that creates a personal distance from the suffering patient, and they can thereby help to protect the carers from the patient's disconcerting impact.

However, as Barratt (1996) has shown, this apparently neutral attitude can serve deeper purposes. With careful anthropological observation in the psychiatric setting, he described the way in which a typical patient progresses through the stages of admission to a psychiatric ward. There are four steps, each characterized by a constellation of specific views and attitudes held by the culture of the ward.

1. At first, the patient is perceived (and dealt with) as an object—one that does not live in the world of ordinary meanings. He is not held responsible for his thoughts and behaviour: it is the "illness" that is responsible. In this way the patient is denied his own volition and agency; without responsibility, he is no longer experienced as a person.

2. Then, after a period of observation, he is dismantled into a set of symptoms and pathologies that can be recorded objectively.[3]

3. This is followed by a reconstruction as he is "worked-up" into a case: the patient's various "objective" signs and symptoms are combined into a picture that is psychiatrically meaningful. He has a diagnosis, a set of treatment interventions, and a prognosis about his future. He *has become* "a schizophrenic".

4. At the end of this processing as an object of scientific study and record, the patient may be reinvested with subjectivity as a person. Interestingly, Barratt described this as deriving *from the reactions of the professionals*, who thereby restore the person in the patient, and he is returned to a world in which he is regarded as having his own volition—that is, he becomes a moral agent once again. The staff can like or dislike the person, agree or disagree with him, approve or disapprove of what he does; thus,

the reactions of the staff restore a reacting subject. In this way, the patient may be rescued from the category of a "case" and restored to being a person.

Many patients do not, of course, make it through that final step.[4] For the patient's personhood to be restored, we must hold him responsible for how he is and what he does. In other words, we must engage with him in a world of meaningful intentions and actions. Significantly, professionals normally believe that they should avoid moral judgements about their patients, but in doing so they inevitably denude patients of their personhood.

Barratt (1996) gives an excellent account of a journey in which at certain stages a person can be an impersonal object of investigation and treatment, while at others he is a responsible human agent.[5] This anthropological observation of the psychiatric process indicated a collective (though unacknowledged) agreement by the whole social group of staff that, for most of his residence, the suffering patient is not a human person/agent.

Meaninglessness

How are we to understand this "anti-human" attitude towards such suffering patients, which is collectivized across the team? What feels inhuman in the patient is the *lack of meaning* in his own expressions and behaviour. Meaninglessness is like a vacuum, and nature abhors it—or, rather, human nature does. In order to grow and develop, the mind needs truth and meaning, as Bion has emphasized: "healthy mental growth seems to depend on truth as the living organism depends on food" (Bion, 1965, p. 38). I am suggesting here that this capacity for truthfulness is closely related to the capacity for developing and sustaining meaning.

Bion described how the mind is impacted on by raw data, which it has to transform into meaningful and significant experiences—a process he termed "alpha-function". This is somewhat akin to the process by means of which the perception of light at a certain wavelength is transformed into an experience of redness. Alphafunction, then, is an essential characteristic of having a mind.

Meaninglessness is thus a failure of alpha-function, where "the appropriate machinery is felt to be, not an apparatus for thinking the thoughts, but an apparatus for ridding the psyche of accumulations of bad internal objects" (Bion, 1962b, p. 112). Evacuation is the kind of process that underlies the countertransference experience with schizophrenic people—the peculiar combination of heartfelt aversion and guilt illustrated above. As Frieda Fromm-Reichmann wrote,

> the schizophrenic patient and the therapist are people living in different worlds. . . . We know little about the language of the unconscious of the schizophrenic, and our access to it is blocked by the very process of our own adjustment to a world the schizophrenic has relinquished. [Fromm-Reichmann, 1939, p. 416]

I am suggesting that the radical difference between the two worlds arises not just from the problem of understanding a different world but, following Bion, from being confronted with a world in which meaning is not achieved, or is destroyed and evacuated.

Bion (1962a) provided us with a model of the development of alpha-function. At the beginning we are all dependent on another mind (that of the caregiver), which we need to contain primitive projections.[6] Bion first described it this way:

> My deduction was that in order to understand what the child wanted the mother should have treated the infant's cry as more than a demand for her presence. From the infant's point of view she should have taken into her, and thus experienced, the fear that the child was dying. It was this fear that the child could not contain. He strove to split it off together with the part of the personality in which it lay and project it into the mother. An understanding mother is able to experience the feeling of dread, that this baby was striving to deal with by projective identification, and yet retain a balanced outlook. [Bion, 1959, p. 104]

The infant is dependent on the "mother" for making sense of the frightening perception, giving it meaning—if it is hunger, "mother" psychologically gives this a meaning, through materially providing satisfaction by offering the breast or a bottle. Psychosis results, according to this model, from a failure of this kind of primary care in which two minds exchange experiences and generate meanings between them. In some cases, the carer makes use of the infant as an object into which are evacuated unmanageable aspects of the *carer's* mind.

This theory of containment and the understanding of the consequences of its failure is now very much part of the psychoanalytic literature (see, for example, Riesenberg Malcolm, 2001). From a developmental perspective, fundamental failures of this early relationship—failures that arise from both sides of the exchange—result in the infant being left with raw sense data and undigested emotional experience. It is this situation that provokes development of an apparatus for evacuation instead of one capable of thinking.

Thus Bion traced the essential problem of schizophrenia to a destruction of mental functions, leaving a mind incapable of having a conflict. Bion stressed that the countertransference experiences evoked in the analyst in these situations are of great importance (Bion, 1954, p. 24). During the conference at which Bion presented his paper, Melanie Klein acknowledged this, saying,

> there is a point I wish to stress—the particular processes of the schizophrenic of splitting his own ego and the analysis of projective identification . . . stir in the analyst very strong counter-transference feelings of a negative kind. [Klein, "Remarks on Countertransference", quoted in Hinshelwood, 2008, pp. 111–112]

Klein was in agreement here as to the destructive processes that underlie schizophrenia, and she thought that the difficulties in managing this might be part of the reason for analysts avoiding the treatment of psychotic people. She also drew attention to the possibility of this situation being "managed" by a kind of reaction-formation where the analyst overemphasizes the positive transference and the excessive idealization of all communication.

This destruction of meaning takes various forms. Bell (1996), in his consideration of the ways in which knowledge is undermined in disturbing situations, has described the process whereby knowledge is replaced by various kinds of "pretenders", including religiosity, the belief that knowledge is merely the accumulation of facts, and a clinging to a selected fact that has acquired a pseudo-certainty (an ideology).

Bion also described the way in which intense splitting in the patient's mind can cause great difficulty for the analyst:

> The patient comes into the room, shakes me warmly by the hand, and looking piercingly into my eyes says, "I think the sessions are not for a long while but stop me ever going out." I know from previous experience that this patient has a grievance

that the sessions are too few and that they interfere with his free time. He intended to split me by making me give two opposite interpretations at once, and this was shown by his next association when he said, "How does the lift know what to do when I press two buttons at once?" [Bion, 1954, pp. 24–25]

The side-effects of science

The discussion above has aimed to provide a better understanding of the nature of the stress that professional carers of schizophrenic people are required to suffer, and this has several components:

» they must care for people living in a "different" assumptive world;

» they are recipients of projected meaninglessness which the patient cannot deal with except by evacuation;

» they must retain their capacity to maintain meaning, protecting it from those who act to destroy it;

» they are subjected to communications intended to split their own minds and so obstruct their capacity to think.

There is little wonder that these noxious effects, unconsciously accomplished and felt, lead to a rejection of these kinds of patients. Psychiatric staff do not, of course, reject them in an overt sense; rather, as we saw above, they reject them as persons, they become objects of study.[7] The culture of a psychiatric team seems specifically adapted to socializing new patients in this depersonalized form.[8] The effect of this culture and its assumptions is to protect the staff from the kind of projective processes that they would risk if they were to take too personal an interest in the patient.[9] This culture can be expressed as a powerful, even proselytizing, professional commitment to scientific understanding of the objective features of brain science, with its lucrative support from the pharmaceutical industry. I need to stress here that I am not opposed to the use of medication and regard it as a very important part of psychiatric care, providing considerable relief to patients and to their carers. What I am referring to is not the benefits of this scientific approach, but its psychosocial side-effects—namely, the compulsion to adopt within psychiatric teams a set of cultural attitudes that objectify and depersonalize the schizophrenic person. I have been struck by the extensive use of what Bell described as an accumulation of facts. This is related to Barratt's second stage in the admission of a schizophrenic person to a mental health service (described above), where the person is reduced to a collection of signs and symptoms.

Ideologies

One of the most pernicious reactions when faced with meaninglessness is a demand for certainty, a desperate need to *know*, when faced with the incomprehensible. Kraepelin's original ideas concerning schizophrenia originating in a nineteenth-century model of science have, over time, acquired the characteristic of ideology. This ideology dictates that psychiatrists must look for signs and symptoms in a dispassionate and emotionally neutral way. The result is a diagnosis, and with it an unrealistic sense of certainty confirmed by teachers and colleagues. Its ideological force is seen both in its hegemony and in its difficulty in managing alternative points of view. It is also true that, in reaction to this, those with an alternative point of view, perhaps one based on a psychoanalytic perspective, can become equally dogmatic and intransigent. However, the excessive insistence (on the importance of meaning) derives some of its force from the pain of confrontation with meaninglessness.

A great deal of benefit can come from knowing, but a great deal may be closed off by the need to know. This discussion of the development of an ideology within a professional group can be compared with the work of Britton and Steiner (1944) with regard to the subtle shifts in the analyst's relation to his own ideas. They described how the analyst can settle upon an interpretation that seems, at least at first, to fit the current situation. However, over time this idea becomes an "over-valued idea": if he is not careful, the analyst may cling to it in order to evade further uncertainty.[10] Like the development of an ideology in the group, they describe a "crystallisation of delusional certainty" (p. 1069) in the analyst's mind when he is anxiously uncertain. From my perspective, this kind of process underlies a group, or culture, which adopts pseudo-certainty in place of loss of meaning.

Multidisciplinary fragmentation

Excessive attachment to what is thought of as "the right idea" leads to fraught relations and intense friction between groups of staff and different disciplines loyal to different "right" ideas. The remarkable frequency of exhortations to multidisciplinary teams to work together signals the tenacious difficulty arising from the various disciplines' differing ideological commitments. The overt result of these unconsciously driven commitments is the serious decline of functional debate.[11] Moreover, when anxiety peaks, ideological commitments may strengthen further.[12]

A team, like any other group, develops its own group culture under the influence of the kind of work it does, which leads to different attitudes towards service delivery within each discipline. Different kinds of work create different cultures, and so there will be differences in the culture of different psychiatric units. Given that a day centre functions by dividing up every day, it may endeavour to establish cultures to reinforce the integrity of the whole centre (perhaps by homogenization). An inpatient unit that takes on the most risky cases may develop a culture of scapegoating, both among the staff and also by transferring the patient, and thus the risk, to another unit.[13]

The well-known slide of multidisciplinary meetings into multidisciplinary fragmentation as the subgroups rally around their own ideological positions leads authorities to urge seamless inter-agency working, although in fact this is nearly impossible to achieve as long as units and agencies cling to ideologies driven by the dynamics described above.

These problems have been with us since the beginning of psychoanalysis. Discussing the relations between psychoanalysis and psychiatry, Freud wrote that

> what is known as scientific controversy is on the whole quite unproductive, apart from the fact that it is almost always conducted on highly personal lines. . . . [A] rejection such as this of all written discussion argues a high degree of inaccessibility to objections, of obstinacy, or, to use the polite colloquial scientific term, of pig-headedness. [Freud, 1916–17, p. 245]

The emotional stress on individuals, which is perhaps inevitable, leads to organizational problems and loss of functioning of the service as a whole. Communication between different groups in the organization declines, and teamwork is further undermined.

It has often been noted with some irony that the fragmented state of the psychiatric service itself reflects the schizophrenic results of the splitting processes in its patients' intrapsychic states. The splitting in the schizophrenic process and the splitting characteristic of the disharmony of group dynamics may indeed have something in common (Bion, 1952), but more detrimental is the opportunity for the patient to perceive the plight of the service as being as serious as his own.

Public responsibility

The quality of the work is then bound to decline further. Mistakes may be made and the service called to account. Myths and imaginings about madness are always rife in the community. Reportage often stresses the alarm and danger the public *should* fear. On the one hand, such media responses are a kind of social container for the impact of the fear and danger that professionals have to withstand, face-to-face. However, on the other hand, public opinion is formed only indirectly, and there is scope for newspaper reports about violent patients to generate uncontained and unrealistic panic. In this social and public context, our mistakes exacerbate and interact with the generalized fear of madness, and these processes make a major contribution to the ensuing public scandals. This phenomenon has increased since the move from incarceration to community care. Despite its enlightened and humanitarian aims, community care has become indelibly linked in the popular imagination with highly inflated risk. The upshot is that the public service that psychiatry offers—to separate individuals who are alarming or even dangerous from the general population—appears to fail the public.

Increased government and media attention and anxiety then lead to increasing rounds of service changes and, especially, risk management strategies. The latter may take the form of manualized procedures. Personal and professional judgement based on experience and training declines, mental health workers feel increasingly deskilled, leading to demotivation. The end result is the haemorrhage of personnel, leading to an increase in temporary and locum employments. This effect of the social context exacerbates the problems deriving from work stress, as described, and so disruption escalates (Hinshelwood, 1998). The medical discipline, clinical psychology, social work, and other professions (including psychodynamic approaches) may engage in similarly "pigheaded" attitudes to each other's points of view.

Staff groups

If one origin of institutional pathology is the stress on the professional carer, can it be tackled at source? Although a culture of silence often closes over these problems, there is increasing awareness of the stress on individuals. One response is to institute staff support groups. This can be an important and healthy strategy, but it is not always so, for there is often a lack of understanding of what such support needs to provide.

At the very simplest, sharing the distress of the work is a support: "a problem shared is a problem halved". However, staff groups can function to create powerful attitudes and exert a coercive pressure on their members, forcing them to adopt common group attitudes, defensive ones as well as healthy ones. The great danger is that the culture of the group can be taken over by a powerful ideological system. This increases the solidarity individuals feel within the team, but the teams themselves pull apart.

Considerable care has therefore to be taken when setting up and running these groups. In my view the group should be geared around a specific focus, one that is relevant to the task, and not just around the individuals' own feelings. The task should not be simply expressive, leading to abreacting the distress of the work, which may create a system for evacuation and the circulation of unthought meanings. The group should reflect on the work and on its impact on staff members. The support group needs to trace the stress back to its roots *in the work* and so work on these problems and the relations that surround them. The group needs to support the *ability to not understand*, to not know, to live in uncertainty and doubt when that is necessary (as it often is in psychiatry).[14] It is necessary to protect the group from being taken over by powerful ideological positions and to maintain openness and leave room for real doubt and questioning. Nor should the group listen only to the senior members or the group conductor, simply accepting their advice, summaries, or even instructions. Socratic scepticism and doubt needs maintenance, and a staff support group is a place where that maintenance can be carried out. Similarly, the group needs to be protected from disintegrating into a therapy group.

Conclusions

In summary, the inevitable stress on professional carers can easily lead to serious organizational problems and loss of functioning of the service as a whole, as communication between different groups breaks down and the capacity for real teamwork is lost.

The schizoid nature of the minds of our patients directly promotes a kind of schizoid functioning of the system that cares for them. This is admittedly a somewhat simplistic notion of a parallel process, and there is a more complex and longer route of influence by which one phenomenon becomes realized in the other. The experience of meaninglessness affects levels and units within the system, and all the disciplines in mental health, with the result that each tends to look for its own certainties in order to ameliorate the unmanageable stress; however, such certainties will be coloured by the different groups' work and perceptions of success/failure, risk, aetiology, and so on. Organically oriented psychiatrists will look to biological causation and treatment, psychodynamic staff will emphasize relationships, cognitive psychologists will press rational strategies on patients. The problem is not that these orientations are incompatible—though they could be—but that they become too easily driven by this need for certainty. Group solidarity then supports each group's convictions as to the nature of the disorder—a biochemical brain problem, or a relational and probably upbringing problem, or a dysfunction in thinking strategies. Thus, the coherent model of schizophrenia that is held by each group serves a function at a deep psychological level *for the individual carers* who are always in danger of drowning in face of the incoherence they encounter at this level of disturbance. The different approaches are not just guides to different forms of practice for the various units and disciplines; they also function as expressions of the tensions in the work between groups. Tenacious clinging to ideologies may protect the individual to some extent, but the cost is high: useful controversy is replaced by "pig-headedness". As a result, groups, units, and disciplines drift apart into fragmented isolation, so that the state of psychiatry comes to resemble the fragmented state of mind of its most vulnerable patients. This may lead to greater anxiety for patients, with an increase in symptoms and an ensuing increase in anxiety for staff.

In this chapter, I have focused on underlying dynamics that can be specifically aroused in psychiatry by the core problem of meanings and their destruction in schizophrenia. I do not wish to dismiss other kinds of stress[15] that are operative in the professions, but I believe the problem of meaning and meaninglessness is specific and rarely emphasized in the literature on mental health.

Notes

1. This was in a private letter from Freud to Stephan Hollós, who had sent Freud a copy of a book he had authored.

2. In consequence, schizophrenic patients do not, in Freud's view, make transferences to a psychoanalyst, and so cannot be analysed. This view has been contested (Fromm-Reichmann, 1939; Rosenfeld, 1965). The non-relationship is now thought to be not a simple lack, but an actively abnormal one, even on casual contact.

3. It is, of course, interesting that this dismembering process, conducted in a conscious scientific way, parallels the unconscious process of the individual. Moreover, the patient comes apart psychically through projection, and various "bits" may be lodged in separate caregivers who concentrate on separate aspects of the patient, such as his biochemistry, his relations, his expressivity, and so on. As a result, the institution also comes apart.

4. I have tried to show (Hinshelwood, 1999) that the attitudes of contemporary orthodox psychiatry that objectify the patient are in themselves a factor that promotes the very chronicity that psychiatrists struggle so hard against. Both staff and the patients themselves collude to diminish the patient's personhood.

5. The patient's loss of self conjoins with the scientific objectifying of him as an object of scientific study. It is not surprising, therefore, that so many schizophrenic persons sink into a static state of chronicity.

6. I shall call this external caregiver "mother" as a short-hand for all the later objects that can give meaning to an infant's cries.

7. This is not only a contemporary problem but stretches back into the history of psychiatry—see, for instance, Laing's critique of Kraepelin's objectifying diagnostic methods in the 1890s (Laing, 1967).

8. It is worth noting the contrast: (1) psychoanalysts may deal with the problem of being confronted with a noxious experience by reassurance and a collusive positive culture in the consulting room, while (2) psychiatric teams resort to objective, depersonalizing methods.

9. In arguing for this protective quality of the professional culture, I draw on the work of Jaques (1955), Menzies Lyth (1979), and many subsequent investigators (including those contributing to Hinshelwood & Skogstad, 2000b), who have demonstrated the collective social support of personal defences against anxieties provoked by a working situation. (See also Obholzer & Roberts, 1994; Trist & Murray, 1990.)

10. Britton and Steiner borrowed Bion's use of the term "selected fact", which emphasizes that the understanding is based on a selection of data.

11. This emotional pressure for multidisciplinary teams to come apart at their seams has been enhanced by the spatial or geographical separation of various units in the move to the community three decades ago.

12. Menzies Lyth (1979) gave an example of a residential school for very deprived children, where the staff and inmates evolved a school system based more on the general unconscious phantasies of replacing parental care for the deprived than on the consciously agreed academic educational task. Another example is given by Miller and Gwynne (1972), who studied residential homes for the physically and incurably disabled. They showed that the job became distorted in the minds of the staff and inmates, to become one of either warehousing hopeless cases or, alternatively, getting the essential human creativity of the victims to flower as if undiminished by disability. Neither set of attitudes—the "warehousing" or the "horticultural"—is completely realistic, and both do some damage to those in need of the care.

13. This differential culture may also apply to different disciplines as well as teams. Stokes (1994) considered the phenomenon in terms of Bion's basic assumption groups—doctors tending to a pairing culture, nurses to a dependency culture, and social workers to a flight–flight one.

14. Such a task unfortunately strikes directly against the culture of risk management that has become so prevalent, perhaps understandably, at the higher levels of our organizations. The grass-roots level of the working team needs some protection by middle managers from the pressures of institutional risk management.

15. In my view, there are indeed a number of other stresses—particularly a generalized strong sense of failure and a specific fear of madness itself (and its contagiousness). These stresses lead to other features of the culture in addition to the development of differential ideologies: they may give rise to demoralization (with problems of absenteeism and retention), stereotyping and scapegoating, routinization, a passive helplessness in relation to supporting authorities, and other deleterious cultural manifestations. (For an account of some of these additional factors and their effects see Hinshelwood, 1998.)

CHAPTER TWELVE

Brilliant stupidity: madness in organizational life—a perspective from organizational consultancy

Tim Dartington

In the play *Enron*, by Lucy Prebble (2009), the main protagonist Jeffrey Skilling (neither hero nor anti-hero) describes life in a bubble:

> Every dip, every crash, every bubble that's burst. That's you. Your brilliant stupidity. This one gave us the railroads. This one the internet. This one the slave trade. And if you wanna do anything about saving the environment or getting to other worlds, you'll need a bubble for that too. Everything I've ever done in my life worth anything has been done in a bubble; in a state of extreme hope and trust and stupidity. [p. 114]

This chapter explores the way that concepts derived from psycho-analytic practice with individuals and groups can contribute to the understanding of disturbed organizational processes. I draw on examples from group relations consultancy and work with human service organizations in the public sector.

A psychoanalytic perspective is helpful in thinking about the context in which leadership is expressed in ways that can promote or sabotage the task of a group or organization. There is much to support the view that there has been a change in the prevailing ethos of our modern world towards one that is hostile to human dependency. As a consequence, the narcissism of leaders tends to go unchecked and may even be idealized. Like individuals, social organizations construct defences against anxiety, particularly the anxieties that are specific to the task at hand. These defences can result in serious dysfunction of the organization as a whole. For public services—and here the NHS is a prime example—struggling to respond to the unmanageable pressures external to the organization, the management can come to act as if it is under siege.

The unconscious dynamics of organizations: a psychoanalytic approach

The transposition of psychoanalytic insights from the consulting room to the organizational context has its historical origin in the creative collaboration of psychologists and psychiatrists in wartime and post-war recovery. The work of Klein is particularly relevant here. She described a primitive state of mind, the paranoid-schizoid position (Klein, 1940, 1946, 1959), which is characterized by terror of annihilation and the use of archaic defences (splitting and projection) to manage this situation. This contrasts with the depressive position (Klein, 1935, 1940), where anxiety and frustration can be managed, enabling integration of the self and the world. In this latter state, paranoid terror of the other transforms into concern for his or her sufferings. The development of Bion's theory of containment (Bion, 1962b) and Winnicott's description of the "holding environment" (Winnicott, 1965) have furthered our understanding of the creative tension between these two positions.

Processes of splitting and projection are never overcome, and under pressure we all resort to these more primitive ways of organizing our experience. This becomes especially apparent when we are under pressure from the organizations we live and work in. Elliot Jaques (1955) and Isabel Menzies Lyth (1960b) laid the foundation for the application of psychoanalytic understanding to the organizational context when, with their understanding of the dynamics of managing/managed, they undertook consultation to work organizations. They showed that the same mechanisms were at work and that working relations in organizations are deeply influenced by the unconscious anxieties of their members.

The tensions associated with paranoid-schizoid and depressive internal dynamics in organizational life should not be misunderstood as moral descriptions—they are tensions necessary for survival and growth. The individual in the organization tries to make sense of the world and, in a turbulent environment, tends to overcompensate for the relentless pressure caused by the person's inability to understand what is going on around him or her. Examples of over-compensation include reward systems that are divorced from achievement and excessive need for an overly positive approach to all issues: "Don't bring me problems, bring me solutions" or, in the modern political vernacular, "The menu, not the mind maps." The distinction between "task" and "anti-task" processes in the functioning of institutions has provided a major theoretical underpinning to thinking in this area (e.g., see Menzies Lyth, 1979). Where the primary task involves the care of vulnerable and dependent people, hostile defences inevitably come into play to block awareness of the demands of vulnerability and also to displace this awareness onto others. Although this may meet psychological needs in the short term, such anti-task activity can be very dysfunctional for the organization.

Good leadership of any enterprise requires the achievement of shared meaning among those involved. In the examples that follow, I focus on the dynamics of "human service" organizations (education, health, social welfare) and foreground a destructive process of psychological splitting that leads to a primitive breakdown of shared meaning—"What you are doing is deviant from what I am doing; I've got it right, you've got it wrong."

Of course, we are all different and have different roles in the organizations within which we work. In hospitals, there are differences in perception of task between doctors and nurses, between nurses in different wards but working with the same patients, and between all of them and the other professionals, and the patients and their families. These differences may go largely unnoticed, except by the patient, who experiences a kind of "Alice in Wonderland" world of changing identity according to all these different and conflicting perceptions.

Here, a shift in focus from the individual to the group may be useful. A group exists where there is evidence of individuals being prepared to "join", to share in the collective emotional life of the group. A familiar example is a theatre audience. The hush as the lights dim is a moment of collective anticipation. It may not be as exciting, but something of this anticipation is there below the surface of any meeting where there is real work going on.

We may also reflect on how the common awareness of a problem or a crisis will draw an aggregate of individuals into a collective identity, with shared beliefs and fantasies of potential disaster and hope of salvation. Bion showed that, in groups that meet regularly, a distinction can be made between those activities that serve the manifest aims of the group (which he termed the work group) and the more hidden activities, which serve more primitive emotional needs (termed "the basic assumption group"). He described three such basic assumptions: the dependency group, where all individuals sacrifice their own cognitive capacities and surrender to the higher wisdom and authority of the leader; the "fight-and-flight" group, which organizes itself around an axis of a feared predator/competitor; and, lastly, the "pairing group", where the group functions as if awaiting a messianic saviour provided by a divine couple. He argued that these defensive organizations protect against deeper psychotic anxieties and, indeed, are motivated by them (Bion, 1961); they are evidence of a group identity at work in the unconscious of members of the group. But this is not the same thing as saying that there is a group mind, separate and distinct from the states of mind of the individuals in the group. It is the individuals who create the group—not the other way round. Much of the time we participate in groups without even being aware of it. For example, two or more people walking together without touching will often nevertheless fall into step without conscious awareness or effort. The individuals in a group are not autonomous psychologically or physiologically in terms of their response to stimuli that are external or internal to the group. Different members of the group—and different parts of an organization—express different aspects of the unconscious processes as they affect the work task. The creation of a "purchaser–provider" relationship in the management and delivery of public services is noteworthy in this context. The separation of powers is to be viewed not simply as an efficient mobilization of market forces, but more as making manifest and promoting a primitive struggle for dominance in our relations with others. This organizational structure provides an effective vehicle for projecting those unwanted parts of ourselves—particularly our own feelings of helplessness—into others, whom we may then view contemptuously as weak.

Post-dependency and narcissism in organizations

Many of the characteristics of contemporary organizations stem from a model that foregrounds efficiency without taking the ordinary frailties of human behaviour into account. Life in organizations has become more frightening as the unpredictability of the future impacts on our consciousness and we realize that there is no longer a steady state, a stability that ensures our survival—if, indeed, there ever was one. Eric Trist (2001) wrote about this kind of continuous organizational turbulence:

> Particularly worrying has been the increase in the level of aggression. No love was now lost: the internal world of these organisations became a darker and more savage place. Socially amplified regression brings exceedingly primitive defences into play, whether in the form of hostile projection or of alienated withdrawal. [p. xxii]

Howard Stein (2001) has described some further characteristics of this darker and savage place:

> Downsizing and managed care are only partly (at most) the result of independent economic exigencies, and are largely driven by anxieties, wishes, fantasies and defenses that come to be codified and enforced in rationalist-economic ideology and social policy. [p. 52]

In his analysis of the decline and fall of General Motors, Stein (1990) outlines some of its causes: the commitment to bad decisions, the advancement of those who detach themselves from reality, and the discouragement of those who are reality-orientated participants and committed to their work. He describes the creation of an "organizational jungle" where individuals become obsessed with rank, management is isolated, and communications are ruptured. This can easily lead to cynicism, corruption, self-deception, and a narcissistic loss of reality in organizational leadership. This is worth reflecting on, when those managing public service organizations are encouraged to be more "business-like" in their approach.

The extraordinary financial rewards that such organizational leaders now expect as their right—because "they are worth it", according to their own processes of governance—are a remarkable assertion of self-worth. Leaders of organizations are transformed into celebrities peddling the myth that it is the work of an individual to "turn around" an organization.

Mark Stein (2007) has drawn attention to the pervasiveness of envy in relations with and around business leaders. His analysis of the role of envy and contempt in the downfall of financial institutions from Barings Bank to Enron brings together a focus on the personal psychological characteristics of key protagonists with the economic and social characteristics of contemporary organizational life.

My working hypothesis is that the organizational narcissism that these authors describe is an effect of the "post-dependency culture" identified by Khaleelee and Miller (1985):

> Hitherto safe institutional structures have become unreliable: not only are they no longer to be relied upon as sources of employment and prosperity, but they are also too fragile to cope with the force of our negative projections. These have to be taken back by the individual, whose props to identity are already undermined either by unemployment or uncertainty of employment, and re-projected on to "society". The force of projection required to defend the individual against the experience of internal chaos aggravates the fear of retribution from the projective receptacles, or, in more ordinary language, the fear of anarchy and violence. [p. 380]

This process has been mapped over succeeding years by OPUS "listening posts". These are free-associative discussion groups designed to catch some of the large group dynamics of society in the microcosm of the small group (Dartington, 2001). The theme of failed dependency has continued over 25 years:

> . . . any search for synthesis is doomed, as something makes it very difficult. There is a fear of contact and others are experienced as a threat; a result is a withdrawal, and the risk of engaging with others is denied by closing up and avoiding social involvement. [Stapley & Rickman, 2010, p. 134]

We may ask what is the undefined "something" that makes healthy social interaction so difficult. In my view, these unconscious dynamics are not perverse exceptions, to be isolated and dealt with severely by "special measures", for sabotage of the task is itself endemic to the culture of organizations. The question, then, is not how do we do away with it, but how do we understand it and live with it?

Erlich (2010) has suggested that corruption in the social realm is critically linked to the presence of chaos and fragmentation: he sees corruption within the social and organizational realm as the equivalent of psychotic regression in the paranoid individual. There is considerable literature on narcissistic leadership. Kernberg (1985) suggests that certain paranoid personalities may appear to function well where externally there is a threat of breakdown— for example, in revolutionary situations. However, leadership by disturbed personalities is bound to end in organizational failure, particularly as such leaders encourage delusional beliefs and dis-courage reality testing. Often the leader deals with this by moving on before his (or her) failures catch up with him—a process com-mon to the careers of football managers, politicians, and business leaders and also senior managers in public services, including the NHS. (Sometimes the hubris is too great, and their careers often end in disgrace: the football manager Brian Clough and senior executives of Enron are examples that come to mind.)

Those with a more clinical orientation may be interested to identify ways in which those who do well in certain organiza-tional contexts may seem, in other contexts, to exhibit pathological symptoms in their sense of self, and indeed there may be evidence for such conjectures. But we do well not to get stuck on interpreta-tions purely on the level of individual pathology when trying to understand such complex social and institutional processes.[1] When managers say, "I have no time to read" or "that is not something I can think about"—common enough expressions—we may begin to suspect that they are defending themselves from the disturbing meaning and significance in their actions. For to know what they are doing—which as individuals they would be able to do—is intolerably painful in their roles, which require them to attempt to improve services while cutting back resources.

In understanding the pathological organization at work, we have to shift our perception from the individual as a person, who may or may not be thought at times to act in a disturbed manner, to the person *in role*. The role in its organizational context might require managers, and those they manage, to ignore what they know and thus to act on a motivated misperception of reality.

Deregulation in the private sector, testament to a neo-liberal faith in the "unseen hand" of the market and the impatience of shareholders, has been matched by the introduction of a persecu-tory audit culture in all public service organizations. Furthermore, human services have to work in a highly politicized environment where Government is always anxious to secure a succession of quick gains. These new features of public service organizations create a culture in which it is increasingly difficult to think.

The gang in the organization: a group relations perspective

To some extent, those who manage organizations have to defend themselves against uncertainty—otherwise they would be over-whelmed—but the omnipotence required for this can get out of hand. When it does, we see the emergence of a kind of "gang"[2] in the organization, a narcissistic leadership—and followership—that acts as if there is a fusion between the self and the desired object: put simply, "If I get my way, everything will be all right; if my view of the world goes unchallenged, everything will be for the best in the best of all possible worlds". A capacity for thinking and self-reflection inevitably challenges such a polarized view.

Taking further the analogies between characteristic distur-bances at an individual level and the pathology of groups, one could say that certain organizations seem to develop a borderline personality,[3] living, on the one hand, in an uneasy space between an institutional integration, continuity, and ordinary dependency and, on the other, a paranoid-schizoid mentality characterized by binary oppositions, win–lose competitiveness, total success or annihilating failure, boom and bust.

For the "gang in the organization", the task is to maintain tri-umphant superiority. Authority is perverted into dominance, and leadership is given to and chosen by the most charismatic and disturbed individuals, who can represent for the group this most disturbed part of its own functioning. The gang in the organization acts in such a way that it only has internal reference and so fails in its capacity for a reality check; however, when things start to go badly wrong, its lack of judgment becomes apparent. A mature organizational culture with a more integrated/depressive mode of functioning can be self-questioning of its ability to complete the primary task, because it is able to accept the possibility of failure.

The working of the gang in the organization can be illustrated with an observation of a group relations conference.[4] In the course of the conference, a sub-group took on the qualities of a gang-like organization. There were 10 people in the sub-group, exactly the same number as the 10 staff in the conference. (It is not unusual for a group within an organization to mirror the management and then parody its worst features.) This sub-group had formed from a sub-set of the members and included several people with other significant relationships in their work roles outside the conference.

At first two women, working together, led the group into a culture of solidarity. They stated without fear of contradiction that there would be no "conflict in the group". As the conference task was to interact with other groups, they *would* interact, but the context of the interaction appeared to be a matter of complete indifference. They decided that they would support each other whatever happened, and in this way they presented themselves to the outside world as completely undifferentiated. It became clear that they were dominated by primitive processes to such an extent that they could act without moral reflection; it was enough that the management had asked them to carry out the activity. They went to meet another group, which they chose at random and which they knew nothing about. This group declined to meet with them *en masse* in this way. Thwarted in their immediate aim, they reacted by taking a hostage. They returned triumphant, celebrating their success.

The impact of their aggressive behaviour on another group did not concern them. They displayed no sense that any ethical questions might arise from their conduct. They felt that they now had an identity, clearly the most important thing for them. They repeated the oldest justification for unacknowledged cruelty—that the ends justify the means. Their anger was unacknowledged, as was their cruelty. To the disinterested observer (the role that the group relations consultant aspires to), the totalitarian atmosphere in the group was very hard to bear. Interestingly, it was a potential outsider, a black man in this otherwise white group, who was able to express doubts about the way they related to other groups. "Why didn't you leave, then?" was the immediate response from one of the leader women. In other words, the only way of dealing with dissent was rejection from the group.

Later, the two women became increasingly preoccupied with the distress of another member of the other group (the one from which they had taken the hostage). As a solution to the problem, they considered offering a merger of the two groups—that is, complete fusion.

A curious detail: the two women who were clearly the leaders of the group (a group that they claimed was leaderless) were employed in social agencies with an overtly reparative task (local authority social services and the ambulance service). Who, then, would dare to point to their underlying aggressive intent?

Those working with troubled families are familiar with a particular paradox: the need for the child to be sufficiently in touch to know the truth while at the same time recognizing the need to subvert it—that is, to enact a lie on behalf of the family. A gang in an organization can function in a similar manner: it seeks the truth but only in order to subvert it in the interests of a narcissistic authority that cannot distinguish between the desire and its fulfilment.

Secrets can also function as a mode of sabotage. A secret makes manifest an exclusive relation, where what is known is kept from those who do not know, stimulating envy and jealousy. The secret can become the location of sexualized fantasies that centre on an anticipated new future, and this intoxicating mixture serves to effectively undermine the primary task. Furthermore, relationships at work that are known about but not acknowledged provide opportunities to subvert the clarity of authority in formal roles. In group relations conferences, external relationships—both working relationships and friendships—are often left unspoken, because of the fear of the attacks (phantasied or real) that any such disclosure would bring. But knowledge is power, and secret knowledge is all the stronger because it cannot be challenged.

Social defences in organizations

Bion (1961) described man as a group animal, whether we liked it or not—very often not. As a result of the basic assumptions that underlie group life, we are never altogether removed from non-rational and dysfunctional behaviour. Menzies (Menzies Lyth, 1960b) describes in detail the ways in which the intimate contact that nurses have with others' vulnerability, both physical and mental, stirs primitive anxieties and dreads, which bring in their wake defensive structures to manage them. At both individual and social levels, defences of this kind can, of course, be protective and contribute to the individual or group's capacity to carry out the necessary tasks, but often these defensive systems have entirely the opposite effect.

Menzies describes how these social defences—for example, the misdirection of responsibility up and down the system—may be dysfunctional, as

> nurses are deprived of positive satisfactions potentially existent in the profession, for example the satisfaction and reassurance that comes from confidence in nursing skill. Satisfaction is also reduced by the attempt to evade anxiety by splitting up the nurse–patient relationship and converting patients who need nursing into tasks that must be performed. . . . Success and satisfaction are dissipated in much the same way as the anxiety. . . . The poignancy of the situation is increased by the expressed aims of nursing at this time—to nurse the whole patient as a person. The nurse is instructed to do that, it is usually what she wants to do, but the functioning of the nursing service makes it impossible. [Menzies Lyth, 1960b, p. 70]

It is famously difficult to get out of a hole if you persist in digging. In one NHS organization tasked to meet the long-term dependency needs of a vulnerable population, the clinical lead came into conflict with two of his colleagues. The conflict had an intransigent quality, a stuckness, leading to a request for external facilitation. The clinical leader was generally recognized as an effective manager—exercising an ego function on the boundary of the service in its relations with the senior management of the Trust. However, his leadership had not been altogether able to resist certain cutbacks and closures, seemingly inevitable at a time of financial stringency for a service unable to deliver quick wins. The predictable tensions arising in a service under siege were demonstrated in the conflict with colleagues, both of whom had experienced a loss of potency when they were displaced from semi-autonomous positions of personal authority in their clinical teams—positions they had envisaged as theirs by right. What was remarkable was the unforgiving nature of their resentment, which had an intransigent quality that was not to be eroded by time. They accepted the logic of the situation, accepted that the clinical leader had done what he could, but continued to harbour a grudge against his "autocratic" and "secretive" management style.

The quality of our understanding of the system we are working in depends on the process of learning that brought us there. Harris and Meltzer (1976) have usefully defined a different, more primitive kind of "learning" that disavows dependency, a process they call learning by "scavenging":

Learning by scavenging . . . is typified by [the activity of] the envious part of the personality, which cannot ask for help nor accept it with gratitude. It tends to view all skill and knowledge as essentially secret and magical in its control of nature and people. It watches and listens for items "thrown away", as it were, where no "please" or "thank you" need enter in, and therefore tends to feel triumphant over the stupidity of others for giving away the formula. [pp. 393–394]

The increased narcissism of leaders—or, rather, the increased acceptance in organizational life and in society more widely of the narcissism of leaders—has left us exposed to the extremes that we are prepare to go to in order to alleviate dependency needs that go unrecognized and unresolved. Post-dependency has also meant post-dependability—an outcome that Khaleelee and Miller (1985) warned against more than 25 years ago.

Management under siege:
lessons from organizational consultancy in the NHS

In consulting to human service organizations in health, social welfare, and education, we might expect that, given their primary task, they are not so suited to a fight–flight basic assumption mentality— or are they? What are the conditions conducive to the emergence and the continuing dominance of fight–flight phenomena in organizations that are in their overt expression intended to be agencies of compassion and therapeutic endeavour?

Such organizations tend to have a powerful identification with a founder. Sometimes there has actually been such a figure; charitable organizations may still bear their powerful evocative name. Even now, when the NHS is experiencing far-reaching changes in its structures and governance, this is described as the most radical change *since its founding*. Alternatively, the founder may have a more mythological existence. However, esteemed founders stimulate repressed envy and oedipal violence.

The capacity to stay with a depressive or even "tragic" state of mind (Symington, 1994) or to live with uncertainty and a capacity for negative capability (French, Harvey, & Simpson, 2002) is rarely considered a valuable quality in a leader. Indeed, the narcissism of leadership in political life has led to a (con)fusion of reputation and celebrity. The narcissist does not want to see beyond the boundary of the self and so has to maintain a stability that preserves the self-referring certainties of his position.

The perversity and corruption of organizations is not a phenomenon in a vacuum. It is characteristic of an open system that is relating—but not very well—to its environment. At an unconscious level, it is possible for the sadistic perpetrators of inhumane practices to justify their actions because they are being carried out on behalf of a wider society: The "turning of a blind eye internally" is only made possible by the deliberate ignorance—or ignoring—that is the ordinary obliviousness of the large group. Such abuses may be exposed in moments of shock and outrage, but soon things return to normal and the abuses continue. In the wider policy field, we hear successive reports by the Inspector of Prisons and critical incident reports in child care; in the wider global context, there are revelations of abuse in the wars in Iraq and Afghanistan. But such perversity and corruption is possible only when there is collusion—a passive acceptance—from the wider environment.

The sense of unreality that continuously threatens those in public services is a direct result of the effects of uncontained anxiety (see chapter 13) originating at the level of political leadership, which courses through the system as NHS management in strategic health authorities and primary care trusts work to implement cuts that are then targeted on their own services. The following discussion of a consultancy illustrates these processes.

A primary care trust with a charismatic and successful CEO was looking to develop its organizational culture, moving from an unwieldy bureaucracy, with different divisions working as "silos", to a small, more proactive matrix organization. It was shedding all its previous responsibilities for the provision of services in order to focus on its commissioning role, in line with the Government-led initiative [termed, in the language of positive thinking, "World Class Commissioning" (WCC)]. My role was as a consultant to this process, over a six-month period.

The management of the NHS is, of course, not known for consistency and continuity, and by the end of the six-month consultancy the management group had been orphaned: the chief executive had left, his deputy (who had commissioned the consultancy) was leaving to join him, the Chair of the Trust (another sponsor of the consultancy) had resigned, and there was a new "interim" CEO, who came with a fearsome reputation (he seemed to have all the qualities of a wicked stepfather).

Our work was with an expanding group of Assistant Directors, described as "the powerhouse of the organization"; we reported to the Board. Their espoused task was to work together in a cohesive and strategic way, avoiding replication and overlap of competing divisions. In fact, they experienced the Board of executive and non-executive directors as divisive and competitive among themselves. "When two directors have a disagreement on how to deal with a problem, there is an argument—but no decision." "It's like going off to do your mum's shopping, and then when you get back she says, 'Oh I don't want this, I wanted that ... why did you get that?'"

Of course, these characteristics had an impact on the consultation, which was aiming to support further the transformation of the organization from separate fiefdoms into a "matrix organization". The project had the formal backing of the CEO and the senior management, but two or three members of the group did not attend any of the regularly arranged consultation sessions, which were intended to be mandatory; they were not challenged about their non-attendance. In remaining loyal to the priorities of their own individual directors, they represented very well the ambivalence of the senior management as regards any process of authorization of this supposed "powerhouse".

Internally the organization worked very hard to maintain a self-image of excellence, which did not allow for exceptions: everything they did had to be the best, and this had the effect of "beating ourselves up over what we are not achieving all the time". The language of hyperbole, of WCC and "Gold Standards", reminded me of trying to get foreigners to understand by shouting at them. They seemed to struggle to understand each other; their vocabulary was full of acronyms whose original meaning was often lost.

The "strategic plan" for the organization was delegated to a consultant, and it was not completed until the last moment: "We need to put something in about finance, can you help? But we need it by close of play tomorrow."

The organization appointed a Project Management Officer to contribute to the effective integration of their collective endeavour: members of the group said, critically, that they had never met him—but it seemed that he had called a meeting and only three of them had attended. Comments on a strategy document concerning accidental injury had grown to 16 MB on the organization's net-worked computers, but they were no nearer to making a decision.

"I'm overwhelmed by the amount of requests for things that I need to do, in a timeframe that is completely unrealistic. . . . Could we say no? . . . I don't want to let the CEO down." The narcissism of the leader in such situations is absolutely dependent on the support of his or her followers.

Abrupt communication had the effect of creating a kind of battlefield, not allowing any possibility for individuals to work through their concerns with each other. Problems were enveloped in an email culture of blame and accusation.

After a difficult session, my colleague described the counter-transference well: "I felt during the afternoon that I was out of touch with their reality—struggling to understand—feeling that my experience and understanding of the day was naïve, irrelevant; at the same time I felt that they are the people who are out of touch—creating a virtual world that has little to do with the realities of delivering services."

It should be recalled that this took place in the context of a growing atmosphere of austerity. "Everything for the next ten years will be about cutting costs." Although trying to see how they would manage this shift of priorities, they were as yet unaware that a change of government would mean that their own management level within the organization would itself be most at risk of being rationalized out of existence.

The experiences brought by the managers to the consultancy discussions were often, in their own words, "maddening". They aspired to plan for longer term objectives but were having to manage short-term fixes. This meant that they "did not have time to think"—and yet all the time they were identifying mistakes that they would then have to rectify. There was a sense that their work was monitored to meet the preoccupations of others, but at the same time they took on invisible tasks—responding to freedom of information requests, for example—that they were required to deal with. Email communication was increasingly peremptory and rude and also sered as a vehicle for procrastination.

As is so often the case, the frustrations in the organization became focused, for a while, on the use of the car park. Decisions about parking spaces were made and reversed. Finally, staff were given an extra day's holiday to compensate for bearing with the difficulties that ensued. This made manifest the reactive and inconsistent pattern of decision-making.

I have described the exhortatory character of the language. They were working to "hit their targets". It was common for employees to refer to their work as the "day job", conveying the day-to-day routine of reactive responses to whatever came up, an action-based culture separated from any overall strategic vision.

As I came to understand their stresses, I saw that they were having to live sometimes on the boundary of what was real and at other times of what was imaginary, or perhaps living on the boundary between these two realities. Their remit was to ensure the best possible health care for a community of 200,000 people. But they had to achieve this by meeting expectations coming directly from central government, through mechanisms of command and control, audit and inspection, creating a culture not of doing things but of *being seen to do the right thing*—not the work itself but its representation in national league tables.

Conclusion

This NHS consultancy clearly illustrates the conditions conducive to the creation of a bubble within which it is desperately important to be internally consistent. The bubble is maintained by keeping up the pressure to achieve an illusion of certainty. For those within the bubble it may appear to have a reality of its own, but it becomes increasingly isolated from the external world and so increasingly incapacitated.

I have suggested that situations such as this provide the soil for the germination of a perverse structure—the "gang"—which is then given the task of maintaining the illusion of well-being, even as the institution as a whole ceases to be viable. It has been argued by Hoggett (1998) that this "internal establishment" offers a perverse protection against the very danger that it represents. Furthermore, the disturbed relationships based on massive projection and splitting are analogous to some very primitive or psychotic processes observed at the individual level.

At the same time, the internal establishment is not all bad. In fact, its achievement is to meet the demands made of it, however persecuting and illogical these are felt to be, while retaining the capacity of the group to meet its own objectives. As it happened, when the WCC performance ratings were announced a year later, the organization had moved twenty places up the national league table. The work of the Board was particularly commended as a collaborative team. It had "invested in designing and establishing a matrix organization, which, it feels, will be more effective".

From an outsider perspective, I was impressed by the capacity of different protagonists to retain their enthusiasm for their work in the organization. This requires a certain cut-off–ness of focus in order to survive but also allows for creativity under fire. Using the example of the US Presidency, Gould (2010) argues that there is a need in organizational leadership for sophisticated use of PS–D dynamics: "the ability to mobilize and integrate paranoid/schizoid capacities in a sophisticated way, along with those of the depressive position, are an essential requisite for mature, enlightened and effective leadership" (p. 173).

Resigning one's individual autonomy to the group may be thought as, potentially, betraying the capacity both to think and behave in an ethical manner. I have described how, in the political world of public services, organizational dynamics, understood as group processes and not only through the preoccupations of the leader, may become an arena for very disturbed modes of functioning. We should therefore also acknowledge the capacity of individuals under pressure to retain—or, if necessary, recover—a sense of identity and purpose when working under the pressure of these dynamics. We may then find continuing evidence to support Bion's belief in the on-going vitality of the work group.

Notes

1. Erlich (2010) has warned against the tendency to regard suicide bombers as sick—they might be well-adjusted individuals, loving and loved by their families, although we need an "unpolitically correct" capacity for empathy to recognize that possibility. Cherie Blair, lawyer but also wife of the then Prime Minister, had to back off from a position of wanting to understand the terrorist mind. This is what she is reported to have said in 2002: "As long as young people feel they have got no hope but to blow themselves up, you are never going to make progress." In the outraged reaction to this common-sense statement, you could observe the closing of minds.

2. This term takes its origin in the psychoanalytic literature from the work of Herbert Rosenfeld, who found references to gangs and mafia-like organizations in the dreams and associations of his more disturbed patients. He came to understand this as representing an *internal* structure that dominated the personality structure, imprisoning the patient "as if one were dealing with a powerful gang dominated by a leader, who controls all the members of the gang to see that they support each other in making the criminal destructive work more effective and powerful" (Rosenfeld, 1971, p. 174). This structure idealized self-sufficiency, hated dependence, and made the patient feel exposed and vulnerable in the face of any awareness of his own ordinary human dependency. Rosenfeld recognized these processes as being both destructive and narcissistic.

3. John Steiner (1987) has described how an internal pathological organization functions "as a defence, not only against fragmentation and confusion, but also against the mental pain and anxiety of the depressive position. It acts as a borderline area between the two other positions, where the patient believes he can retreat if either paranoid or depressive anxieties become unbearable" (p. 71).

4. Group Relations conferences are experiential training events lasting for anything from a day to two weeks (the "Leicester Conference" on authority and leadership in organizations). They provide a context for the members of the conference to explore their own functioning in the here-and-now of group situations.

CHAPTER THIRTEEN

The dynamics of containment

David Bell

The title of this chapter serves to capture a dimension of mental health care that I think we all know about at some level, albeit implicitly rather than explicitly. It refers to both the inner world and external reality and, crucially, the relationship between them. Transactions across this boundary generate the most primitive anxieties even in the relatively well, as we all know from the experience of moving house, moving country, or major changes in role. But what for others is a tremor is, for those who are mentally ill, more akin to the feeling of an impending earthquake, a psychic catastrophe that reawakens all the terrors of breakdown.

A supervisee brought the following material. A not very ill patient was late for her session. She described her journey. On the way she had a lovely walk; she met a friend, they talked; it was a beautiful day, wonderful scenery. And so she went on. The analyst thought of her as involved in a happy world, excluding him; he experienced himself as looking on at this happy scene, feeling that he had been kept waiting because, in comparison, he was rather uninteresting. He felt a pressure to make a comment conveying this to the patient. But instead he stayed with his uncomfortable feeling and refrained from making what he thought of as the expected interpretation. He remembered that this patient was socially isolated, and very inhibited, dominated by a cruel superego that made her feel uninteresting and worthless. The analyst could now see that she had projected this superego into him and was trying to nudge him into an enactment that would serve to attack the pleasure she had experienced on her walk. Understanding this enabled him to contain the pressure and think about it, and this provided the possibility of development. For, as it turned out, the capacity to enjoy the countryside and her conversation with her friend rested upon important developments in the analysis.

* * *

Mrs B suffered an acute paranoid breakdown and was continuously persecuted by the idea that "they" were coming to get her. She arrived on the ward, accompanied by her relatives, who were exhausted with trying to reassure her, to no avail. The charge nurse went to greet her, but as he arrived she was continuously muttering to herself "They are coming to get me . . . Cannot stay here . . . they will come . . . they are coming to get me."

"Who are coming to get you?" said the charge nurse, fixing her with his gaze.

"They are," she responded.

"Oh no they won't," he responded ". . . because I am in charge."

The patient immediately calmed down, seemed to feel understood and safer, and went calmly on to the ward.

These two anecdotes, one from an analysis, the other from an observation on a ward, serve to introduce my topic. The contexts were, of course, very different, but in both situations the capacity to contain something was essential to the therapeutic outcome.

Like many psychoanalytic terms, the word "containment" has both an everyday meaning and a more technical psychoanalytic one, the latter providing a deepening of the concept and also locating it within a theoretical structure and a model of the mind. Although it is clear that appropriate support—that is, containment—of mental health staff provides them with a basis of confidence and morale, which is perhaps one of the most vital therapeutic factors in work with the mentally ill, it is largely absent from all documents dealing with policy, strategic planning, and so on. This is increasingly so as the "thinking" that underlies these projects degrades into performance targets, measured competencies, and the like.

Many years ago, when I was a young doctor working at the Maudsley Hospital, Alexis Brook (a well-known expert in the psychodynamics of institutions) came to give a lecture on the nature of institutions. He started by asking us "What is a hospital?" and we gave the predictable answers such as "a place where patients are looked after". After we had given various suggestions, he pointed out that something essential had been overlooked: a hospital is a place where *staff* get looked after.

This might strike us as strange and perhaps even indulgent, and the fact that it does so in itself reveals much about the lack of place for such thinking in our present culture. But it does indicate an important truth. That is, if the staff feel well supported and valued, they in turn will value their work, and so the patients will be well cared for. This brings to mind the model of a mother looking after a baby, who needs the support of those around her, such as the immediate family and social context, to provide her with a basis for managing the intense emotional engagement with her infant.

In approaching the concept of containment within a service, it is important to bear in mind the many different levels within the system, which interact with each other in complex ways. In the Introduction to the book, it was suggested that these different levels can be pictured as like Russian dolls, each outer system containing the ones inside. These levels may act to support each other, providing levels of containment within the system; alternatively, they can interact in more destructive ways.

Over the last 20 years or so, important changes have occurred in the NHS and more widely in the public sector. In the earlier period, the outermost level (i.e., government) was distant, and, though it clearly had a determining effect, it was relatively—at least manifestly—unobtrusive. Now, however, it is ever-present, hovering like a kind of menacing superego penetrating into every pore of the relationships within the system. Whereas intermediate management structures previously could serve as buffers, absorbing pressures from above and containing them, they now act as fully porous conduits distributing anxiety that is amplified as it resonates throughout the system, flooding those at lower levels in such a manner that they cannot carry out their task. A previous government Inspector of Prisons described similar processes within the prison service (personal communication). On visiting a prison, he asked the Prison Governor what he regarded as the main aim of his prison. The Governor answered immediately, "To reach my performance target of saving over one million pounds before the end of this financial year."

So what do we mean by the term "containment"? The need to contain things in the mind is part of our ordinary common-sense psychology: "keeping things in mind", "keep your hair on", "look before you leap" are well understood idiomatic expressions that emphasize the importance of thinking instead of acting and, more than this, the value of sustaining even unpleasant states of mind and resisting the pressure to "do something" at least long enough to allow their nature to become known, reflected upon, thought about. We all recognize these capacities and value them as part of everyday life, but psychoanalysis has given these terms a breadth and depth. Since the beginning, psychoanalytic theory has stressed the centrality of sustaining thought and resisting the temptation to act, as so well captured in Freud's (1911b) quotation of Shaw as the capacity "To be able to choose the line of greatest advantage instead of yielding in the direction of least resistance."[1] One of Freud's most remarkable attributes, perhaps characteristic of very great minds in general, is the extraordinary development of the capacity to think and to sustain this painful process over long periods, without peremptory closure.

When we say "thinking" rather than "acting", it is important to bear in mind that there are two different kinds of action. There is external action, and here we may think of that type of action which, instead of being the outcome of thought, serves as a replacement for it. However, Freud also put firmly on the map a new kind of action that similarly serves to obviate unpleasant or difficult thoughts—*internal actions* (see Wollheim, 1971). These actions would include defence mechanisms such as symptomatic forgetting, denial, repression, displacement, minimizing significance, and so forth, all serving to restrict what can be thought. Central to the psychoanalytic endeavour is its capacity to widen the possibility of what can be thought about—that is, contained in mind. The psychoanalytic method of free exploration of all that comes into mind serves exactly this purpose.

The work of Melanie Klein considerably extended our understanding of the internal factors that might support the mind's capacity to think. She described how in early life the world is largely divided in a simple binary way between good and bad.

This is a method of dealing with powerful anxieties that cannot be tolerated. Unbearable thoughts and feelings cannot be contained within the mind and are instead projected, creating a frightening external world. As the child establishes a secure relation to a good, albeit idealized, internal object, his anxiety lessens, and a qualitative change occurs in his way of being in the world. The feeling of internal security removes the need for such violent projection, and so his world, internal and external, becomes more integrated. Integration, however, brings profoundly painful feelings deriving particularly from the awareness of separation and feelings of guilt.[2] But if these can be borne—that is, contained within the mind—this lays the basis for feelings of confidence, faith in the world, and development. Every new crisis in life provides further opportunities for development, but it also brings with it the possibility of regression into illness and more paranoid-schizoid ways of functioning.

Central here is the distinction between the depressive position, a state of mind characterized by its capacity for integration and containment, and the schizoid mode of functioning, where reflective thought is severely compromised by the mind's urgent need to deal with overwhelming anxieties.

A particular strength of the Kleinian account of human development is that the theory of the depressive position links the capacity to bear mental pain with the capacity to sustain empathic identification with the other, and thus concern for his or her sufferings—in other words, to enter a moral world. This moral world centres on a relation to reality, internal and external, and a struggle for truthfulness.

Although the above account provides a framework for understanding the development of the capacity for containment, it does so only implicitly. It was Bion who moved this function from implicitness to explicitness, bringing to the centre of psychoanalytic scrutiny the process of containment itself, which is closely bound up with his model of the development of thinking. "Thinking" in Bion's sense expresses the capacity to contain thoughts in the mind.

Bion's model rests upon an understanding of a dynamic relation between two psychic elements: the "container" and the "contained". He provides us with a phenomenology of the vicissitudes of this relationship and an account of their development. Bion's model of container–contained not only refers to processes in one individual, or even between two, but has a much wider reference to group, institutional, and social processes in general. Certain types of social structure, for example, serve to provide containment of violence, whereas other types promote it.

Having established the model of containment, different types of failure of this relation can be studied, and this is perhaps most easily explicated in terms of group functioning.

Any group acts as a container both of the people who are its members and of the field of thoughts and emotions that these individuals bring. Bion (1962a, 1970)[3] studied the fate in a group of a new idea that is felt to be disturbing, communicated to the group by an individual, whom one might think of as the messenger. There are a number of possible outcomes:

» The group may exclude the new idea. Here, the container extrudes the contained—the messenger is expelled because the message he brings cannot be borne.

» The group may succumb to the dangerous idea but dissolve its identity. Here, the contained destroys the container.

» The group may accept the idea but crush it and strip it of its nature, so that its unique qualities are destroyed. Here, the container suffocates the contained.

» The group may *adapt* to a new idea, be changed by it but exist in a dynamic relation with it. Here, the container and contained have a symbiotic relationship, which might lead to growth and development.

These processes are exactly mirrored at the individual level. In this, the container is an individual mind and the contained is a disturbing thought or feeling—which suffers similar outcomes. Expulsion of the idea occurs through projection, creating a paranoid world; cutting oneself off creates dissociative states and feelings of unreality. Breakdown occurs when thoughts and feelings simply cannot be managed. The patient may say he feels he is "falling to pieces".[4] In a certain sense, this is an accurate "endopsychic perception", for what is being described here is the experience of a powerful force impacting on a rigid container that is then felt to shatter into fragments.

Where the new thought/emotion can be thought about and held in mind so that it can become known, the container and contained are affected by each other in ways that can promote development.

Bion suggests that the origin of this capacity is to be found in the mother–infant relationship, but the detail of this need not detain us here. What is essential is that this model provides a kind of prototype of mental functioning both within the individual and in relation to those around him or her.

The disturbed patient is afflicted by thoughts and feelings that he or she cannot manage and is thus impelled to act upon all those around him or her. The way these interactions are managed will have important implications for both the patient and those involved in the patient's care. Good mental health professionals know this and carry out this work quite intuitively—for example, as in the situation cited above where the nurse intuitively contained the patient's paranoid terror without challenging it.

With this theoretical background in mind, we can start to build up a picture of the factors that might support containment and those that, on the other hand, might undermine it. Crucial here are the quality of the support structures at various levels that can provide the basis for feelings of morale and confidence in one's role. As discussed above, menacing superegos hovering in the corridors will have the opposite effect.

Where containment fails, the result, not infrequently, is enactment—that is, action replaces thought. This may find expression in irrational management plans.

Miss B, a young married woman, was internally dominated by a cruel, primitive superego, which she felt watched her every move. She experienced any attempt at self-control as in the service of this superego, and so she could not distinguish between it and ordinary ego functions that sought to protect her from danger: in other words, the ego masqueraded as the superego. This resulted in a wholesale projection of her sane awareness of the danger of her actions into her analyst. Left free of any concern for herself, she took increasingly dangerous risks—such as driving while under the influence of sedatives—with what appeared to be complete equanimity, while her analyst grew increasingly horrified as the momentum of her self-destructiveness gathered pace. She said that she experienced the ending of sessions as "like a guillotine". This was a very apt description since, having projected important ego functions into her analyst, she left the session in a "headless" state. The situation deteriorated to such an extent that it became necessary to admit her to hospital.

On the ward she behaved in a very provocative way to the nurses. She would leave the hospital without telling them where she was going, leaving them with an overwhelming anxiety that she was about to carry out a very self-destructive attack. For example, she might say, seemingly calmly, that she was "going to the shops", as if this was a quite ordinary and banal event, while at the same time conveying that she would be near the pharmacy where, by implication, she might buy some paracetamol. At other times, she would telephone the ward from outside but not speak when a nurse answered and would then hang up. The nurses found this unbearably tantalizing. This resulted in an escalation of the need of the staff to control her, and she was restricted from leaving the ward. The situation then further deteriorated, and the nurses became worried that she might carry out a serious attack upon herself at any moment. In the end, she was restricted to a small room where she was continuously observed. She then became acutely anxious and declared in a terrified voice, "I can't stand this place. I'm being imprisoned."

The patient has "actualized" (Sandler, 1976) her inner situation. What started out as an inner conflict between aspects of herself, an intra-psychic situation, has now been transported into a conflict between herself and the nursing staff—namely, an interpersonal situation. The superego that watches her all the time is of course inescapable, but temporary escape is achieved through projecting it elsewhere in this way. It is not her own superego but, instead, the nurses on the ward who are felt to be imprisoning her.

It is also important to note that the patient's provocative manner did engender a good deal of hostility towards her, which was never really owned by the staff. Although keeping her under continuous observation manifestly served a wish to protect the patient from suicide, I think it also, at a deeper level, satisfied a hatred that had been recruited in the staff and that was associated with some excitement.

These situations are not uncommon. Many patients use admission to psychiatric wards to provide themselves with an immediate context for these projective procedures, and this is particularly the case in suicidal patients. Although, in the last instance, no one can be absolutely prevented from committing suicide, it is easy for staff to become identified with an omnipotence that dictates that it is entirely their responsibility. They come to believe that they are the only ones who are capable of *really* understanding the patient. The determination to save the patient acquires a religiosity, the staff believing themselves to be specially selected for this mission. Hostility that is denied and split off to this extent can quite suddenly return and with a vengeance, breaking down any residual capacity to contain it. Yesterday's poor suffering patient, who only needs help and understanding and constant support, becomes tomorrow's hopeless case, who should be immediately discharged or given high doses of medication or even ECT. Such measures may even bring an apparent improvement in the patient, one based not on any real development but brought about through the gratification of the patient's need for punishment, relieving him or her, temporarily, of the persecuting omnipotent guilt.

It was Tom Main (1957)[5] who originally studied these processes in detail, showing how the splits in the patient's mind are re-lived in the ward as divisions among the staff. The "saintly" group, described above, who endlessly suffer on behalf of the patient and who believe the patient to be only a victim of his or her damaging early relationships, have their counterpart in another group of staff who see the patient only as manipulative and "attention-seeking", who must be "confronted". The extent to which such processes enact the split aspects of the patient's mind is the extent to which the possibility of the system's containment of them has broken down

Where these staff disturbances remain unacknowledged, the situation can quickly escalate, with catastrophic results as the container—the ward—suffers a kind of institutional breakdown. It is important not to underestimate the effects of this kind of catastrophe on the staff, most especially in terms of persecuting guilt and feelings of worthlessness.

> Ms C was referred to be considered for admission by a psychiatric team who had become very worried at the possibility of her suicide. From what I could gather, threats of suicide had become one of her principal modes of communication. When I went to meet her in the waiting room, she had the air of someone who is very seriously disturbed. She was sitting in the waiting room with her head bowed low, and she apparently did not see or hear me arrive. I had to attract her attention. What ensued was a very disturbing experience. For much of the time, she disowned any knowledge about herself, claiming she had come "because they

sent me". When I commented on how difficult she found the interview, she replied with a defiant air, "Well anyone would in this situation, wouldn't they?"

Throughout the interview I felt acutely aware of her dangerous suicidality, while she remained almost entirely cut off from it and apparently superior. However, when I pointed out that she was doing everything she could to stop me from helping her and went on to say that she might succeed, she looked at me, smiled, and said, "You've pulled the rug out from under my feet." She added that getting treatment was "her only lifeline". Although in a certain sense this was true, what I want to convey here is the way that, right from the beginning of the consultation, it was I who was to carry responsibility for her condition. The waiting-room situation where I had to try, in a rather awkward way, to attract her attention was emblematic of what was to transpire. When she said to me that getting help was her lifeline, this was not a moment of contact and reassurance. It filled me with anxiety. I felt that if I didn't accept her for treatment then and there, it would be me who was pulling away the lifeline, me who would be responsible for her suicide. She had projected her wish to live into me, and now I, as the representative of that wish, was being taunted with the terror of her suicide. I carried not only the responsibility for her life but also the threat of an omnipotent persecuting guilt. The smile was a smile of perverse triumph at my impossible position. It did emerge later that this was an enactment of an internal situation in which she herself felt continuously threatened and mocked. Any reference that she made to mental pain was quickly followed by a contemptuous attack on the part of herself that experienced this vulnerability, which was labelled as "whinging and whining".

A marked feature of this kind of situation, where perverse elements are so predominant, is the presence of negative therapeutic reactions. Just when the patient has made some real progress, there is a sudden deterioration with a real risk of suicide. It is as if the progress that brings awareness of the extent of disturbance and vulnerability provokes a furious counterattack by an internal organization that regards this contact with sanity as a betrayal (see Rosenfeld, 1971). It is important to distinguish this sort of negative therapeutic reaction from that where the pull towards suicide is primarily a result of unbearable guilt and despair, which has different management implications.

> Ms D at first appeared rather similar to Ms C, in that she, too, filled the staff with unbearable anxiety as to her suicidal capacity. Although at first perverse psychopathology seemed to predominate, this gave way to a more clearly melancholic picture. She had made innumerable mutilating attacks on her skin by slashing it. Her skin seemed to represent her sexual body, which she regarded as disgusting. She felt full of "bad disgusting thoughts", particularly of abusing children. She felt that she could only rid herself of this identification with her abusing parent through quite literally cutting it out of her body. She had managed, however, to spare her face and hands, and this appeared to represent a limited capacity to hold on to something good in herself. However, once on the ward, she tended to project into the staff all awareness of these good aspects of herself, while she herself sank further and further into a melancholic state. The fact that in this case the staff felt able to maintain a belief in her—that is, to contain it—despite being constantly provoked, turned out to be of great therapeutic importance. Here, the primary motive for projection outside herself of her wish to live was more for "safekeeping", perverse mockery being much less evident. After some improvement, she, like Ms C, also showed a marked negative therapeutic reaction and became more acutely ill. Although there were some perverse elements, the predominant difficulties arose from the unbearable psychic pain. Here, the staff were called upon to contain her wish to live and the intense feelings arising from her awareness of the damage done to her good objects, which to some extent really was irreparable.

I would like to close with an example that I think shows how different levels within a system can serve not to mitigate the disturbing effects of a particular patient but, instead, to amplify them as they resonate through different levels within the system.

> Mr F was a 38-year-old eastern European man who came from a very severely disturbed background, though he disowned knowledge of this himself. He was admitted to hospital after a series of episodes of self-harm, including self-cutting, overdosing, and

a serious attempt at drowning which required resuscitation. The diagnosis was of "treatment-resistant depression".

As he was clearly a very difficult patient to manage, I was asked to carry out a consultation with the team. I learnt that Mr F was relentlessly negative, saying that he had nothing to live for, that his life was entirely meaningless. Mr L, his special nurse, saw it as his job to persuade him otherwise, but without any success.

Special care was provided for the patient on a daily basis. In discussion, it emerged that there was, so to speak, a "politically correct" way of talking about him—that is, as someone who was very ill, suffering, who needed special care. But there was another, much more negative view, which it was very difficult to own.

However, as it became possible to talk more freely, the staff spoke of the hatred that Mr F stirred up in them. The nurse who was "specialling" him described how he himself had to arrange all his meetings with the patient. The patient would reluctantly agree to come, but always added, ". . . if *you* think there is any point". The staff felt extremely burdened with the day-to-day responsibility for keeping him alive, and they found it very difficult when the patient said he enjoyed being on the ward; he said it was "like being in a country spa". It also emerged that a number of the nursing staff worried more about this patient than any other patient and, furthermore, that this worry invaded their personal lives to the degree that even when they were not on duty they thought about him and even phoned up the ward to make sure he was still alive. Each of them felt very alone with this worry, as if it were their own very personal responsibility.

The crucial moment in discussion came when the senior consultant, Dr J, felt able to describe her distaste at a scene she was frequently exposed to when the patient's wife visited the ward. They would exhibitionistically caress each other sexually in the middle of the ward. This was done just sufficiently to make it clear what they were doing, but not so much that it could be censured. We understood this in the following way. The very public excited "intercourse" that was taking place on the ward made manifest the malignant continual "intercourse" that was taking place between the patient and the staff. Projecting his wish to live to the degree that the staff continually felt responsible for keeping him alive had become a source of addictive excitement for Mr F. This excitement seemed to derive from two sources: from being rid of the burden of his wish to stay alive, but also from a perverse triumphant mockery of that wish, which the staff had to suffer, since the wish was now located in them.

As I have discussed, some patients, having projected their wish to live, feel relieved and can allow others to help them. In this situation, it is the nurse's (and it is usually the nurse) capacity to contain—that is, to hold on to—this vital aspect of the patient that proves of greatest importance as regards therapeutic development. But this is not the case here, where there is a more malignant relationship. The more the staff own the patient's wish to live, the more the patient, so to speak, is free of it. It is typical of these patients that they tend to overwhelm the staff's capacity to cope, to the degree that anxiety about the patient so invades their personal life that some may even feel that they cannot have holidays. In this situation, the container is so severely damaged by that which it is called upon to contain that it can no longer function, and if this goes unrecognized the results will be steady deterioration of the patients and staff on the ward.

In order to be able to provide appropriate care for a patient like Mr F, it is necessary that those looking after him do *not* feel that they, individually, have to take full responsibility for whether he lives or dies—that is, that care is taken so that no one person is subject to this omnipotent demand to contain the uncontainable. While it is, of course, inevitable that staff will end up feeling this to some extent, the point here is that this must not be supported externally. Precaution needs to be taken so that no individual member of staff is psychologically isolated with the patient, and this can be achieved by ensuring that the team regularly discuss their involvement with the patient. This is vital in order to avoid the splitting processes described by Main (1957), where different staff members come to contain widely split-off aspects of the patient. For example, one staff member is idealized while another is denigrated, or one staff member is drawn into unrealistic hopes for the future of the patient while another sinks into despair.

There was, however, a further difficulty in the situation described, and this derived from the more general context. There had been a suicide in the hospital within the last year, though on a different ward (but a patient under the care of the same consultant). As far as I could gather, there was nothing to suggest that this could have been avoided. However, the formal enquiry that dealt with the matter had been extremely difficult. The consultant told me that she had to explain in her report what she would do differently in the future to avoid this outcome. She told me: "In reality I felt there was nothing I would do differently, as I believed we had done all we could. But there was no place for this idea: it was assumed that there must have been a failure in the way the patient was managed." Here, one can see how the external system, in insisting that the staff were at least to some extent responsible for this outcome, acted to support the omnipotent persecution that was so evident—each member of staff felt that if Mr F did kill himself, then the responsibility would be laid at his or her door. As we looked further into this, we discovered that the patient himself was aware of this, since the person who had killed himself was known to him.

Concluding comments

It has been my intention to show that containment is a central part of all work with psychiatric patients. This is, as I suggested, implicit in all our work, but the psychoanalytic account of this process, particularly as developed by Bion, offers us a proper theory and model of the dynamics of containment and indicates what kind of processes might support or obstruct it.

A World Health Organization study in the 1950s compared a number of different psychiatric hospitals in terms of outcome. The different outcomes did not seem to result directly from the treatment approach but were more linked to an indescribable quality that they termed "morale" (WHO, 1953).

It seems to me that in our current health service the professional occupies a very beleaguered position, one that is very damaging to morale. As I described in the Introduction, in earlier times the immediate context of patient and mental health worker could, to some extent, be insulated from anxieties emanating from higher up in the system. This situation has now radically altered. While the previous state of affairs led to some realistic concern about the tendency to pass responsibility upwards through the system, the current situation has brought a different kind of problem, which is very much more damaging. The capacity of the outer/higher levels within the system to contain anxiety has been very seriously undermined: a minister sneezes and, somewhere on a ward, a nurse finds herself, so to speak, rushing for a handkerchief. Performance targets, constant systemic upheavals, and anxiety about survival cause anxiety to flood downward through the system, considerably damaging the possibility of therapeutic work. Nowhere is this tendency more destructive than in the consequences of the marketization/commodification of the NHS which is currently gathering pace.

Elsewhere (Bell, 1996), I discussed the manner in which the commodification of the public sector made manifest a peculiar form of thinking, which I characterized as "Primitive Mind of State". In this primitive world,

> There are "good" hospitals or schools and "bad" ones. The "bad" ones will be destroyed because they will not get the custom of the mythically empowered consumer, while the "good" ones will survive. The only way the "bad" ones might survive is by transforming themselves and becoming "good", something that is their own responsibility; and they can expect no help from the nanny state to get them out of the mess they have got themselves into!
>
> There really is something very persuasive about this sort of argument—it appeals to our wish to live in a simple world of "good" and "bad". The question of a careful exploration, and understanding of why a particular hospital is "bad" does not really arise: it is bad . . . because it is bad. A careful exploration would introduce all sorts of unpleasant complexities which go against the simple appeal of "taking your custom elsewhere". One might cite the effects of chronic starvation of resources, lack of opportunities for staff development, chronic severe depletion of that vital ingredient for any therapeutic life, morale. "Good" and "Bad" become, in the transitory shifting nature of the market forces, categories existing only on a horizontal plane that is in the here and now—they have no history. "Good" must survive; "Bad" will go to the wall—as it deserves to. In this primitive world, the market-place is deified as the only source of human freedom and responsibility. [p. 54]

The ruthless primitive morality evinced here has the qualities of an archaic superego structure; for those working in health services, their daily existence is characterized by the experience of constant threat. Under pressure to meet targets, and to make cuts, forced to sell themselves in a world where the representation of services takes precedence over their reality, they find themselves flooded with the constant anxiety of survival. This is a world where, as Mark Fisher (2009) has so aptly put it, "All that is solid melts into PR."

It can sometimes feel as though there is an unholy alliance between the pressure coming from above and pressure coming from the newly "empowered" customer (patient)—the mental health worker feels caught in the jaws of this pincer movement. Of course, it is a very good thing that patients are becoming more active in their own management, but it needs to be noted that this "empowerment" of the consumer/patient does not extend to having any say in the cutting of resources or having to accept a postcode lottery of services. Sometimes this "empowerment" can slide into something more perverse, particularly where complaints procedures can unwittingly provide opportunities for a more destructive part of the patient to wreak vengeance upon the staff.

Insisting that mental health personnel accept a level of responsibility that is quite unrealistic seems increasingly to be a part of mental health policy. Such policies, based less on thought and more on the wish to project unmanageable anxiety into those faced with an already very difficult task, sets the scene for a deterioration in the real care of these patients. Management plans come to serve the function of defending the self against any possible blame, rather than enabling acceptance of the complexities of the task. An attitude of enquiry is transformed into a preoccupation with protecting oneself from the inquisition.

Beyond any other factor, staff morale, which creates the foundation of the staff's capacity to contain, is the vital therapeutic ingredient, a morale that needs to be robust and, as I have explained, not dependent on any individual patient getting better.

One last caveat. In the above I have emphasized the necessity of space for thought, whether at the individual, group, or institutional level, but I am not suggesting some kind of endless reflective thinking without action. We should not think instead of acting, nor act instead of thinking—that is, we should not think "action-lessly", nor act "thought-lessly". But, as I have suggested, our capacity to think, to contain what needs to be contained, depends upon a multitude of factors functioning at different levels within the system.

I would like to end by quoting from a poem of Bertolt Brecht's, which I think describes some of the features of a container that can stand the blast of experience:

In a dream last night
I saw a great storm
It seized the scaffolding
it tore down the iron cross-clasps
What was made of wood
stayed and swayed.

Notes

1. I am reminded here of a patient who was compulsively attracted to love objects whose overriding interest derived from the fact of their availability (the path of least resistance) as opposed to their worth to him (maximal advantage)!

2. It needs to be borne in mind that this is not a sequential process and that the appearance that this is the case is only an artefact of writing which is necessarily linear, whereas in reality these different aspects of the depressive position are all bound up with each other.

3. What follows is based on Bion's model but is derived from a number of sources. The works cited (Bion, 1962a, 1970) are the main references to Bion's theory of the relation "container–contained" but do not refer to all the vicissitudes discussed here.

4. The term "endopsychic perception" is used by Freud (1911c [1910]) to refer to the minds perception of its own activities.

5. Tom Main considerably advanced our knowledge of the processes that are required for containment in an institutional setting. He was fond of saying, "Don't just do something, stand there"!

REFERENCES

Anzieu, D. (1989). Beckett and Bion. *International Review of Psychoanalysis, 16*: 163–169.

Armstrong, D. (2005). *Organization in the Mind: Psychoanalysis, Group Relations, and Organizational Consultancy*. London: Karnac.

Barkun, M. (1974). *Disaster and the Millennium*. New Haven, CT: Yale University Press.

Barratt, R. (1996). *The Psychiatric Team and the Social Definition of Schizophrenia*. Cambridge: Cambridge University Press.

Bell, D. (1996). Primitive mind of state. *Psychoanalytic Psychotherapy, 10*: 45–58.

Bennetts, L. (2001). One nation, one mind? *Vanity Fair* (December).

Berke, J. (1979). *I Haven't Had to Go Mad Here*. London: Penguin.

Bick, E. (1962). Child analysis today. *International Journal of Psychoanalysis, 43*: 328–332.

Bick, E. (1968). The experience of the skin in early object-relations. *International Journal of Psychoanalysis, 49*: 484–486.

Bion, W. R. (1952). Group dynamics: A review. *International Journal of Psychoanalysis 33*, 235–247.

Bion, W. R. (1954). Notes on the theory of schizophrenia. In: *Second Thoughts: Selected Papers on Psycho-Analysis* (pp. 23–35). London: Heinemann, 1967. [Reprinted London: Karnac, 1984.]

Bion, W. R. (1956). Development of schizophrenic thought. In: *Second Thoughts: Selected Papers on Psycho-Analysis* (pp. 36–42). London: Heinemann, 1967. [Reprinted London: Karnac, 1984.]

Bion, W. R. (1957). Differentiation of the psychotic from non-psychotic personalities. In: *Second Thoughts: Selected Papers on Psycho-Analysis* (pp. 43–64). London: Heinemann, 1967. [Reprinted London: Karnac, 1984.]

Bion, W. R. (1959). Attacks on linking. In: *Second Thoughts: Selected Papers on Psycho-Analysis* (pp. 93–109). London: Heinemann, 1967. [Reprinted London: Karnac, 1984. Also in E. Bott Spillius (Ed.), *Melanie Klein Today, Vol. 1: Mainly Theory* (pp. 84–98). London: Routledge, 1988.]

Bion, W. R. (1961). *Experiences in Groups*. London: Tavistock.

Bion, W. R. (1962a). *Learning from Experience*. London: Heinemann. [Reprinted London: Karnac, 1984.]

Bion, W. R. (1962b). A theory of thinking. In: *Second Thoughts: Selected Papers on Psycho-Analysis* (pp. 110–119). London: Heinemann, 1967. [Reprinted London: Karnac, 1984.]

Bion, W. R. (1963). *Elements of Psycho-Analysis*. London: Heinemann. [Reprinted London: Karnac, 1984.]

Bion, W. R. (1965). *Transformations*. London: Heinemann. [Reprinted London: Karnac, 1984.]

Bion, W. R. (1967a). Commentary. In: *Second Thoughts: Selected Papers on Psycho-Analysis* (pp. 120–166). London: Heinemann. [Reprinted London: Karnac, 1984.]

Bion, W. R. (1967b). *Second Thoughts: Selected Papers on Psycho-Analysis*. London: Heinemann. [Reprinted London: Karnac, 1984.]

Bion, W. R. (1970). *Attention and Interpretation*. London: Tavistock.

Bion, W. R. (1975). *A Memoir of the Future*. London: Karnac, 1991.

Bion, W. R. (1982). *The Long Week-End, 1897–1919: Part of a Life*. Abingdon: Fleetwood Press.

Blackwell, D., Bell, D., & Dartington, T. (1993). Clinical commentary XVI. *British Journal of Psychotherapy, 10* (2): 253–269.

Bleuler, E. (1911). Dementia praecox oder die Gruppe der Schizofrenien. In: G. Aschaffenburg (Ed.), *Handbuch der Psychiatrie*. Leipzig and Vienna. [*Dementia Praecox or the Group of Schizophrenias*, trans. J. Zinkin. New York: International Universities Press, 1950.]

Bonaparte, M. (1947). *Myths of War*. London: Imago.

Bott, E. (1976). Hospital and society. *British Journal of Medical Psychology, 49*: 97–140.

Braginsky, B. M., Grosse, M., & Ring, K. (1966). Controlling outcomes through impression management: An experimental study in the manipulative tactics of mental patients. *Journal of Consulting and Clinical Psychology, 3*: 295–300.

Britton, R. (1989). The missing link: Parental sexuality in the Oedipus complex. In: R. Britton, M. Feldman, & E. O'Shaughnessy (Eds.), *The*

Oedipus Complex Today: Clinical Implications (pp. 83–101). London: Karnac.

Britton, R. (1998). Oedipus in the depressive position. In: *Belief and Imagination: Explorations in Psychoanalysis*. London: Routledge.

Britton, R., & Steiner, J. (1994). Interpretation: Selected fact or overvalued idea? *International Journal of Psychoanalysis, 75*: 1069–1078.

Brown, G. W., Bone, M., Dalinson, B., & Wing, J. K. (1966). *Schizophrenia and Social Care: A Comparative Follow-Up Study of 339 Schizophrenic Patients*. Maudsley Monograph No. 17. Oxford: Oxford University Press.

Carrington, L. (1944). Down below. *VVV, 4* (February).

Chaslin, P. (1912). *Elements de Sémiologie et Clinique Mentales*. Paris: Asselin et Houzeau.

Chiesa, M. (2000). At a crossroad between institutional and community psychiatry: An acute psychiatric admission ward. In: R. Hinshelwood & W. Skogstad (Eds.), *Observing Organisations: Anxiety, Defence and Culture in Health Care* (pp. 54-67). London: Routledge.

Clark, D. H. (1965). The therapeutic community: Concept, practice and future. *British Journal of Psychiatry, 131*: 553–564.

Clifford, P. (1988). Out of the cuckoo's nest: The move of 12 Ward from Bexley Hospital to 215 Sydenham Road. In: T. Lavender & F. Holloway (Eds.), *Community Care in Practice*. London: Wiley.

Cohler, J., & Shapiro, L. (1964). Avoidance patterns in staff–patient interaction on a chronic schizophrenic ward. *Psychiatry, 27*: 377–378.

Coleridge, S. T. (1816). *The Pains of Sleep*. In: *Samuel Taylor Coleridge: Selected Poems*. London: Penguin, 1996.

Cooper, D. (1967). *Psychiatry and Anti-Psychiatry*. London: Tavistock.

Coser, R. L. (1963). Alienation and the social structure. In: E. Freidson (Ed.), *The Hospital in Modern Society*. New York: Free Press.

Dartington, T. (2001). The preoccupations of the citizen: Reflections from the OPUS Listening Posts. *Organisational and Social Dynamics, 1* (1): 94–112.

Donati, F. (2000). Madness and morale: A chronic psychiatric ward. In: R. Hinshelwood & W. Skogstad (Eds.), *Observing Organisations: Anxiety, Defence and Culture in Health Care* (pp. 29–43). London: Routledge.

Dundes, A. (1997). *From Game to War, and Other Psychoanalytic Essays on Folklore*. Lexington, KY: University Press of Kentucky.

Dupont, J. (1988). Ferenczi's "Madness". *Contemporary Psychoanalysis, 24*: 250–261.

Eliot, G. (1879). *Impressions of Theophrastus Such*. Edinburgh: William Blackwood and Sons.

Eliot, T. S. (1950). *The Cocktail Party*. London: Faber & Faber.

Eliot, T. S. (1969). *The Elder Statesman*. London: Faber & Faber.

Erikson, K. T. (1957). Patient role and social uncertainty: A dilemma of the mentally ill. *Psychiatry, 20*: 263–274.

Erlich, S. (2010). A beam of darkness: Understanding the terrorist mind. In: *Psychoanalytic Perspectives on a Turbulent World* (pp. 3–15). London: Karnac.

Feldman, M. (1989). The Oedipus Complex: Manifestations in the inner world and the therapeutic situation. In: J. Steiner (Ed.), *The Oedipus Complex Today: Clinical Implications* (pp. 103–128). London: Karnac.

Fisher, J. (1993). The impenetrable other: Ambivalence and the oedipal conflict in work with couples. In: S. Ruszczynski (Ed.), *Psychotherapy with Couples: Theory and Practice at the Tavistock Institute of Marital Studies* (pp. 142–166). London: Karnac.

Fisher, J. (1999). *The Uninvited Guest: Emerging from Narcissism Towards Marriage*. London: Karnac.

Fisher, J. (2009). The Macbeths in the consulting room. *Fort Da, 15* (2): 33–55.

Fisher, M. (2009). *Capitalist Realism: Is There No Alternative?* Winchester: Zero Books.

Fontana, A. F., Klein, E. B., Lewis, E., & Levine, L. (1968). Presentation of self in mental illness. *Journal of Consulting and Clinical Psychology, 32*: 110–119.

Foulkes, S. H. (1973). The group as matrix of the individual's mental life. In: *Selected Papers: Psychoanalysis and Group Analysis* (pp. 223–233). London: Karnac, 1990.

French, R., Harvey, C., & Simpson, P. (2002). Leadership and negative capability. *Human Relations, 55* (10): 1209–1226.

Freud, S. (1905c). *Jokes and Their Relation to the Unconscious. Standard Edition*, 8.

Freud, S. (1905d). *Three Essays on the Theory of Sexuality. Standard Edition*, 7: 123–230.

Freud, S. (1911b). Formulations on the two principles of mental functioning. *Standard Edition*, 12: 213–226.

Freud, S. (1911c [1910]). Psycho-analytic notes on an autobiographical account of a case of paranoia (Dementia paranoides). *Standard Edition*, 12: 1–79.

Freud, S. (1916–17). *Introductory Lectures on Psycho-Analysis. Standard Edition*, 15–16.

Freud, S. (1919h). The "Uncanny". *Standard Edition*, 17: 217–256.

Freud, S. (1920g). *Beyond the Pleasure Principle. Standard Edition*, 18: 3–64.

Freud, S. (1923f). Josef Popper-Lynkeus and the theory of dreams. *Standard Edition*, 19: 259–264.

Freud, S. (1924f [1923]). A short account of psycho-analysis. *Standard Edition*, 20: 189–210.

Freud, S. (1930a). *Civilization and Its Discontents. Standard Edition*, 21: 57–145.

Freud, S. (1933a). *New Introductory Lectures on Psycho-Analysis. Standard Edition*, 22.

Fromm-Reichmann, F. (1939). Transference problems in schizophrenics. *Psychoanalytic Quarterly, 8*: 412–426.

Gaddini, E. (1969). On imitation. In: A. Limentani (Ed.), *A Psychoanalytic Theory of Infantile Experience: Conceptual and Clinical Reflections* (pp. 18–34). London: Routledge, 1992.

Goffman, E. (1961). *Asylums*. New York: Doubleday.

Goffman, E. (1969). The insanity of place. *Psychiatry, 32*: 357–387.

Gould, L. (2010). Barack Obama's post partisan dream: Leadership and the limits of the depressive position. In: H. Brunning & M. Perini (Eds.), *Psychoanalytic Perspectives on a Turbulent World* (pp. 159–178). London: Karnac.

Graves, R. (1955). *The Greek Myths* [combined vol.]. London: Penguin, 1992.

Griffiths, R. (1988). *Community Care: Agenda for Action. A Report to the Secretary of State for Social Services*. London: HMSO.

Haigh, R. (1999). The quintessence of a therapeutic environment: Five universal qualities. In: P. Campling & R. Haigh (Eds.), *Therapeutic Communities: Past, Present and Future*. London: Jessica Kingsley.

Harris, M., & Meltzer, D. (1976). A psycho-analytical model of the child-in-the-family-in-the-community. In: *Sincerity and Other Works: Collected Papers of Donald Meltzer*, ed. A. Hahn. London: Karnac, 1984.

Hedges, L. E. (1994). A shattered self. In: *Working the Organizing Experience: Transforming Psychotic, Schizoid, and Autistic States* (pp. 3–22). Northvale, NJ: Jason Aronson.

Heimann, P. (1942). A contribution to the problem of sublimation and its relation to the processes of internalization. *International Journal of Psychoanalysis, 23*: 8–17.

Hinshelwood, R. D. (1979). Demoralisation and the hospital community. *Group Analysis, 12*: 84–95.

Hinshelwood, R. D. (1986). The psychotherapist's role in a large psychiatric institution. *Psychoanalytic Psychotherapy, 2*: 207–215.

Hinshelwood R. D. (1987). Social dynamics and individual symptoms. *International Journal of Therapeutic Communities, 8*: 265–272.

Hinshelwood, R. D. (1998). Creatures of each other: Some historical considerations of responsibility and care and some present undercurrents. In: A. Foster & V. Roberts (Eds.), *Managing Mental Health in the Community: Chaos and Containment in Community Care*. London: Routledge.

Hinshelwood, R. D. (1999). The difficult patient: The role of "scientific" psychiatry in understanding patients with chronic schizophrenia or severe personality disorder. *British Journal of Psychiatry, 174*: 187–190.

Hinshelwood, R. D. (2008). Melanie Klein and countertransference: A historical note. *Psychoanalysis and History, 10*: 95–113.

Hinshelwood, R. D., Pedriali, E., & Brunner, L. (2010). Action as a vehicle of learning. *Organisational and Social Dynamics 10*: 22–39.

Hinshelwood, R. D., & Skogstad, W. (2000a). The method of observing organisations. In: R. Hinshelwood & W. Skogstad (Eds.), *Observing Organisations: Anxiety, Defence and Culture in Health Care* (pp. 17–26). London: Routledge.

Hinshelwood, R. D., & Skogstad, W. (2000b). *Observing Organisations: Anxiety, Defence and Culture in Health Care*. London: Routledge.

Hinshelwood, R. D., & Skogstad, W. (2000c). Reflections on health care cultures. In: R. Hinshelwood & W. Skogstad (Eds.), *Observing Organisations: Anxiety, Defence and Culture in Health Care* (pp. 155–166). London: Routledge.

Hoggett, P. (1998). The internal establishment. In: P. B. Talamo, F. Borgogno, & S. Merciai (Eds.), *Bion's Legacy to Groups* (pp. 9–24). London: Karnac.

Hoggett, P. (2010). Government and the perverse social defence. *British Journal of Psychotherapy, 26* (2): 202–212.

Jaques, E. (1953). On the dynamics of social structure: A contribution to the psychoanalytical study of social phenomena. *Human Relations, 6*: 3–24.

Jaques, E. (1955). Social systems as a defence against persecutory and depressive anxiety. In: M. Klein, P. Heimann, & R. E. Money-Kyrle (Eds.), *New Directions in Psycho-Analysis*. London: Tavistock Publications.

Jones, E. (1931). *On the Nightmare*. London: Hogarth Press & Institute of Psychoanalysis.

Joseph, B. (1989). *Psychic Equilibrium and Psychic Change: Selected Papers of Betty Joseph*. London: Routledge.

Kennard, D. (1998). *An Introduction to Therapeutic Communities*. London: Jessica Kingsley.

Kernberg, O. F. (1985). Regression in organisational leadership. In: A. Colman & M. Geller (Eds.), *Group Relations Reader 2* (pp. 89–108). Washington, DC: A. K. Rice Institute.

Khaleelee, O., & Miller, E. (1985). Beyond the small group: Society as an intelligible field of study. In: M. Pines (Ed.), *Bion and Group Psychotherapy* (pp. 354–385). London: Routledge.

Klein, M. (1930). The importance of symbol-formation in the development of the ego. In: *Contributions to Psychoanalysis, 1921–1945*. New York: McGraw-Hill, 1964.

Klein, M. (1935). A contribution to the psychogenesis of manic-depressive states. In: *Love, Guilt and Reparation and Other Works. The Writings of Melanie Klein, Vol. 1* (pp. 262–289). London: Hogarth Press. [Reprinted London: Karnac, 1992.]

Klein, M. (1940). Mourning and its relation to manic-depressive states. In: *Love, Guilt and Reparation and Other Works. The Writings of Melanie Klein, Vol. 1* (pp. 344–369). London: Hogarth Press, 1975. [Reprinted London: Karnac, 1992.]

Klein, M. (1946). Notes on some schizoid mechanisms. In: *Envy and Gratitude and Other Works. The Writings of Melanie Klein, Vol. 3* (pp. 1–24). London: Hogarth Press, 1975. [Reprinted London: Karnac, 1993.]

Klein, M. (1952). Some theoretical conclusions regarding the emotional life of the infant. In: *Envy and Gratitude and Other Works. The Writings of Melanie Klein, Vol. 3* (pp. 61–93). London: Hogarth Press, 1975. [Reprinted London: Karnac, 1993.]

Klein, M. (1957). Envy and gratitude. In: *Envy and Gratitude and Other Works 1946–1967. The Writings of Melanie Klein, Vol. 3* (pp. 176–235). [London: Hogarth Press, 1975. [Reprinted London: Karnac, 1993.]

Klein, M. (1958). On the development of mental functioning. In: *Envy and Gratitude and Other Works 1946–1967. The Writings of Melanie Klein, Vol. 3* (pp. 236–246). London: Hogarth Press, 1975. [Reprinted London: Karnac, 1993.].

Klein, M. (1959). Our adult world and its roots in infancy. In: *Envy and Gratitude and Other Works 1946–1967. The Writings of Melanie Klein, Vol. 3* (pp. 247–263). London: Hogarth Press, 1975. [Reprinted London: Karnac, 1993.]

Knowlson, J. (1996). *Damned to Fame: The Life of Samuel Beckett*. London: Bloomsbury.

Laing, R. D. (1967). *The Politics of Experience*. London: Penguin.

Laing, R. D., & Esterson, A. (1964). *Sanity, Madness, and the Family*. London: Tavistock.

Laplanche, J., & Pontalis, J.-B. (1973). *The Language of Psychoanalysis*. London: Hogarth Press.

Larousse. (1959). *The New Larousse Encyclopedia of Mythology*. London: Hamlyn.

Le Bon, G. (1895). *The Crowd: A Study of the Popular Mind*. New York: Dover.

Ludwig, A. M., & Farrelly, F. (1966). The code of chronicity. *Archives of General Psychiatry, 15*: 562–568.

Main, T. F. (1957). The ailment. *British Journal of Medical Psychology, 30*: 129–145. [Reprinted in: *The Ailment and Other Psychoanalytic Essays*. London: Free Association Books, 1989.]

Meltzer, D. (1967). *The Psycho-Analytical Process*. Strathtay: Clunie Press.

Meltzer, D. (1978a). *The Kleinian Development*. Strathtay: Clunie Press.

Meltzer, D. (1978b). A note on introjective processes. In: *Sincerity and Other Works: Collected Papers of Donald Meltzer* (pp. 458–468), ed. A. Hahn. London: Karnac, 1994.

Meltzer, D. (1983). *Dream-Life: A Re-examination of the Psychoanalytical Theory and Technique.* Strathtay: Clunie Press.

Meltzer, D. (1986). *Studies in Extended Metapsychology: Clinical Applications of Bion's Ideas.* Strathtay: Clunie Press.

Meltzer, D. (1992). *The Claustrum: An Investigation of Claustrophobic Phenomena.* Strathtay: Clunie Press.

Meltzer, D. (1994). Three lectures on W. R. Bion's *A Memoir of the Future.* In: A. Hahn (Ed.), *Sincerity and Other Works: Collected Papers of Donald Meltzer* (pp. 520–550). London: Karnac.

Meltzer, D. (1995). Donald Meltzer in discussion with James Fisher. In: S. Ruszczynski & J. Fisher (Eds.), *Intrusiveness and Intimacy in the Couple.* London: Karnac.

Meltzer, D., Bremner, J., Hoxter, S., Weddell, D., & Wittenberg, I. (1975). *Explorations in Autism: A Psycho-Analytic Study.* Strathtay: Clunie Press.

Meltzer, D., & Williams, M. H. (1988). *The Apprehension of Beauty.* Strathtay: Clunie Press.

Menzies Lyth, I. (1960a). A case study in the functioning of social systems as a defence against anxiety: Report on a study of the nursing service of a general hospital. *Human Relations, 13*: 95–121.

Menzies Lyth, I. (1960b). The functioning of social systems as a defence against anxiety. In: *Containing Anxiety in Institutions: Selected Essays* (pp. 43–85). London: Free Association Books.

Menzies Lyth, I. (1979). Staff support systems: Task and anti-task in adolescent institutions. In: *Containing Anxiety in Institutions: Selected Essays* (pp. 222–235). London: Free Association Books.

Miller, E. J., & Gwynne, G. V. (1972). *A Life Apart.* London: Tavistock.

Money-Kyrle, R. (1968). Cognitive development. *International Journal of Psychoanalysis, 49,* 691–698. [Reprinted in: D. Meltzer & E. O'Shaughnessy (Eds.), *The Collected Papers of Roger Money-Kyrle* (pp. 416–433). Strathtay: Clunie Press, 1978.]

Money-Kyrle, R. (1978). *The Collected Papers of Roger Money-Kyrle.* Strathtay: Clunie Press.

Morgan, M. (2005). On being able to be a couple. In: F. Grier (Ed.), *Oedipus and the Couple.* London: Karnac.

Moss, M. C., & Hunter, P. (1963). Community methods of treatment. *British Journal of Medical Psychology, 36:* 85–91.

Novakovic, A. (2002). Work with psychotic patients in a rehabilitation unit: A short term staff support group with a nursing team. *Journal of Group Analysis, 35* (4): 560–573.

Novakovic, A. (2011). Community meetings on acute psychiatric wards:

Rationale for group specialist input for staff teams in the acute care services. *Journal of Group Analysis, 44* (1): 52–67.

Obholzer, A., & Roberts, V. Z. (1994). *The Unconscious at Work: Individual and Organizational Stress in the Human Services.* London: Routledge.

O'Shaughnessy, E. (1992). Psychosis: Not thinking in a bizarre world. In: R. Anderson (Ed.), *Clinical Lectures on Klein and Bion* (pp. 89–101). London: Routledge.

O'Shaughnessy, E. (2006). A conversation about early unintegration, disintegration and integration. *Journal of Child Psychotherapy, 32:* 153–157.

Parsons, T. (1951). Illness and the role of the physician: A sociological perspective. *American Journal of Orthopsychiatry, 21:* 452–460.

Pelled, E. (2007). Learning from experience. Bion's concept of reverie and Buddhist meditation: A comparative study. *International Journal of Psychoanalysis, 88:* 1507–1526.

Penrose, R. (1971). *Picasso.* Harmondsworth: Penguin.

Pines, M. (1983). The contribution of S. H. Foulkes to group therapy. In: M. Pines (Ed.), *The Evolution of Group Analysis.* London: Routledge.

Popper-Lynkeus, J. (1899). *Fantasien eines Realisten* [Fantasies of a realist]. Vienna. [*Fantasises d'un Réaliste.* Paris: Gallimard, 1987.]

Prebble, L. (2009). *Enron.* London: Methuen.

Racker, H. (1968). *Transference and Countertransference.* New York: International Universities Press.

Rapoport, R. N., & Rapoport, R. (1957). "Democratization" and authority in a therapeutic community. *Behavioural Science, 2:* 128–133.

Rapoport, R. N., Rapoport, R., & Rosow, I. (1960). *Community as Doctor.* London: Tavistock.

Rees, J. (2000). Food for thought: The canteen of a mental hospital. In: R. Hinshelwood & W. Skogstad (Eds.), *Observing Organisations: Anxiety, Defence and Culture in Health Care* (pp. 44–53). London: Routledge.

Resnik, S. (1986). *L'esperienza psicotica.* Turin: Bollati Boringhieri.

Resnik, S. (1995). Introduction. In: *Mental Space* (pp. 1–11), trans. D. Alcorn. London: Karnac.

Resnik, S. (1999). *Temps des Glaciations.* Toulouse: Erès Editions. [*Glacial Times: A Journey Through the World of Madness,* trans. D. Alcorn. London: Routledge, 2005.]

Resnik, S. (2001). *The Delusional Person: Bodily Feelings in Psychosis.* London: Karnac.

Riesenberg Malcolm, R. (2001). Bion's theory of containment. In: C. Bronstein (Ed.), *Kleinian Theory: A Contemporary Perspective.* London: Whurr.

Riolo, F. (2007). Psychoanalytic transformations. *International Journal of Psychoanalysis, 88:* 1375–1389.

Roberts, V. (1994). The organization of work. In: A. Obholzer & V. Z.

Roberts (Eds.), *The Unconscious at Work: Individual and Organizational Stress in the Human Services* (pp. 28–38). London: Routledge.

Rosenfeld, H. A. (1952). Notes on the psycho-analysis of the superego conflict in an acute schizophrenic patient. In: *Psychotic States: A Psychoanalytical Approach* (pp. 63–103). London: Hogarth Press, 1965. [Reprinted London: Karnac, 1982.]

Rosenfeld, H. A. (1960). On drug addiction. In: *Psychotic States: A Psychoanalytical Approach* (pp. 128–143). London: Hogarth Press, 1965. [Reprinted London: Karnac, 1982.]

Rosenfeld, H. A. (1964). On the psychopathology of narcissism: A clinical approach. In: *Psychotic States: A Psychoanalytical Approach* (pp. 169–179). London: Hogarth Press, 1965. [Reprinted London: Karnac, 1982.]

Rosenfeld, H. A. (1965). *Psychotic States: A Psychoanalytic Approach.* London: Hogarth Press, 1965. [Reprinted London: Karnac, 1982.]

Rosenfeld, H. A. (1971). A clinical approach to the psychoanalytic theory of the life and death instincts: An investigation into the aggressive aspects of narcissism. *International Journal of Psychoanalysis, 52*: 169–178.

Rosenfeld, H. A. (1987a). *Impasse and Interpretation.* London: Routledge.

Rosenfeld, H. A. (1987b). Projective identification and the psychotic transference in schizophrenia. In: *Impasse and Interpretation* (p. 220–240). London: Routledge.

Rosenfeld, H. A. (1987c). A psychoanalytic approach to the treatment of psychosis. In: *Impasse and Interpretation* (pp. 3–27). London: Routledge.

Ruszczynski, S. (2005). Reflective space in the intimate couple relationship: The "marital triangle". In: F. Grier (Ed.), *Oedipus and the Couple.* London: Karnac.

Sandler, J. (1976). Actualisation and object relationships. *Journal of the Philadelphia Association for Psychoanalysis, 3*: 59–70.

Sandler, J. (1983). Reflections on some relations between psychoanalytic concepts and psychoanalytic practice. *International Journal of Psychoanalysis, 64*: 35–45.

Sarbin, T. R., & Mancuso, J. C. (1970). Failure of a moral enterprise: Attitudes of the public toward mental illness. *Journal of Consulting and Clinical Psychology, 35*: 159–173.

Scott, R. D. (1973). The treatment barrier. *British Journal of Medical Psychology, 46*: 45–67.

Scott, R. D. (1974). Cultural frontiers in the mental hospital service. *Schizophrenia Bulletin, 10*: 58–73.

Scott, R. D., & Ashworth, P. L. (1965). The "axis value" and the transfer of psychosis. *British Journal of Medical Psychology, 38*: 97–116.

Scott, R. D., & Ashworth, P. L. (1967). Closure at the first schizophrenic breakdown: A family study. *British Journal of Medical Psychology, 40*: 109–145.

Scott, R. D., & Ashworth, P. L. (1969). The shadow of the ancestor: A historical factor in the transmission of schizophrenia. *British Journal of Medical Psychology, 42*: 13–32.

Scott, R. D., Ashworth, P. L., & Casson, P. D. (1970). Violation of parental role structure and outcome in schizophrenia. *Social Science and Medicine, 4*: 41–64.

Scott, R. D., Casson, P. D., & Ashworth, P. L. (1967). *A New Method and Concept for Presenting and Analysing Hospitalisation Data for Psychiatric Admissions.* Unpublished paper.

Segal, H. (1950). Some aspects of the analysis of a schizophrenic. *International Journal of Psychoanalysis, 31*: 268–278.

Segal, H. (1956). Depression in the schizophrenic. *International Journal of Psychoanalysis, 37*: 339–343.

Segal, H. (1957). Notes on symbol formation. *International Journal of Psychoanalysis, 38*: 391–397.

Shelley, M. (1818). *Frankenstein or The Modern Prometheus.* Oxford: Oxford University Press, 1988.

Skogstad, W. (2000). Working in a world of bodies: A medical ward. In: R. Hinshelwood & W. Skogstad (Eds.), *Observing Organisations: Anxiety, Defence and Culture in Health Care* (pp. 101–121). London: Routledge.

Sommer, R., & Osmond, H. (1962). The schizophrenic no-society. *Psychiatry, 25*: 244–255.

Spillius, E. B. (1994). Developments in Kleinian thought: Overview and personal view. *Psychoanalytic Inquiry, 14*: 324–364.

Spillius, E. B., & O'Shaughnessy, E. (2011). *Projective Identification: The Fate of a Concept.* London: Routledge.

Stanton, A., & Schwartz, M. (1954). *The Mental Hospital.* New York: Basic Books.

Stapley, L., & Rickman, C. (2010). Global dynamics at the dawn of 2010. *Organisational and Social Dynamics, 10* (1): 118–141.

Stein, H. (1990). *Narcissistic Process and Corporate Decay: The Theory of the Organization Ideal.* New York: New York University Press.

Stein, H. (2001). *Nothing Personal, Just Business: A Guided Journey into Organizational Darkness.* Westport, CT: Quorum.

Stein, M. (2007). Oedipus Rex at Enron: Leadership, Oedipal struggles and organizational collapse. *Human Relations, 60* (9): 1387–1410.

Steiner, J. (1987). The interplay between pathological organizations and the paranoid-schizoid position and depressive positions. *International Journal of Psychoanalysis, 68*: 69–80.

Steiner, J. (1993). *Psychic Retreats: Pathological Organizations in Psychotic, Neurotic and Borderline Patients.* London: Routledge.

Stock, D. (1962). Interpersonal concerns during the early sessions of therapy groups. *International Journal of Group Psychotherapy, 12*: 14–26.

Stokes, J. (1994). The unconscious at work in groups and teams. In: A. Obholzer & V. Roberts (Eds.), *The Unconscious at Work: Individual and Organizational Stress in the Human Services*. London: Routledge.

Symington, N. (1994). *Emotion and Spirit*. London: Karnac.

Symington, N. (2007). A technique for facilitating the creation of mind. *International Journal of Psychoanalysis, 88*: 1409–1422.

Szasz, T. (1961). *The Myth of Mental Illness*. New York: Hoeber.

Towbin, A. P. (1966). Understanding the mentally deranged. *Journal of Existentialism, 7*: 63–83.

Trist, E. (2001). Prologue. In: G. Amado & A. Ambrose (Eds.), *The Transitional Approach to Change* (pp. xxi–xxvii). London: Karnac.

Trist, E., & Murray, H. (1990). *The Social Engagement of Social Science, Vol. 1: The Socio-Psychological Perspective*. London: Free Association Books.

Tudor Will, G. E. (1952). A sociopsychiatric nursing approach to intervention in a problem of mutual withdrawal on a mental hospital ward. *Psychiatry, 15*: 193–217.

Tudor Will, G. E. (1957). Psychiatric nursing, administration and its implications for patient care. In: M. Greenblatt, D. J. Levinson, & R. H. Williams (Eds.), *The Patient and the Mental Hospital*. Glencoe, IL: Free Press.

Tustin, F. (1981). *Autistic States in Children* (revised edition). London: Routledge, 1992.

WHO (1953). *Expert Committee on Mental Health: 3rd Report*. Geneva: World Health Organization.

Wing, J. K., & Furlong, R. (1986). A haven for the severely disabled within the context of a comprehensive psychiatric community service. *British Journal of Psychiatry, 149*: 449–457.

Winnicott, D. W. (1965). *The Maturational Processes and the Facilitating Environment*. London: Hogarth Press.

Wollheim, R. (1971). *Freud*. London: Fontana/Collins.

INDEX